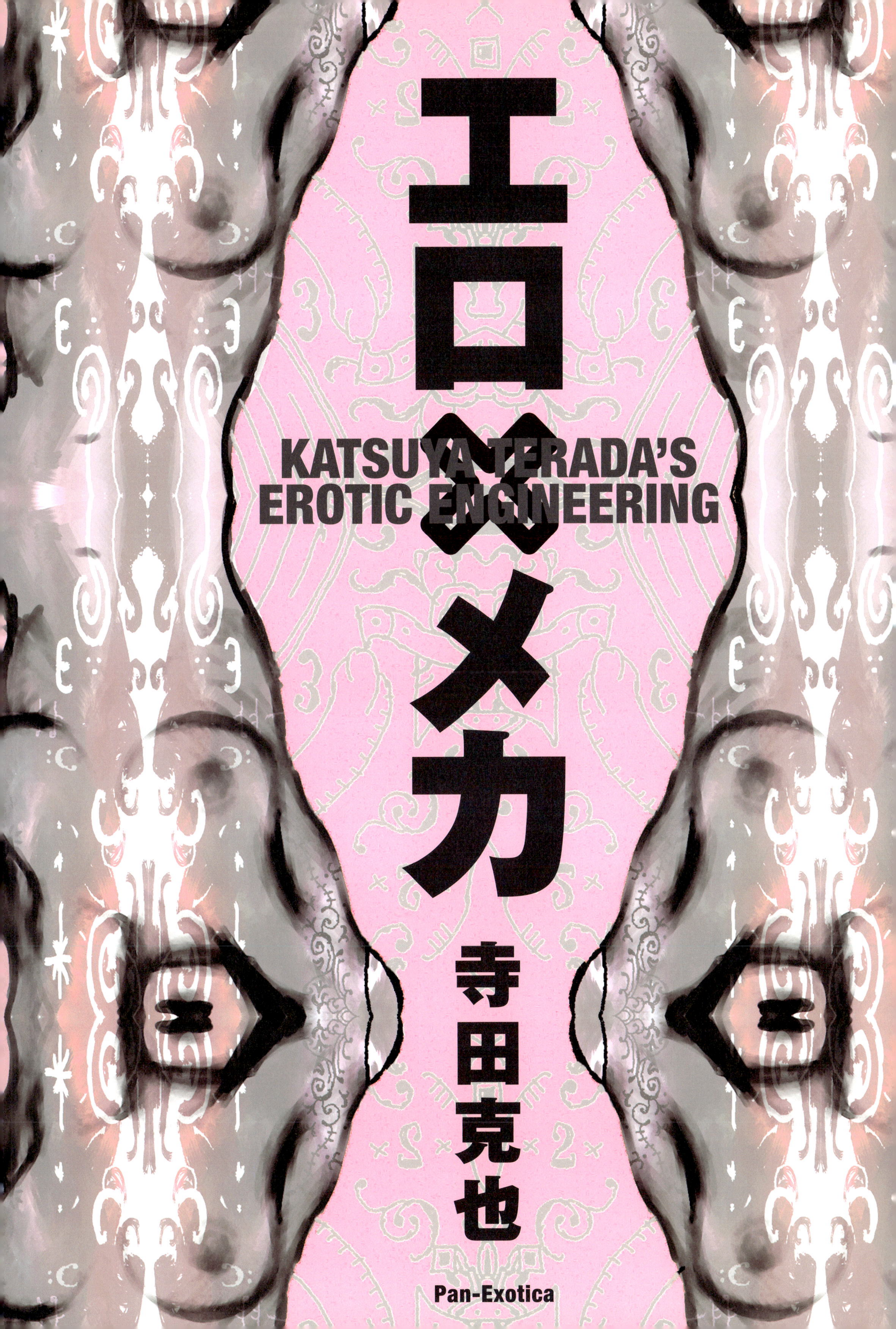
エロメカ
KATSUYA TERADA'S
EROTIC ENGINEERING
寺田克也
Pan-Exotica

Printed and bound in Japan

エロ×メカ I
EROTIC ENGINEERING I

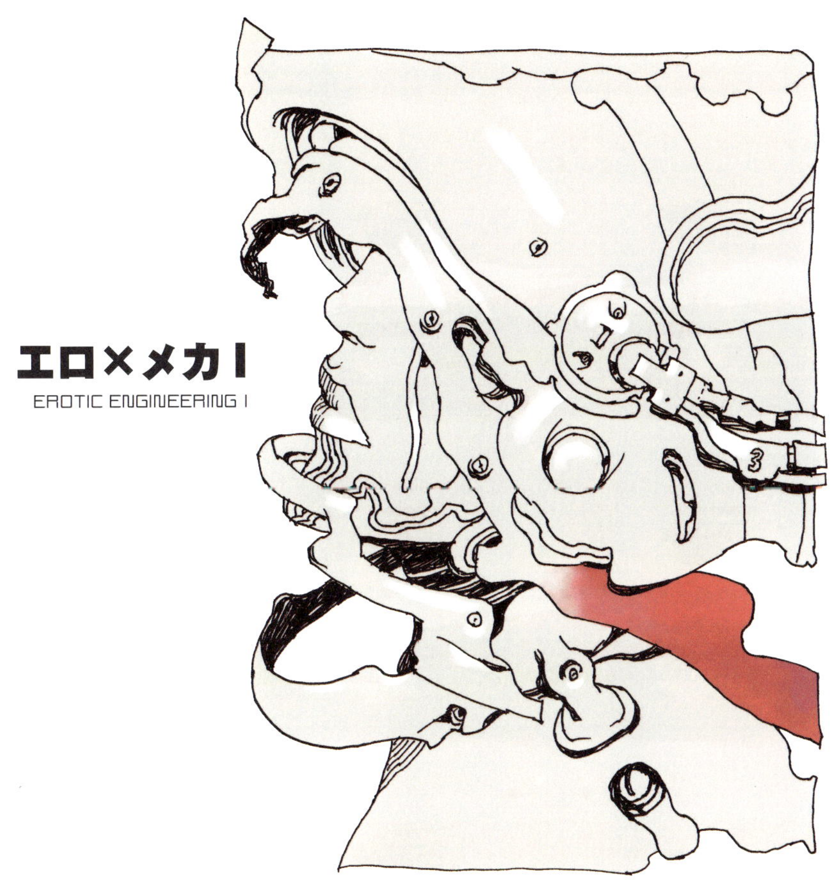

狙ったアナルは逃さない、とばかりに浣腸ガンを手にクールな瞳で迫ってくる全裸の女性に出会ってみたいものだなあ、と思ったがよく考えたら怖い。アナルに思い入れはありません。

When I begin to think how nice it would be to meet a totally naked woman with an enema syringe who looks like she would never let an anus that she has aimed at get away, I get frightened at the thought. I do not have any emotional attachment to anuses.

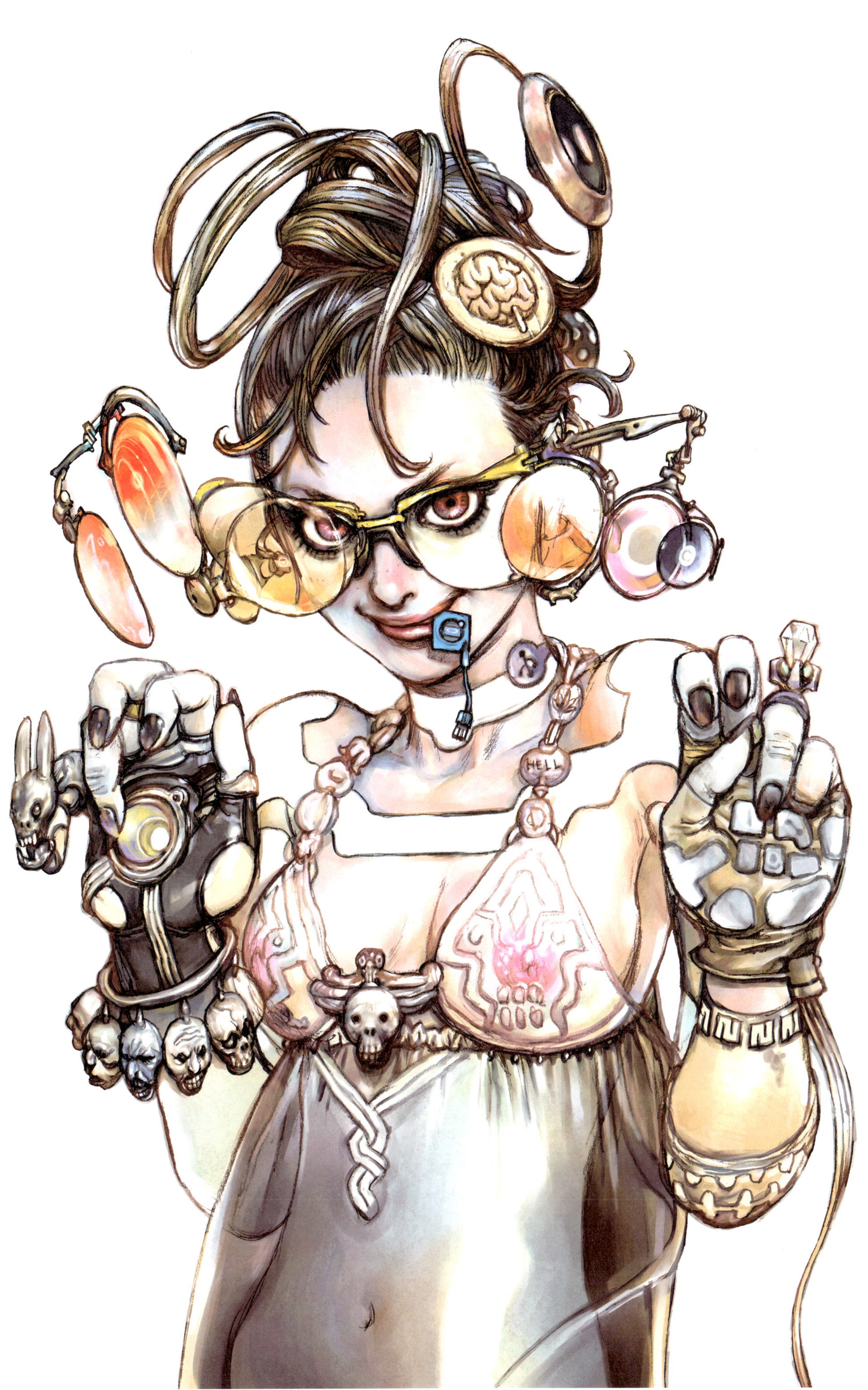
HELL

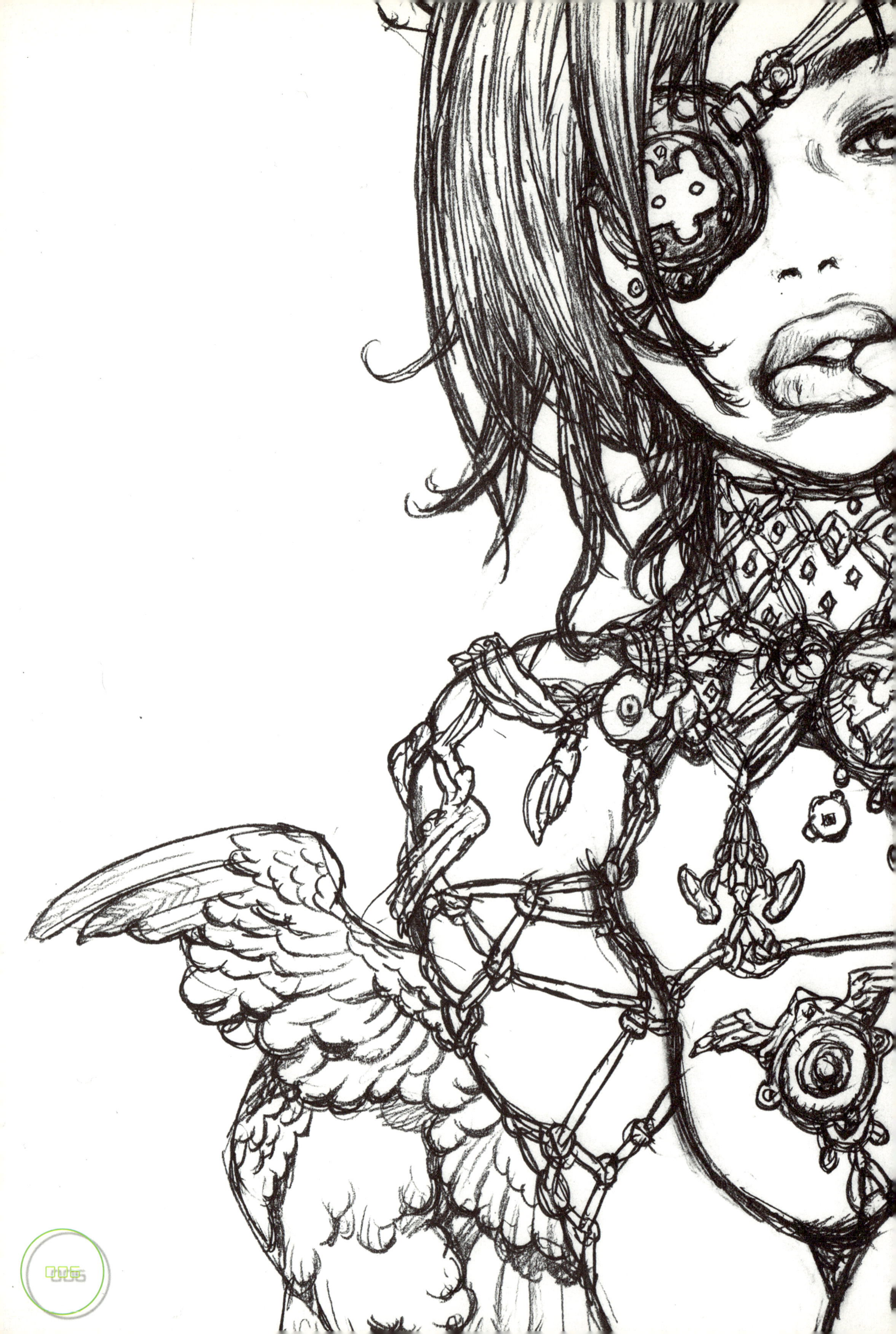

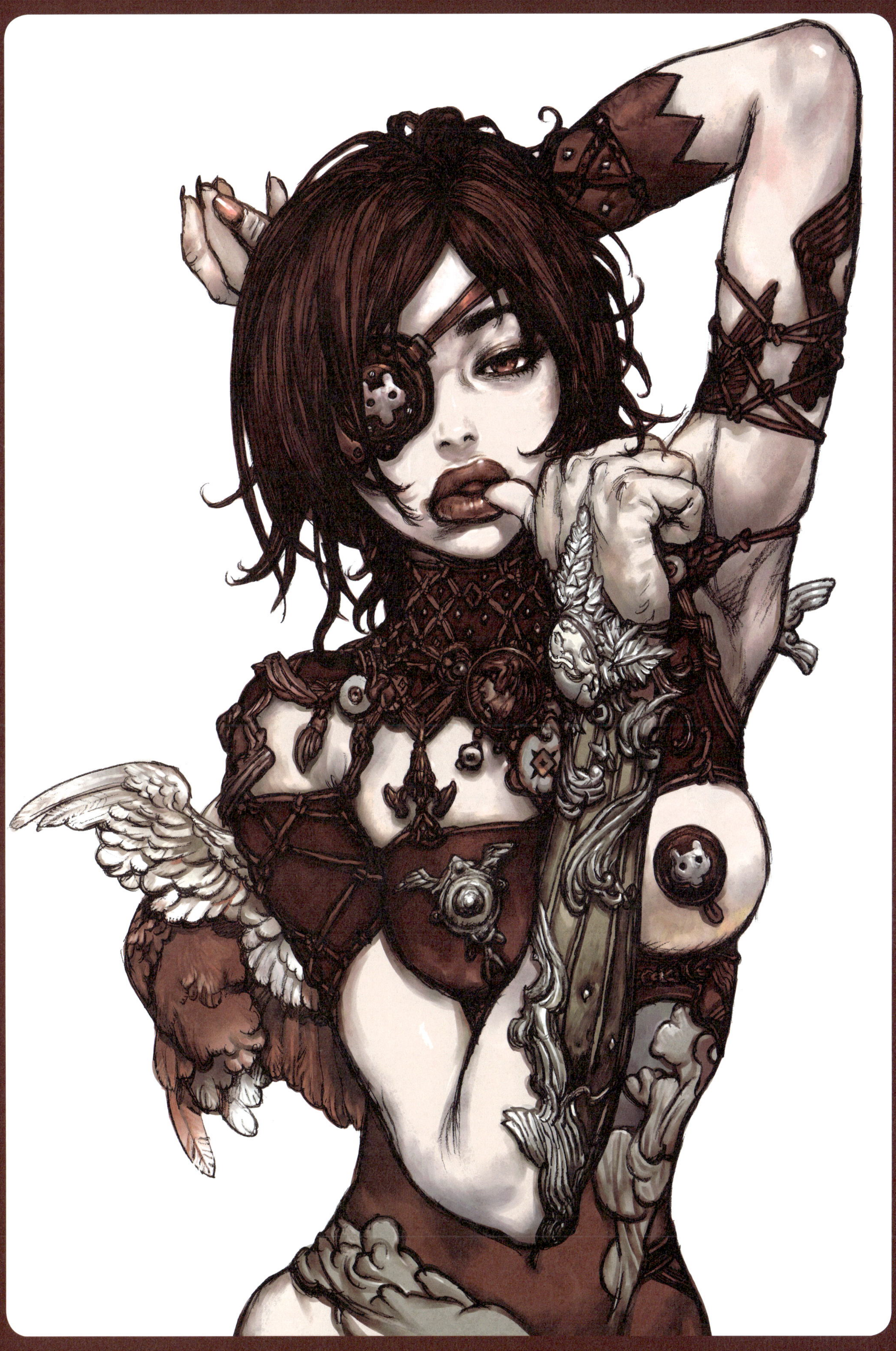

女性はみな天使のごとき存在なわけですが、
だからこそ、その翼を強引に毟り取って地べたに留まらせたいという男の欲望が
「天の羽衣」とかのおとぎ話に集約されているのだなあ。

Women are all like angels, but even so, the universal desire of men to rip off their wings and make them stay on the ground is summarized in the fairy tale that is called "The Heavenly Feather Robe" [Hagoromo].

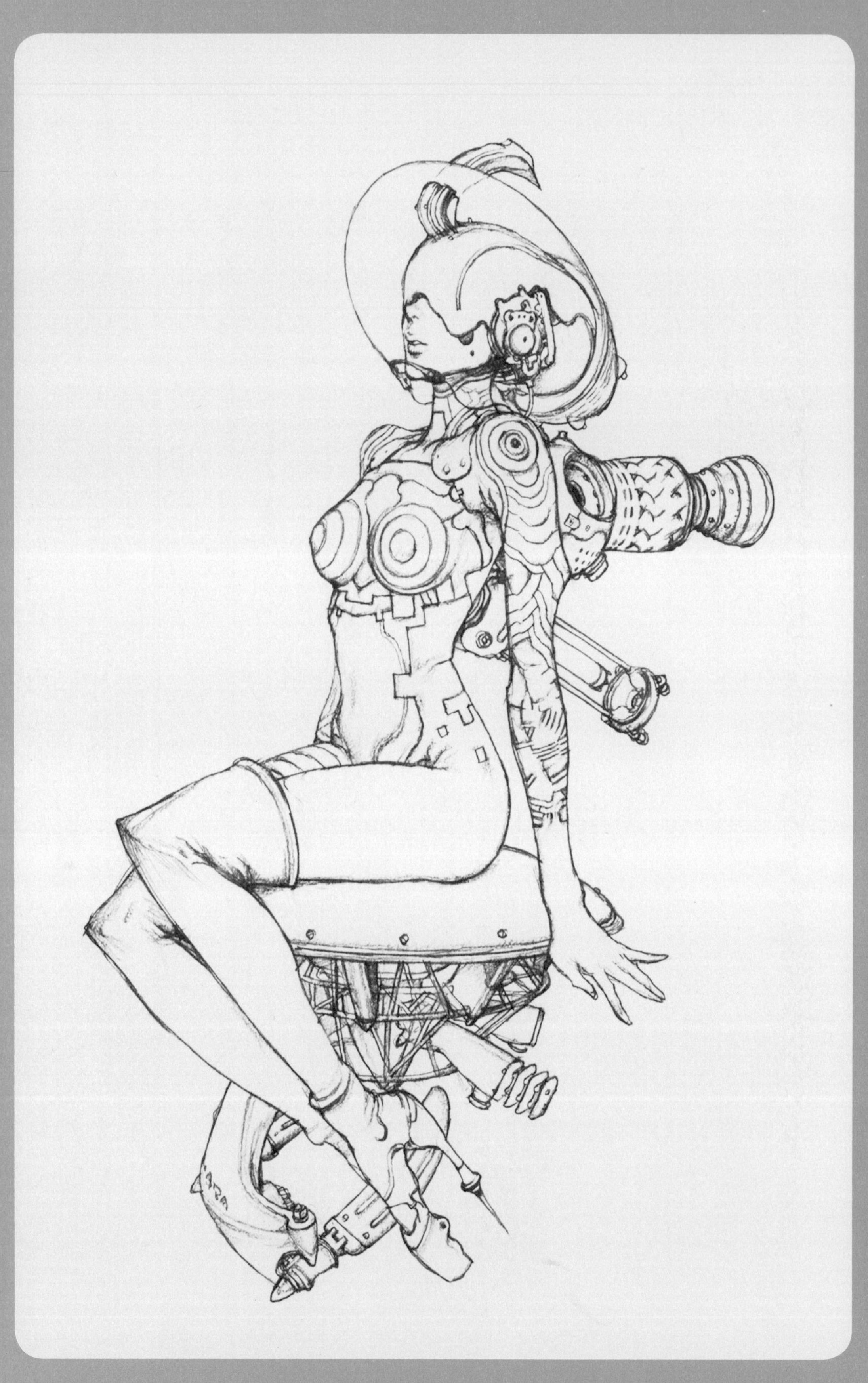

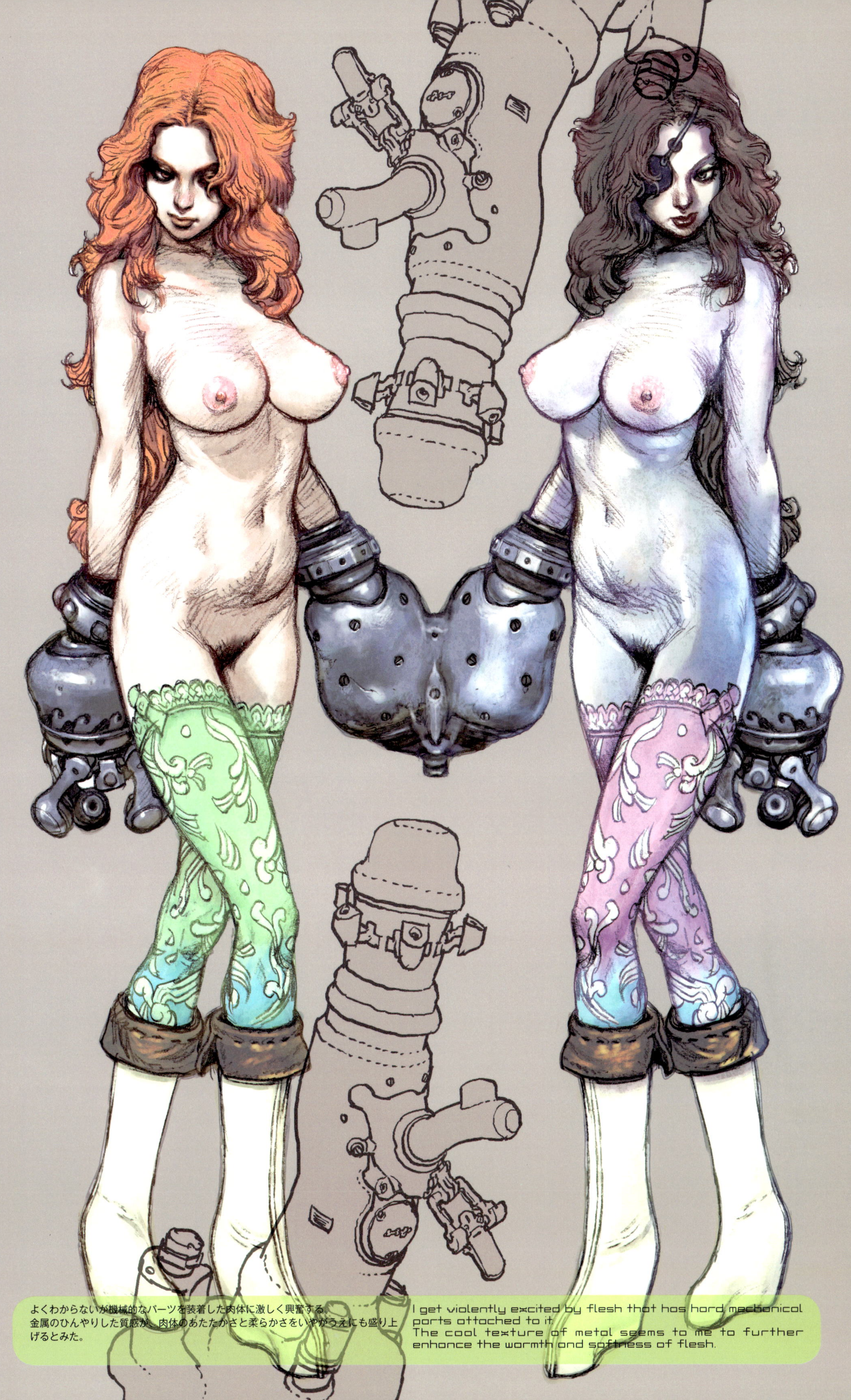

よくわからないが機械的なパーツを装着した肉体に激しく興奮する。
金属のひんやりした質感が、肉体のあたたかさと柔らかさをいやがうえにも盛り上げるとみた。

I get violently excited by flesh that has hard mechanical parts attached to it.
The cool texture of metal seems to me to further enhance the warmth and softness of flesh.

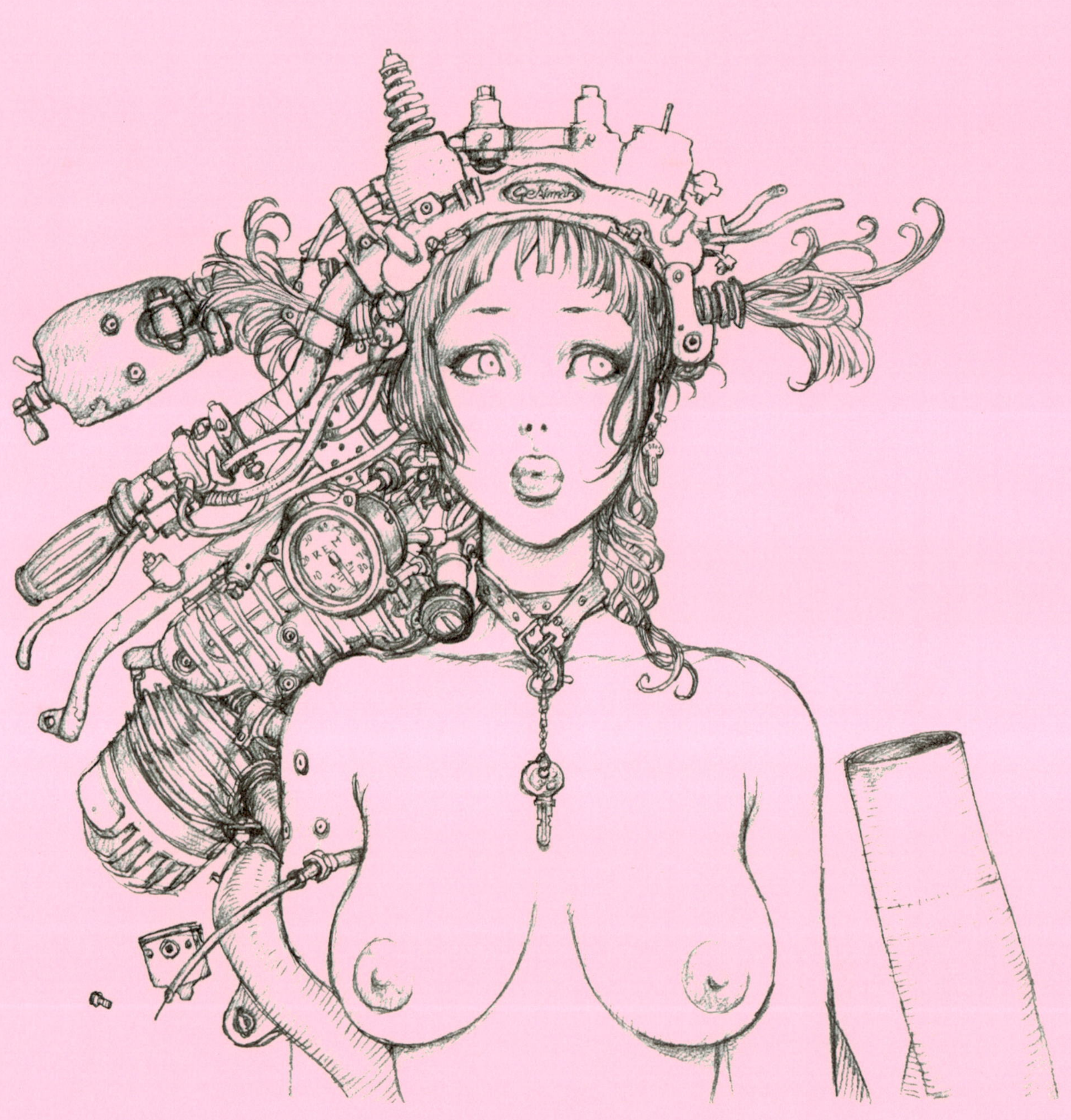

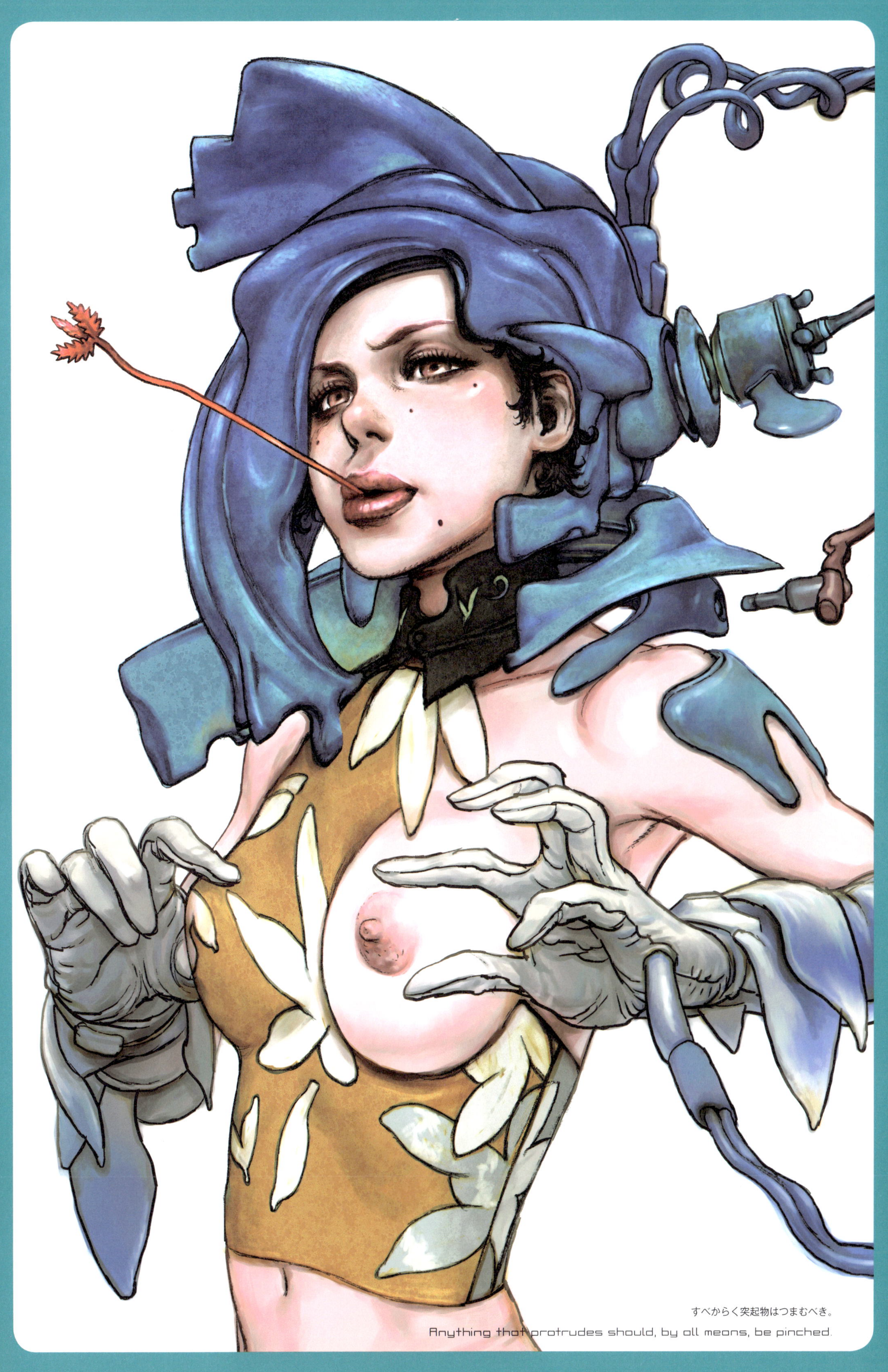

すべからく突起物はつまむべき。

Anything that protrudes should, by all means, be pinched.

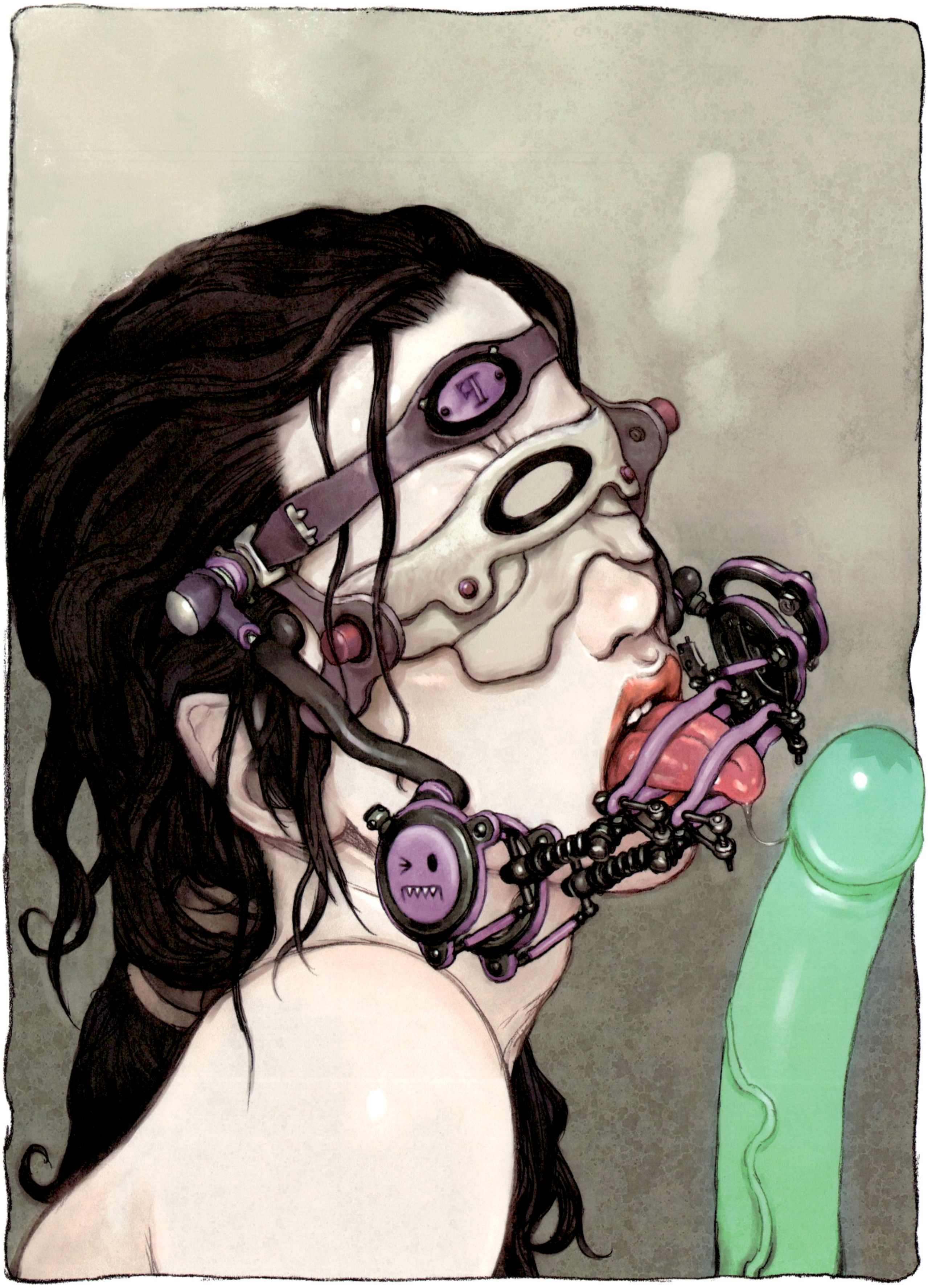

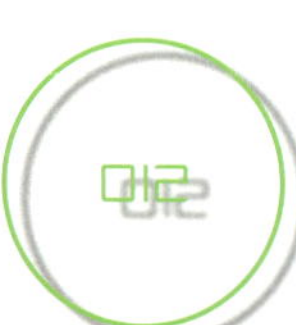

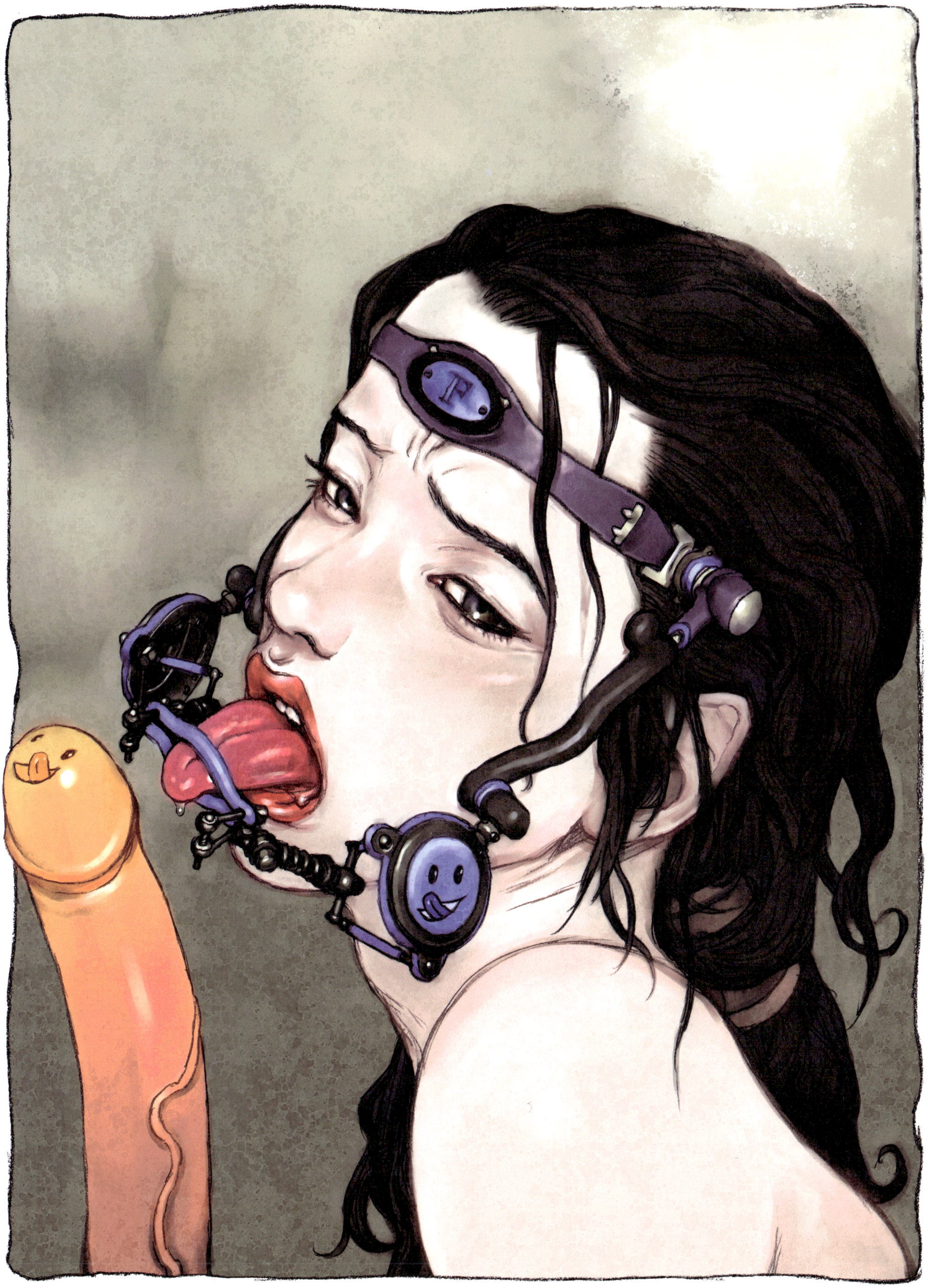

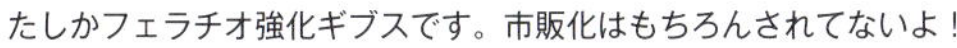

たしかフェラチオ強化ギブスです。市販化はもちろんされてないよ！

This is definitely a plaster cast prosthetic device for power-enhancement of fellatio. Of course, it has not been merchandised!

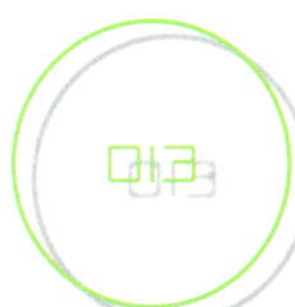

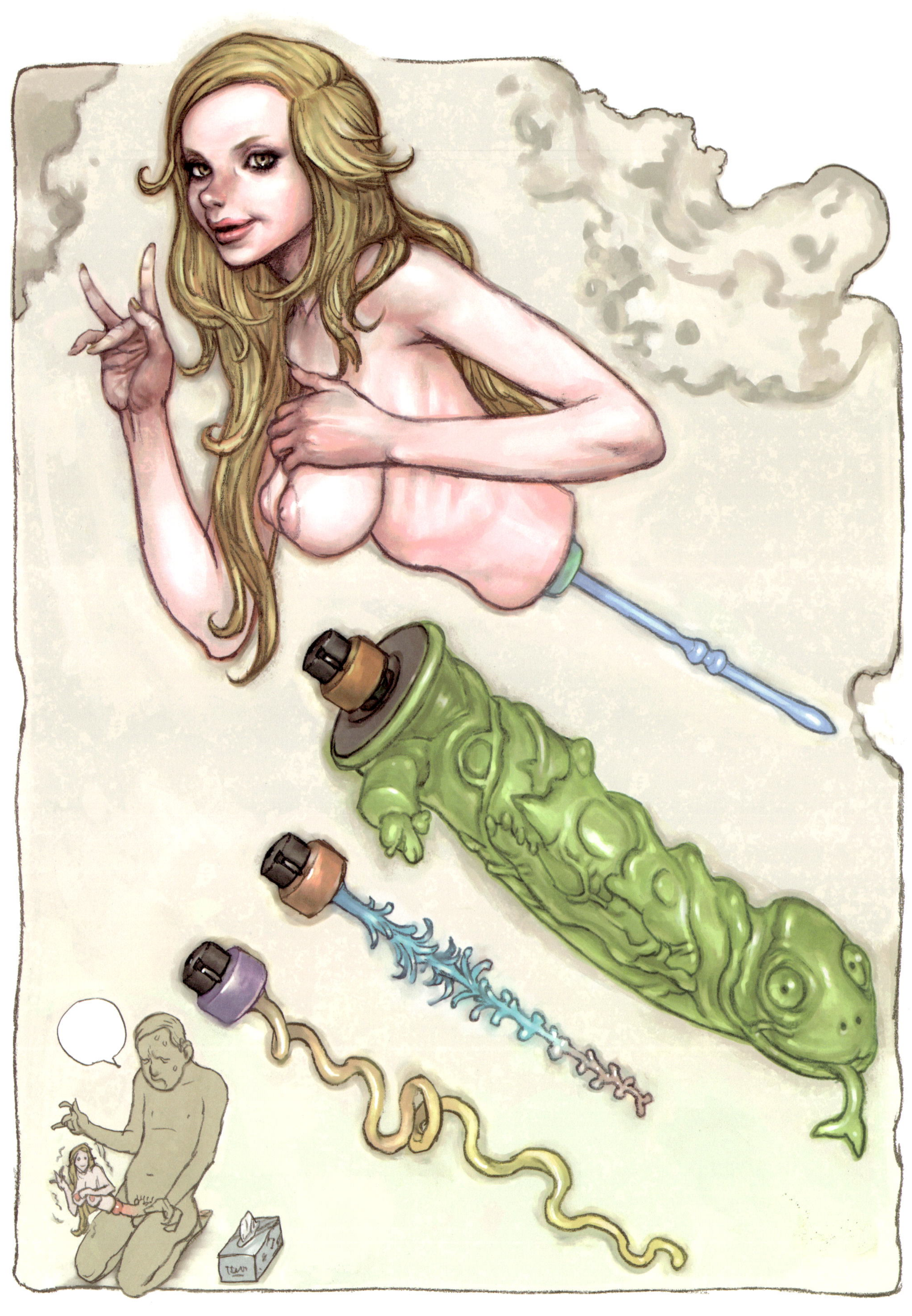

一人暮らしの寂しい野郎用の交換アタッチメント付き体温計。好きなアタッチメントで体温を計っていこー！
性的なプレイに使っちゃダメだ！

This is a thermometer with alternate attachments for lonely guys who live alone. Take your temperature with the attachment of your choice! But you must not use it as a sex toy.

女性用の下半身だけのダッチハズバンド。ヒーター内蔵で冬もホカホカだ！ 特に股間はアッツアツだぜ！
もちろん商品化はされてないが。

This is a Dutch-husband of only the lower body for the use of women. It has a heater installed inside, so it is pleasantly warm even in winter! And the crotch is particularly hot! Of course, it has not been merchandised.

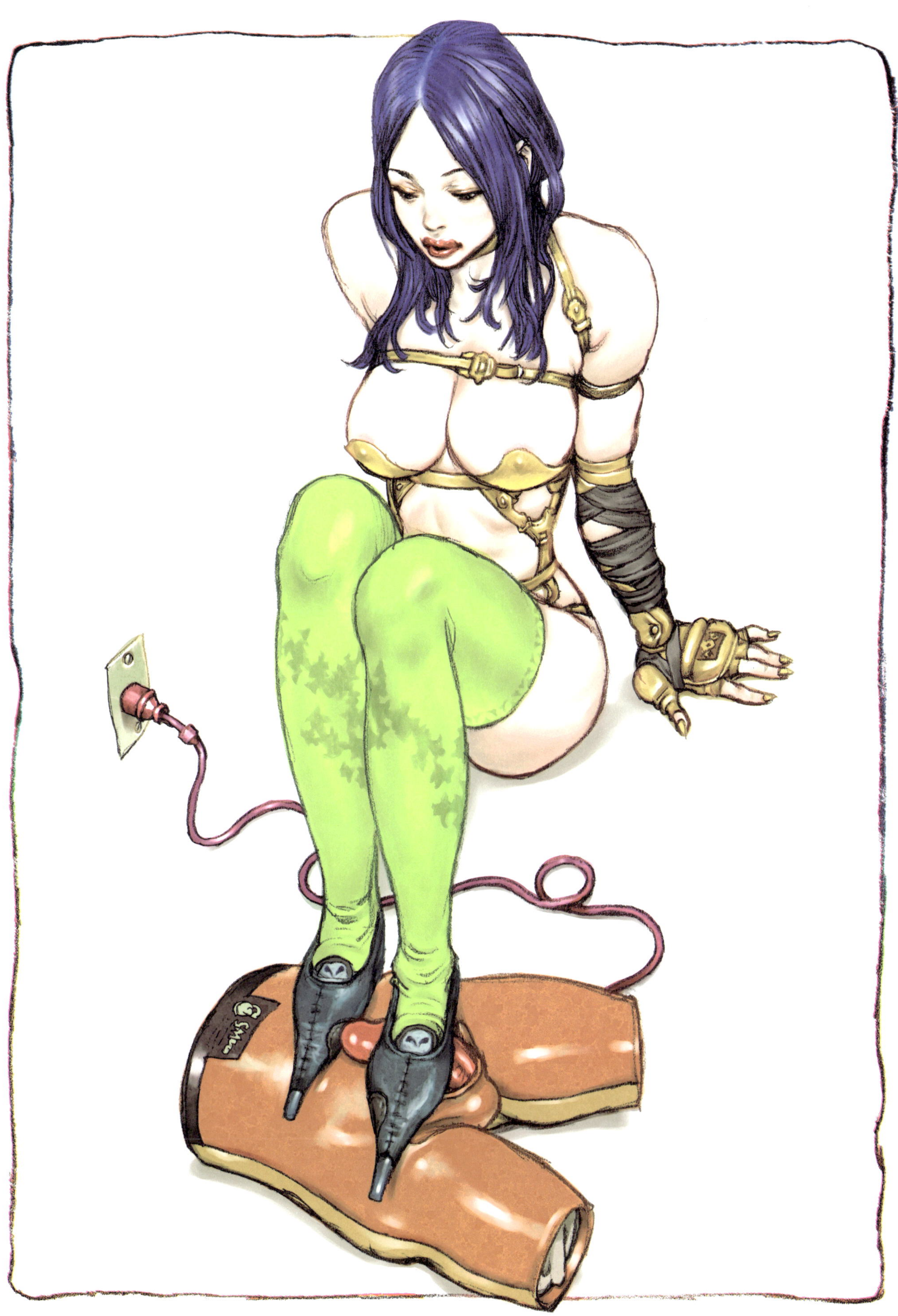

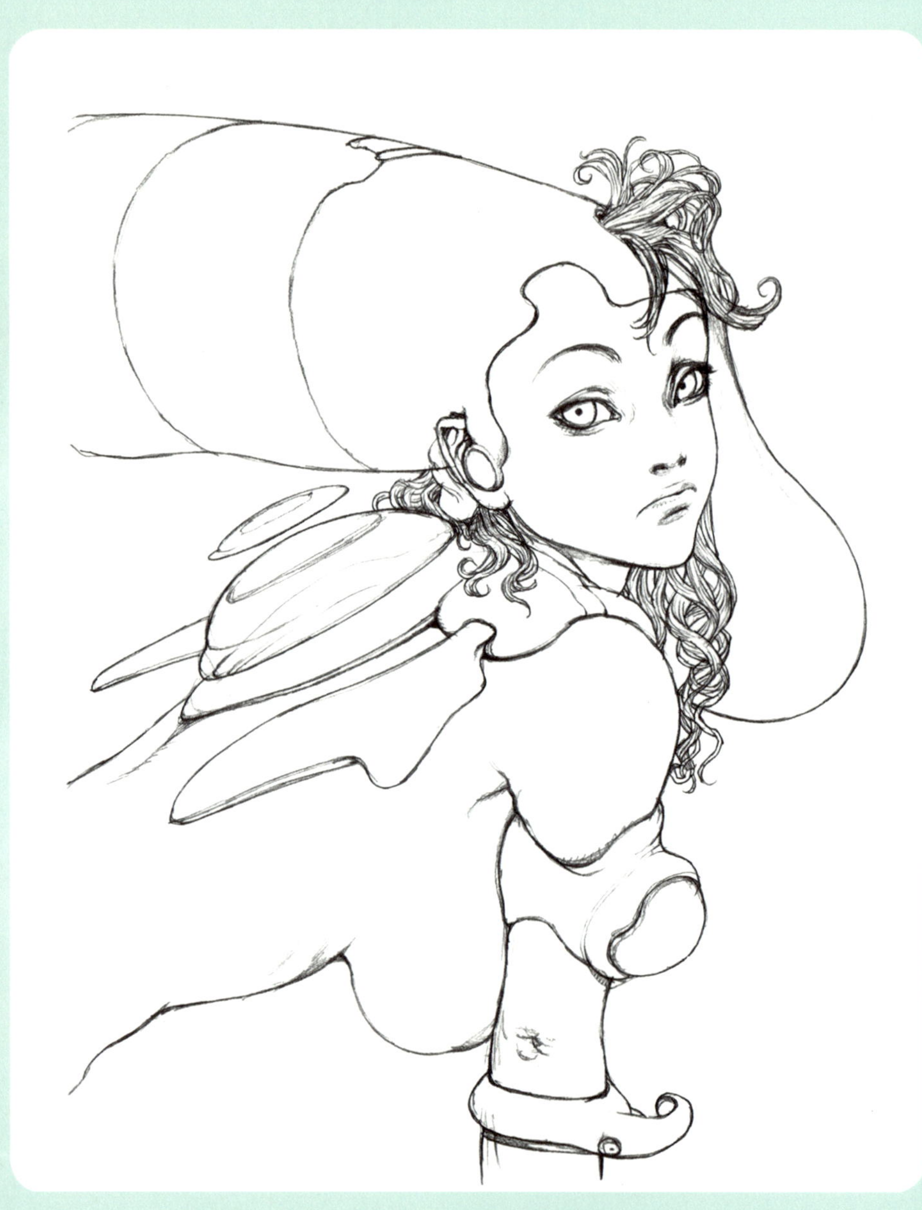

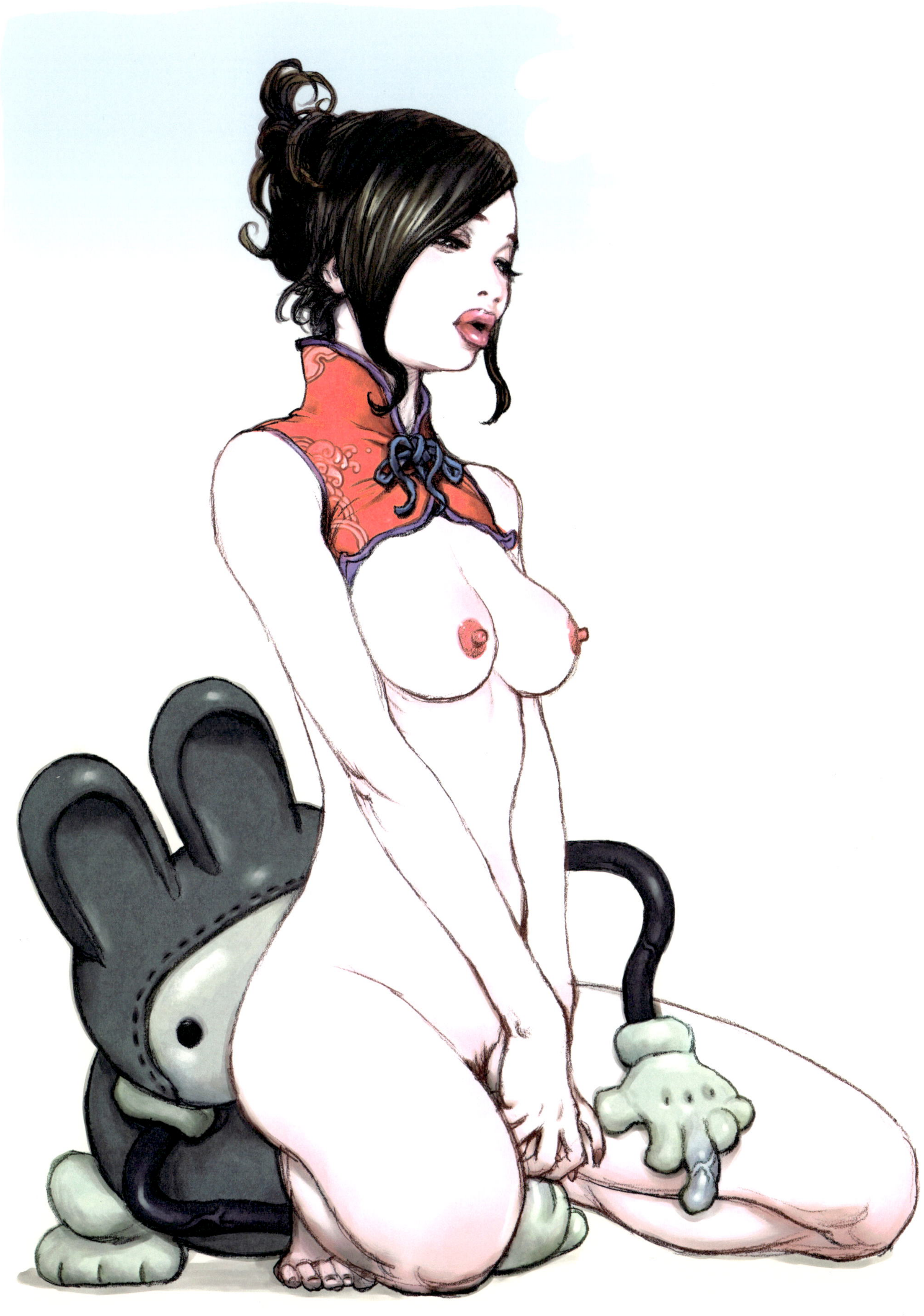

なにを考えて描いたのか忘れたが、かわいいフリしてエロい物を描きたかったんだろう。

I forget what I was thinking about when I painted this picture, but I think that I just wanted to paint something erotic of a girl acting innocent.

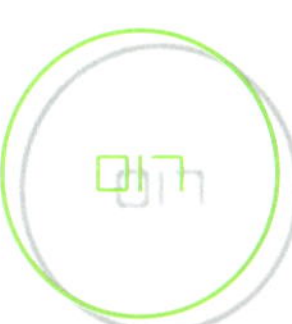

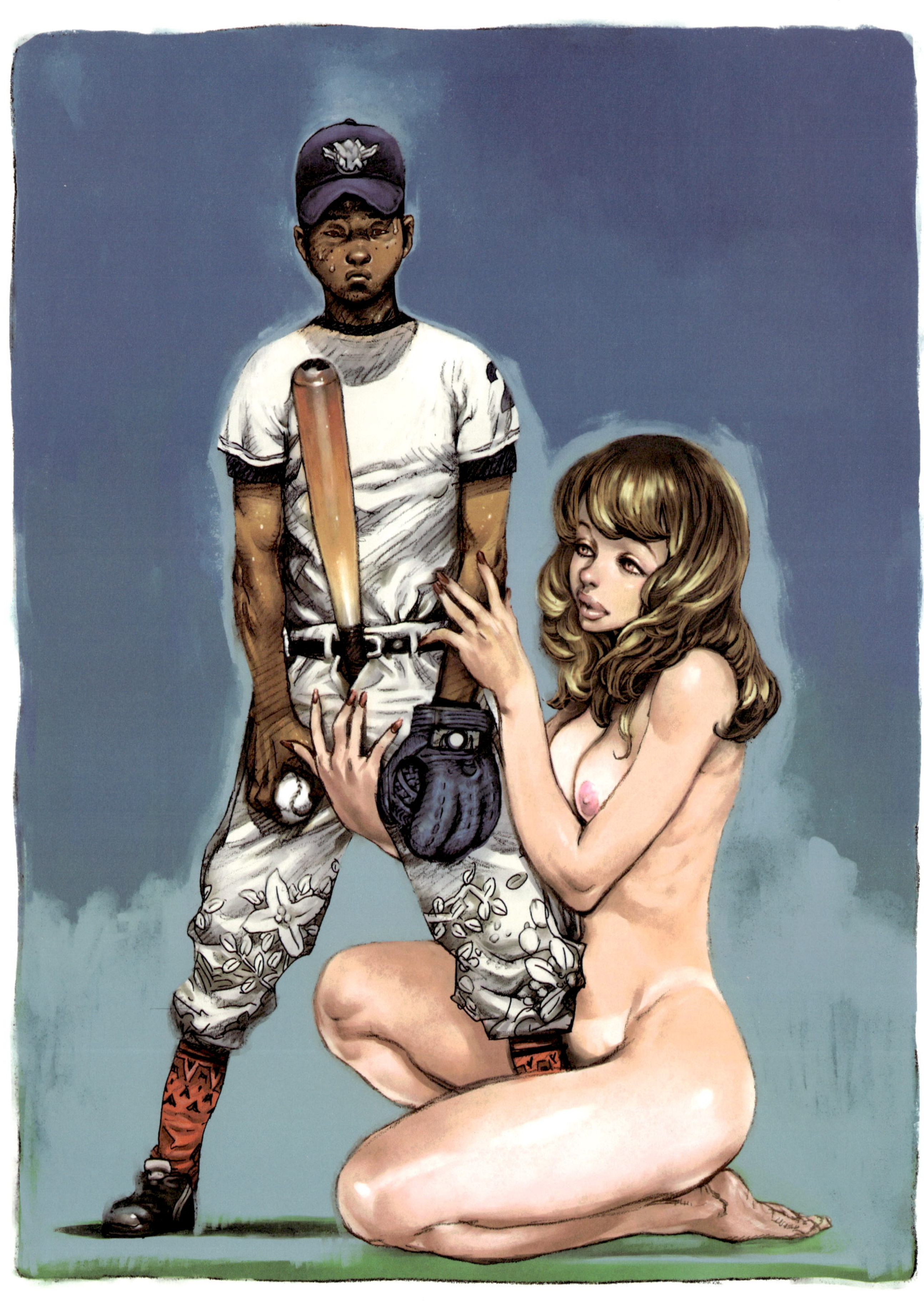

ニッポン人は野球が大好き！ 未成年がカラダ壊すまで頑張らせるのが大好きです！！ てゆーかコレは高校球児型、夜のバッティングマシーンです。淫行じゃないので安心だ！

Japanese people all love baseball! They really adore adolescents who work so hard at the sport that they even make themselves ill! What I mean to say here is that this is a night-time batting machine for high school baseball-freak boys. Don't worry, because it isn't for sexual intercourse.

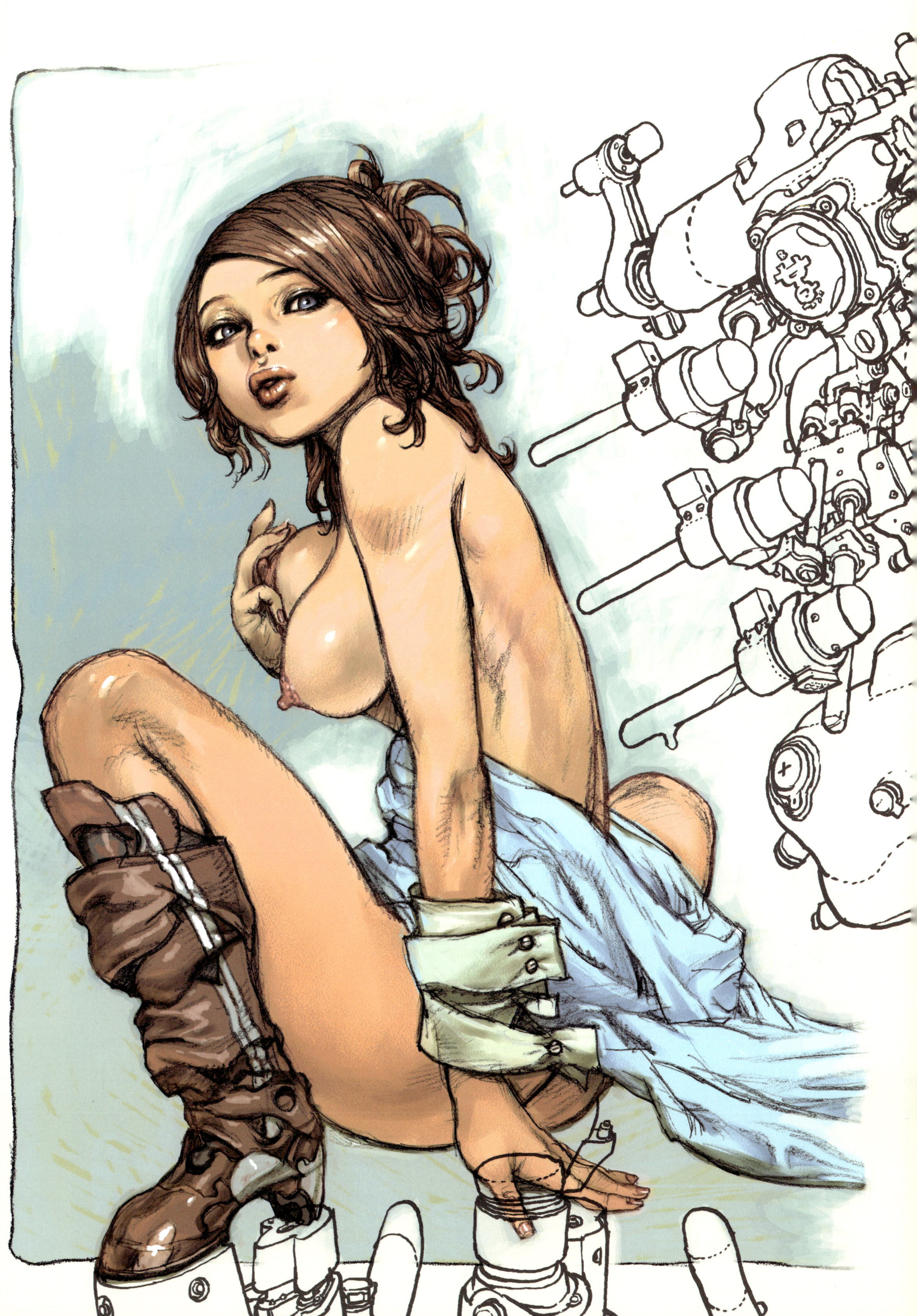

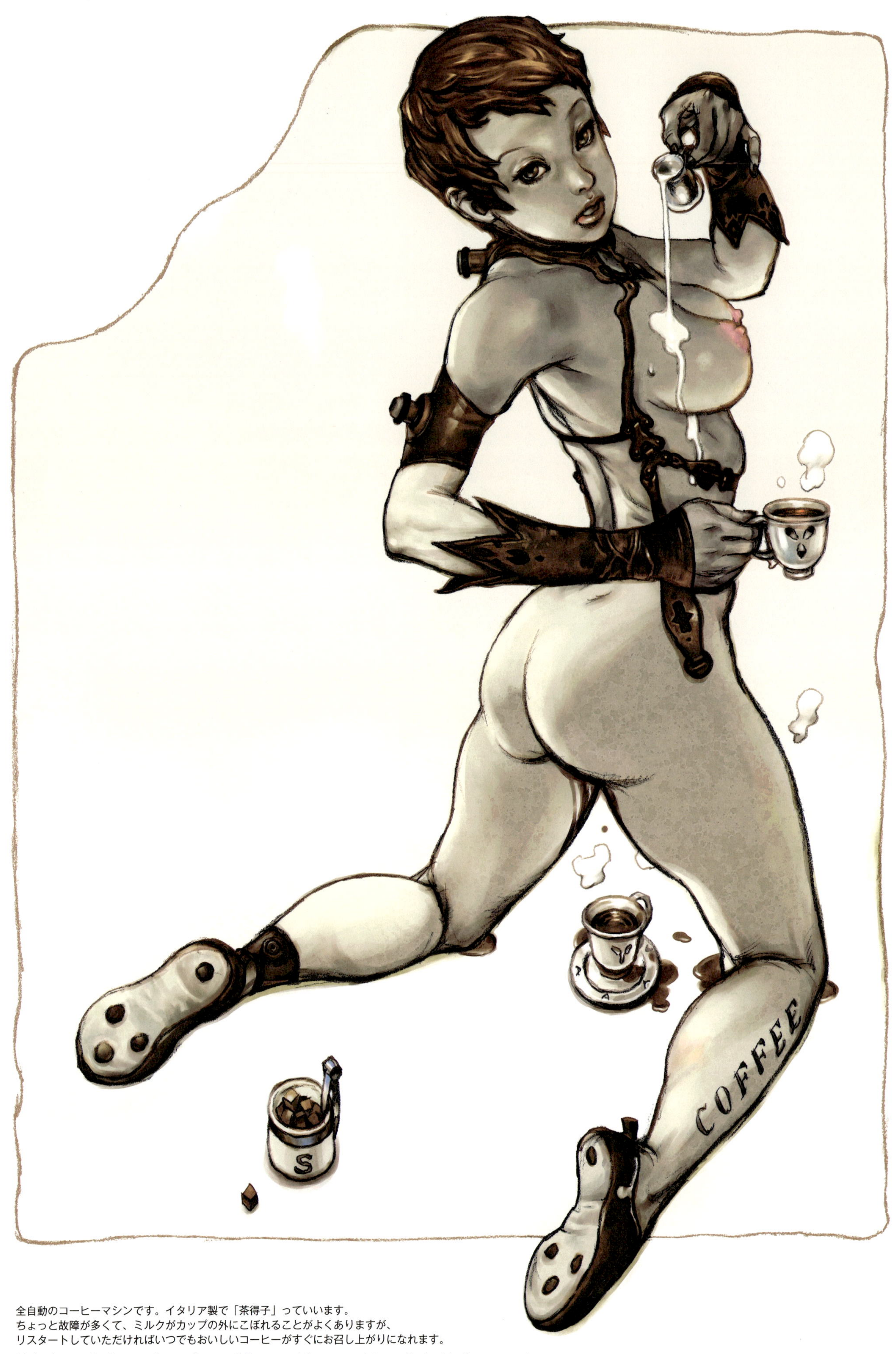

全自動のコーヒーマシンです。イタリア製で「茶得子」っていいます。
ちょっと故障が多くて、ミルクがカップの外にこぼれることがよくありますが、
リスタートしていただければいつでもおいしいコーヒーがすぐにお召し上がりになれます。

This is a fully automatic coffee-making machine. It is Italian-made and its name is "saeco." It often breaks down and milk frequently makes the cup overflow, but if you restart it, you can always and immediately have a nice drink of delicious coffee.

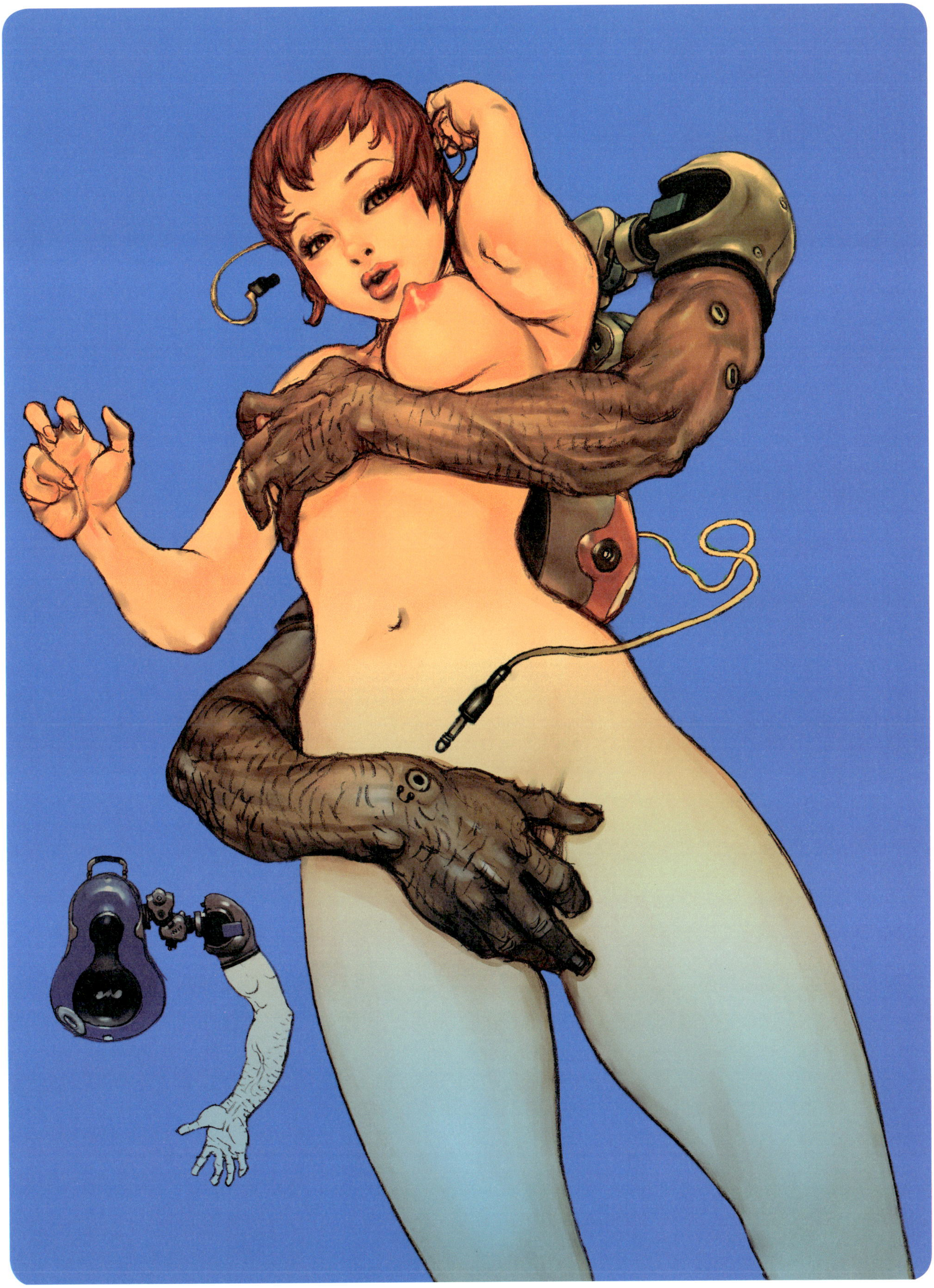

リュックのストラップが、たくましい男性の腕型！ 筋骨隆々の男腕にしっかりホールドされてみませんか？

Backpack straps that are in the shape of a muscular man! How about trying being held tightly by such masculine bulging muscled arms?

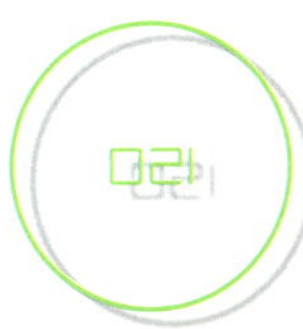

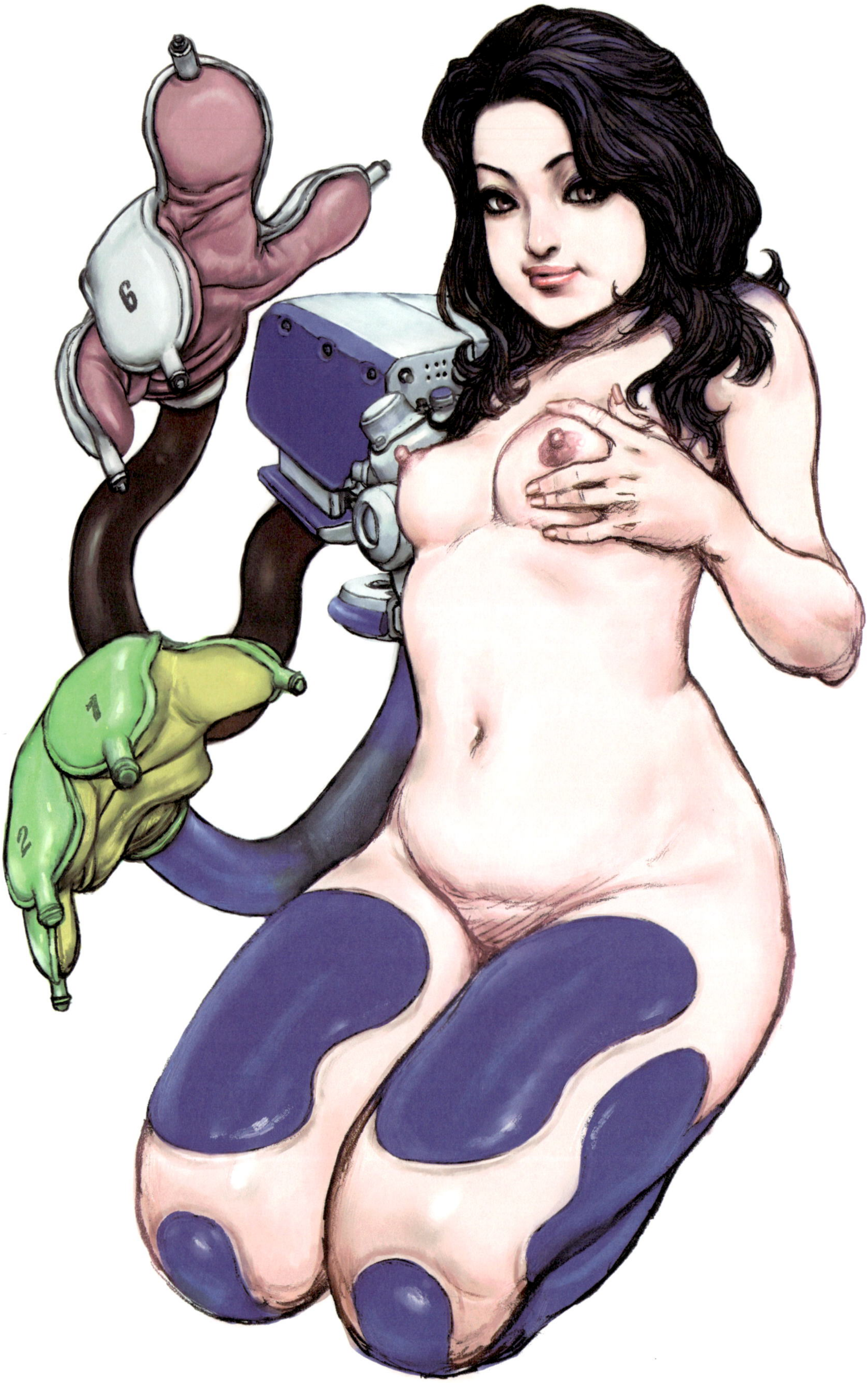

ひざまくらとかしてもらって、やさしく頭を撫でたり揉んでもらうと、ほとんどの中年男性は泣き始めるのではないか。そんな女性型アンドロイドひざまくら「なで子ちゃん」の紹介です。

Don't most middle-aged men start crying when they put their head in a woman's lap and she gently caresses and massages them. This is an introduction to such a female lap-android named "Nade-Ko-chan" [Little Massage Girl].

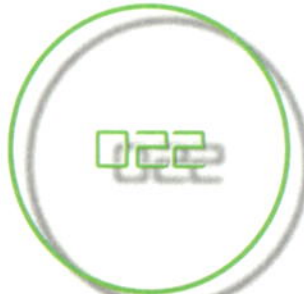

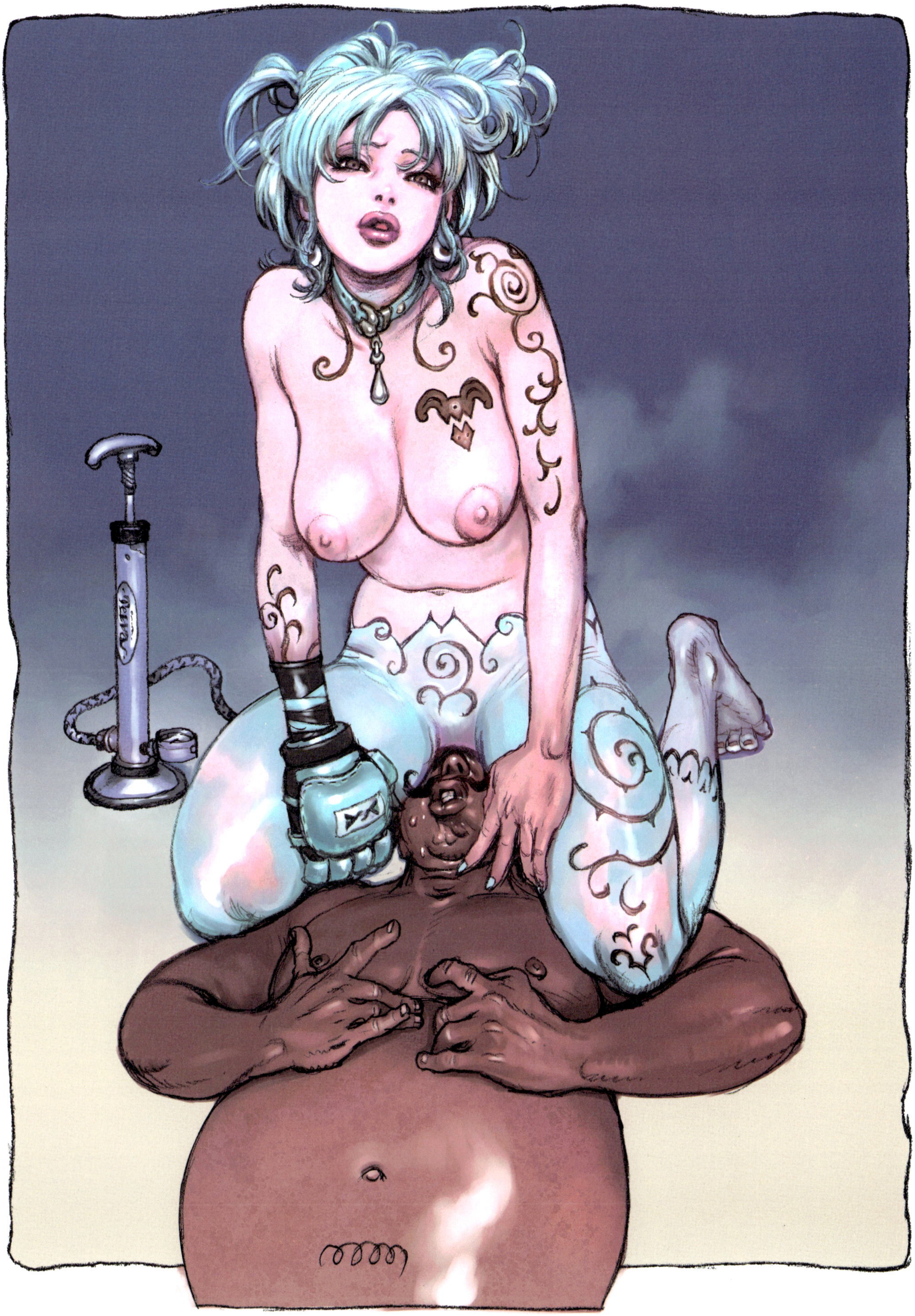

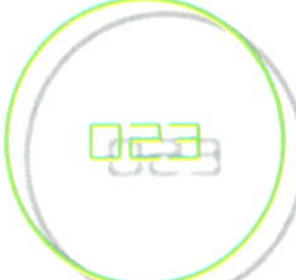
023

個人的な性癖としては縛ったり縛られたりとかでより興奮、ってのはない（ハズ）なんだが
絵的なエロい拘束表現は好きなんである。
ただし裏筋金入りの和姦派としては、あくまでも納得づくの拘束に燃えるのであって無理強いはどんな局面でも不愉快である。

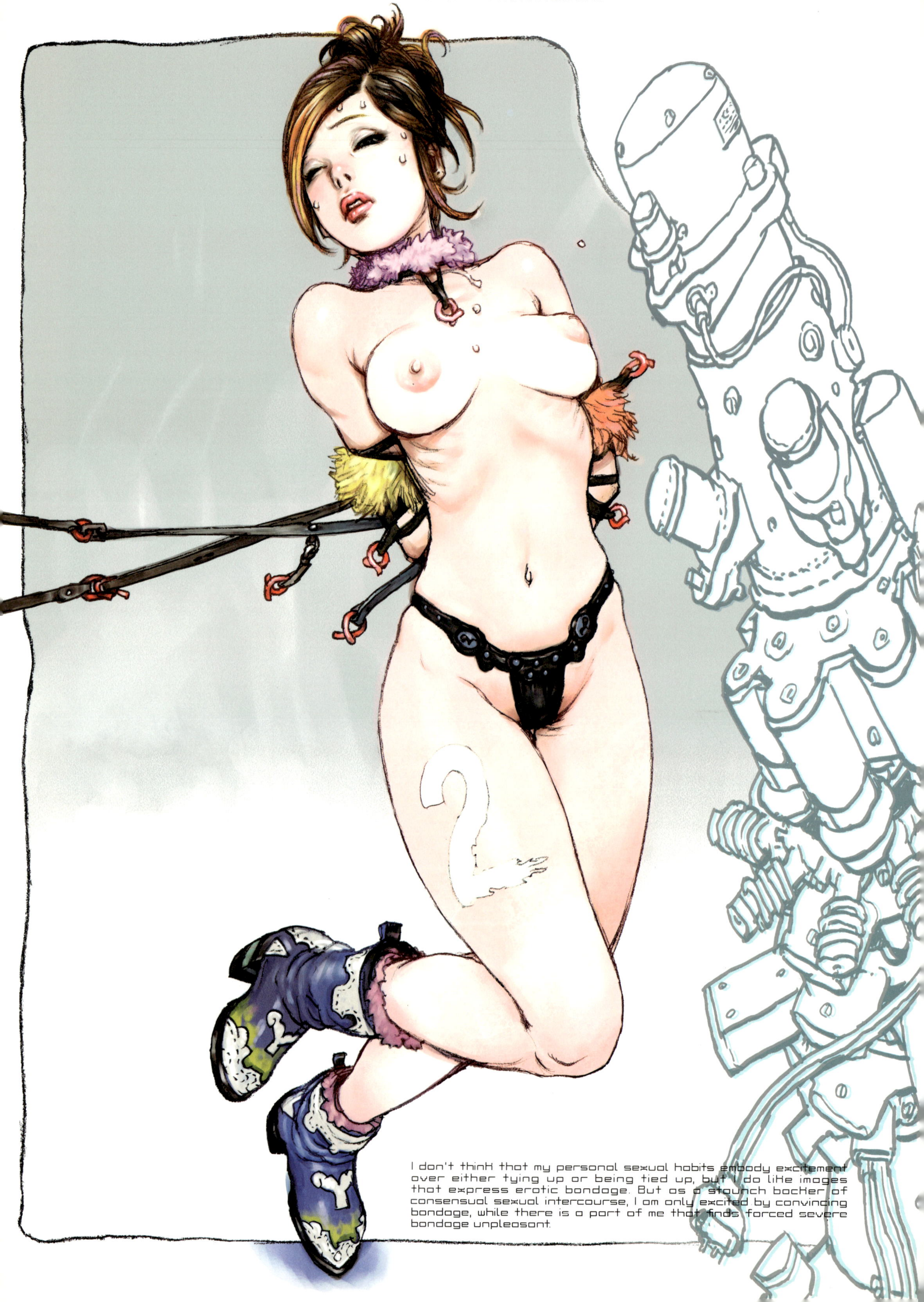

I don't think that my personal sexual habits embody excitement over either tying up or being tied up, but I do like images that express erotic bondage. But as a staunch backer of consensual sexual intercourse, I am only excited by convincing bondage, while there is a part of me that finds forced severe bondage unpleasant.

シゴトに疲れるとネットで拾ってきた肌色の写真をスケッチしたりトレースしたりして遊ぶ。
ネットには無修正がフリーであふれてて、時代は無修正だなーと思った。
てゆーか無修正に見慣れてくると、モザイクとか乗ってるほうがなんか不思議だ。

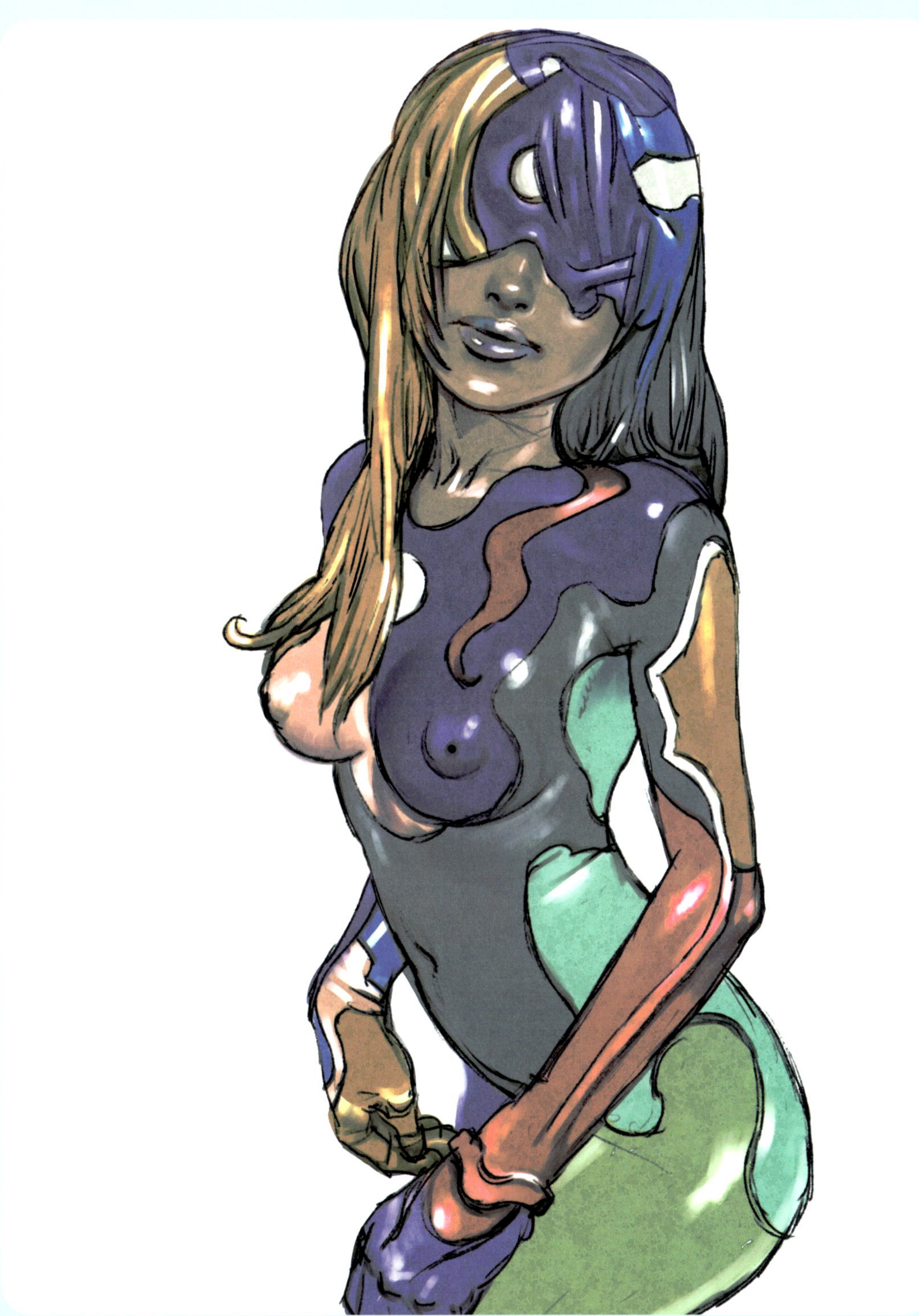

When I get tired of work, I pick up flesh-colored photos from the internet and enjoy myself sketching and tracing them.
The internet is full of uncensored images, giving me the feeling that this is the age of no censorship.
Or maybe it would be best to say that when you get used to no censorship, it makes images with mosaics seem strange.

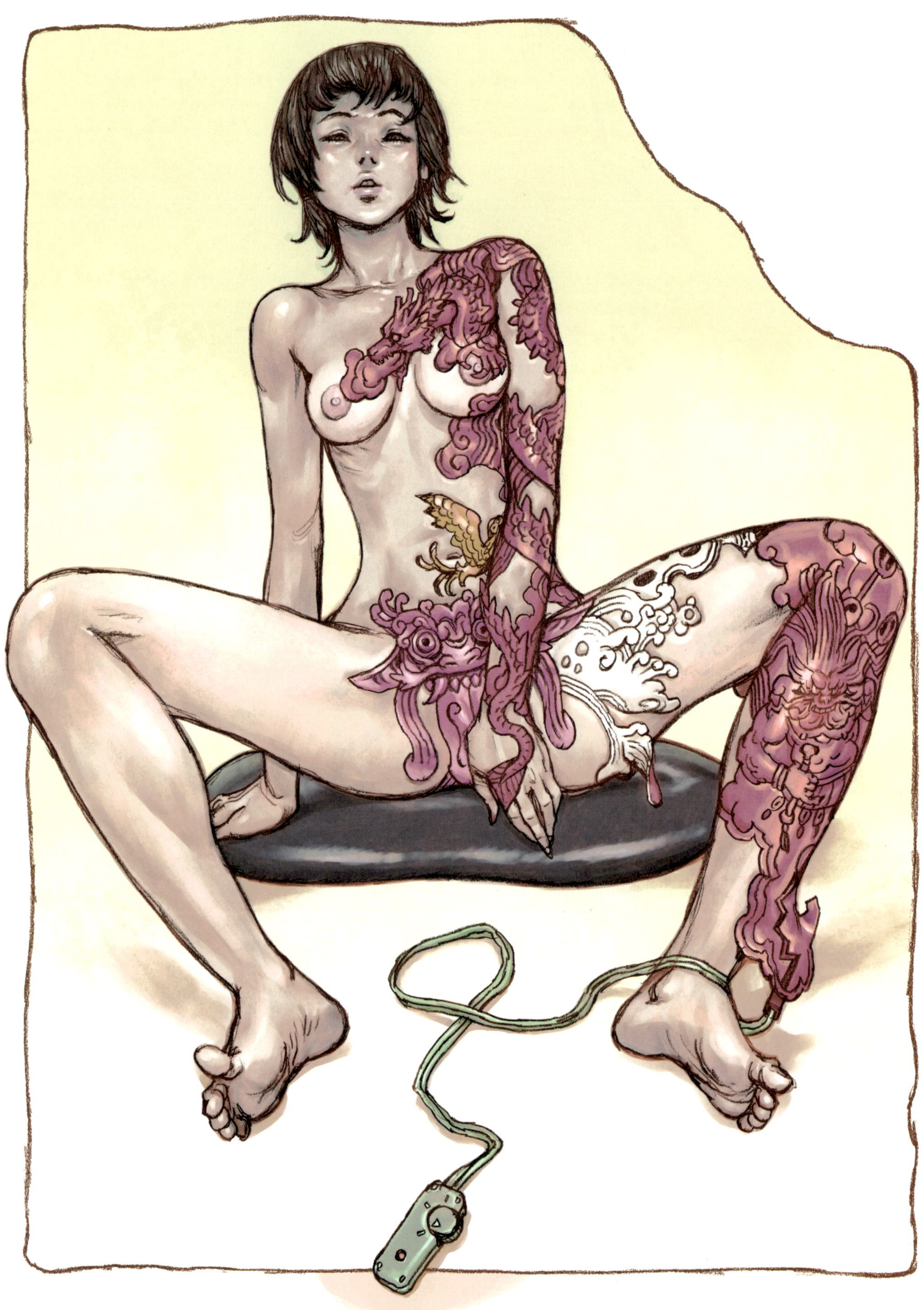

コンニャクを筆頭に、オナホだ、TENGA だと男のオナニーへの飽くなき探求心の持つ熱量は凄いので
なんとか発電に使えないものかと昔から考えてた。エコだし。このご時世ですしね。

Using devil's tongue jelly [Konnyaku] or Ono-ho [Onanism hole] or TENGA for masturbation by men has always been an endless source of passionate curiosity for me, and I used to wonder whether it couldn't be used to generate electricity. It's a very ecological idea. And with the times as they are today.

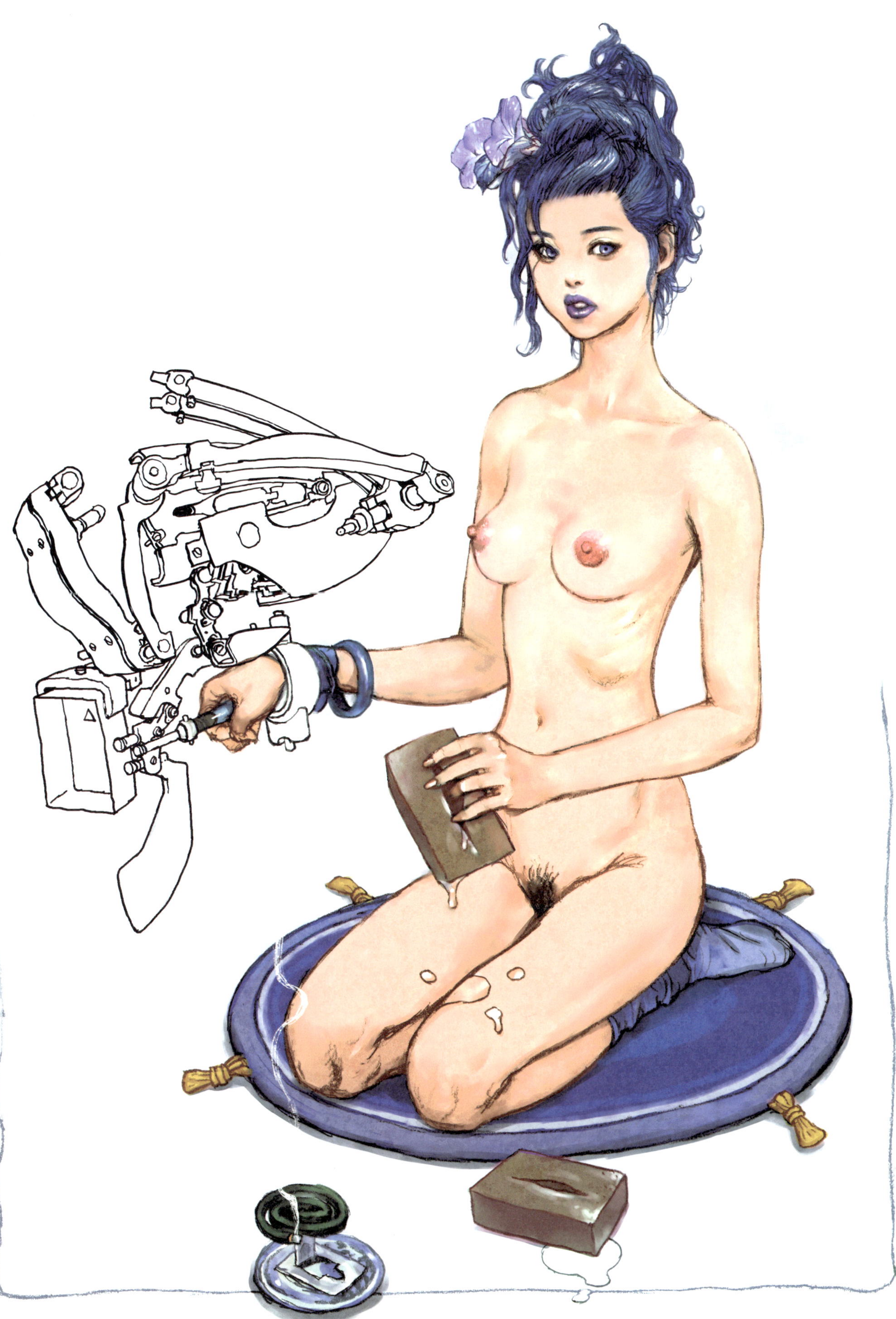

オレのリビドーの目覚めは永井豪「マジンガーZ」のあしゅら男爵のシャワーシーンなわけですが
キャラに燃えたのは「あばしり一家」の十兵衛です。イメージとしてはこんなカンジだ！
半裸でアクションとか無防備過ぎて最高だ。これは「映画秘宝」のカバーとして描いた絵ですが
表紙ではおっぱい出せないので、ブラつけてましたがこの本の為に取ってみた。
今でこそ本屋に並ぶ本の表紙からおっぱいが消えましたが、オレが子供の頃は通学路にふつーに
にっかつロマンポルノのポスターが貼ってあった。たまらなかった。

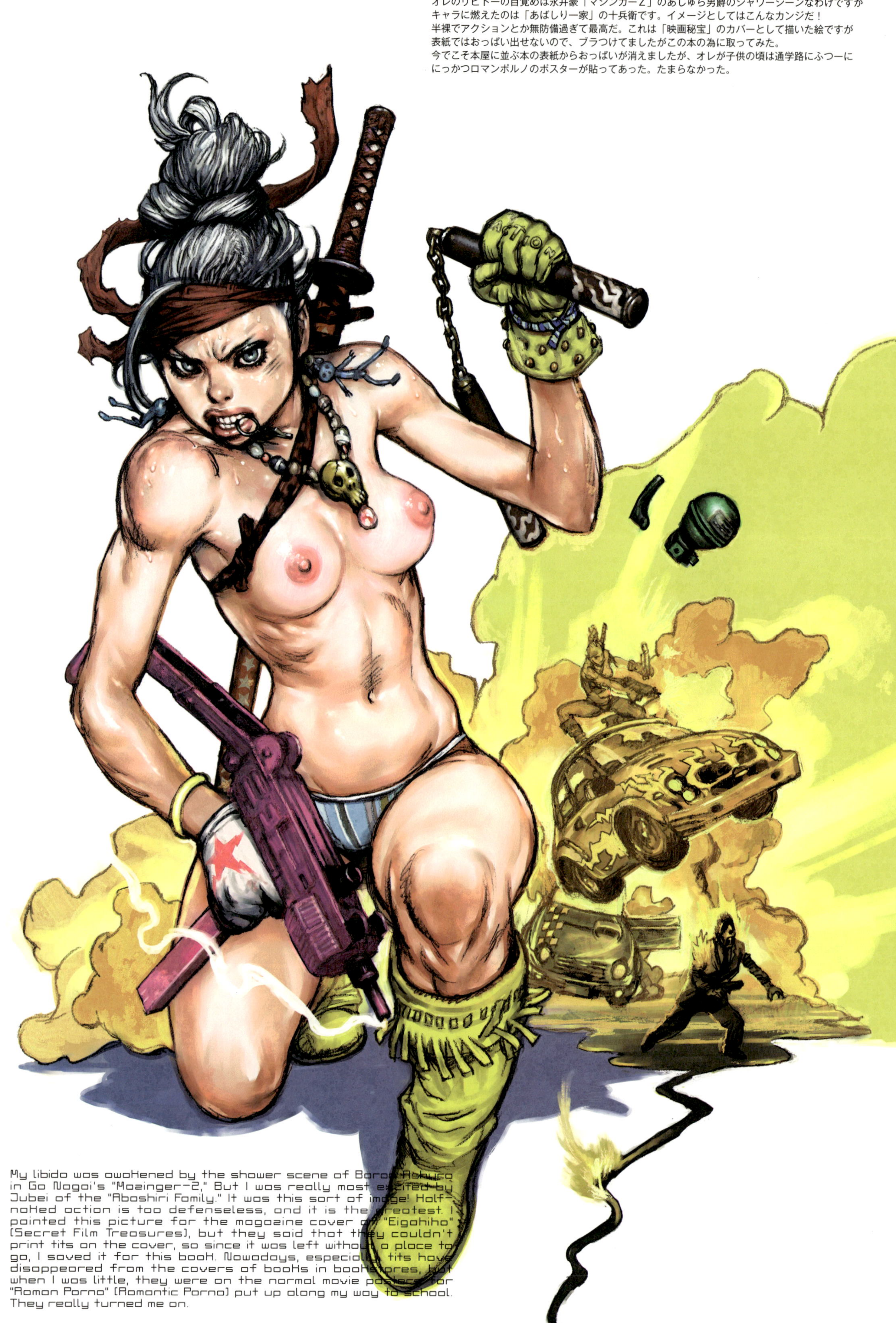

My libido was awakened by the shower scene of Baron Ashura in Go Nagai's "Mazinger-Z," But I was really most excited by Jubei of the "Abashiri Family." It was this sort of image! Half-naked action is too defenseless, and it is the greatest. I painted this picture for the magazine cover of "Eigahiho" [Secret Film Treasures], but they said that they couldn't print tits on the cover, so since it was left without a place to go, I saved it for this book. Nowadays, especially, tits have disappeared from the covers of books in bookstores, but when I was little, they were on the normal movie posters for "Roman Porno" [Romantic Porno] put up along my way to school. They really turned me on.

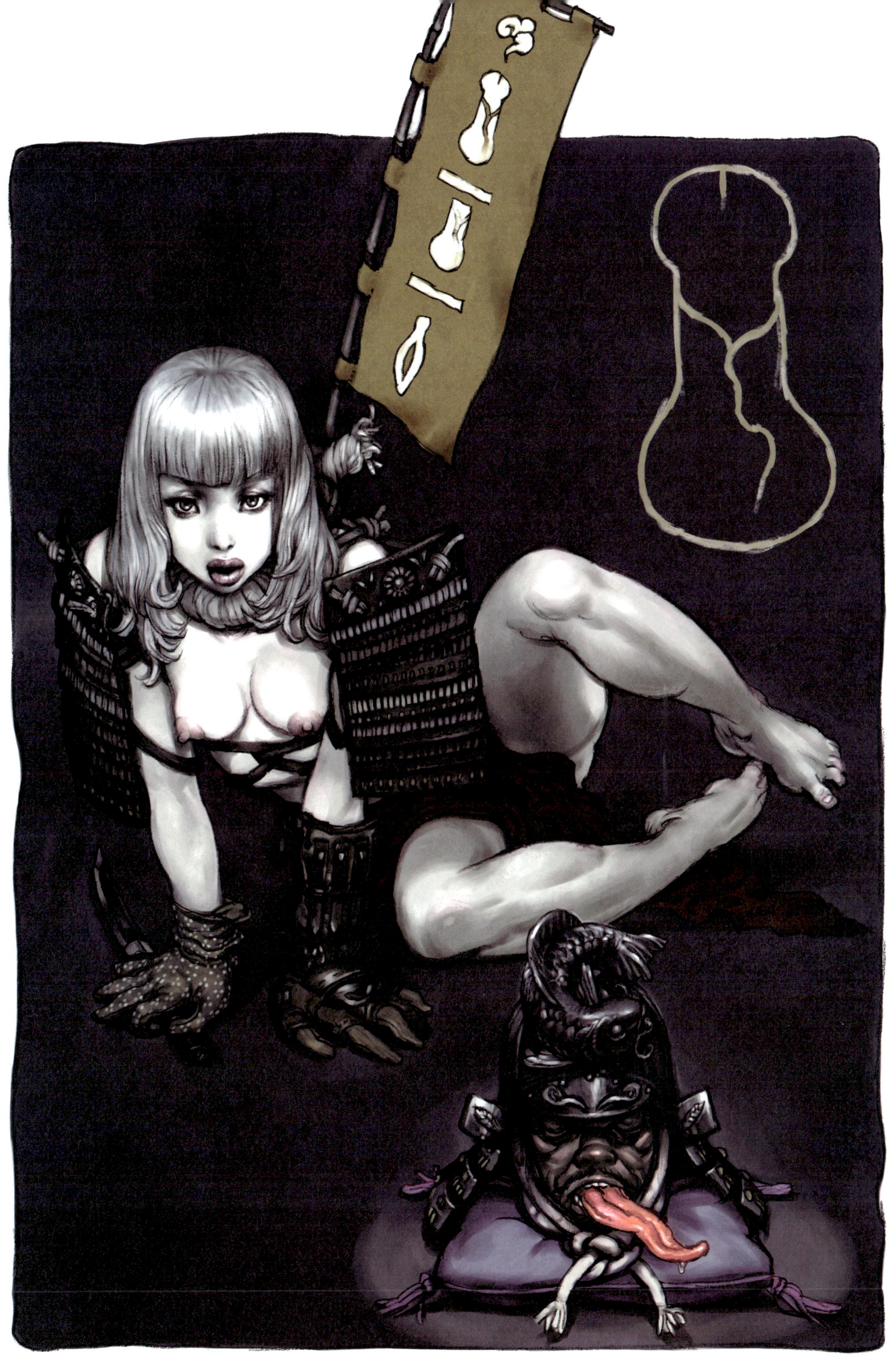

ニッポンはサムライの国です！ まー人口の８割は農民だったので現在生きてる日本国民のほとんども農民の血筋だと思うんだけど、ちいさいことはおいといて世界は侍が大好き！
武者姿でエロはなおさら好きだ！ 死してなお舐めようとする大和魂に世界が嗚咽と我慢汁を流したといいます。

Japan is a nation of samurai! Well, but I think that since more than 80% of the population used to be farmers, the majority of the nations citizens still have farmer's blood in their veins. But, leaving such details aside, the world totally loves the samurai! They love eroticism even more when it is done dressed as a samurai! The Yamato Spirit of trying to lick even in the face of death is said to elicit groans and draw out pre-cum.

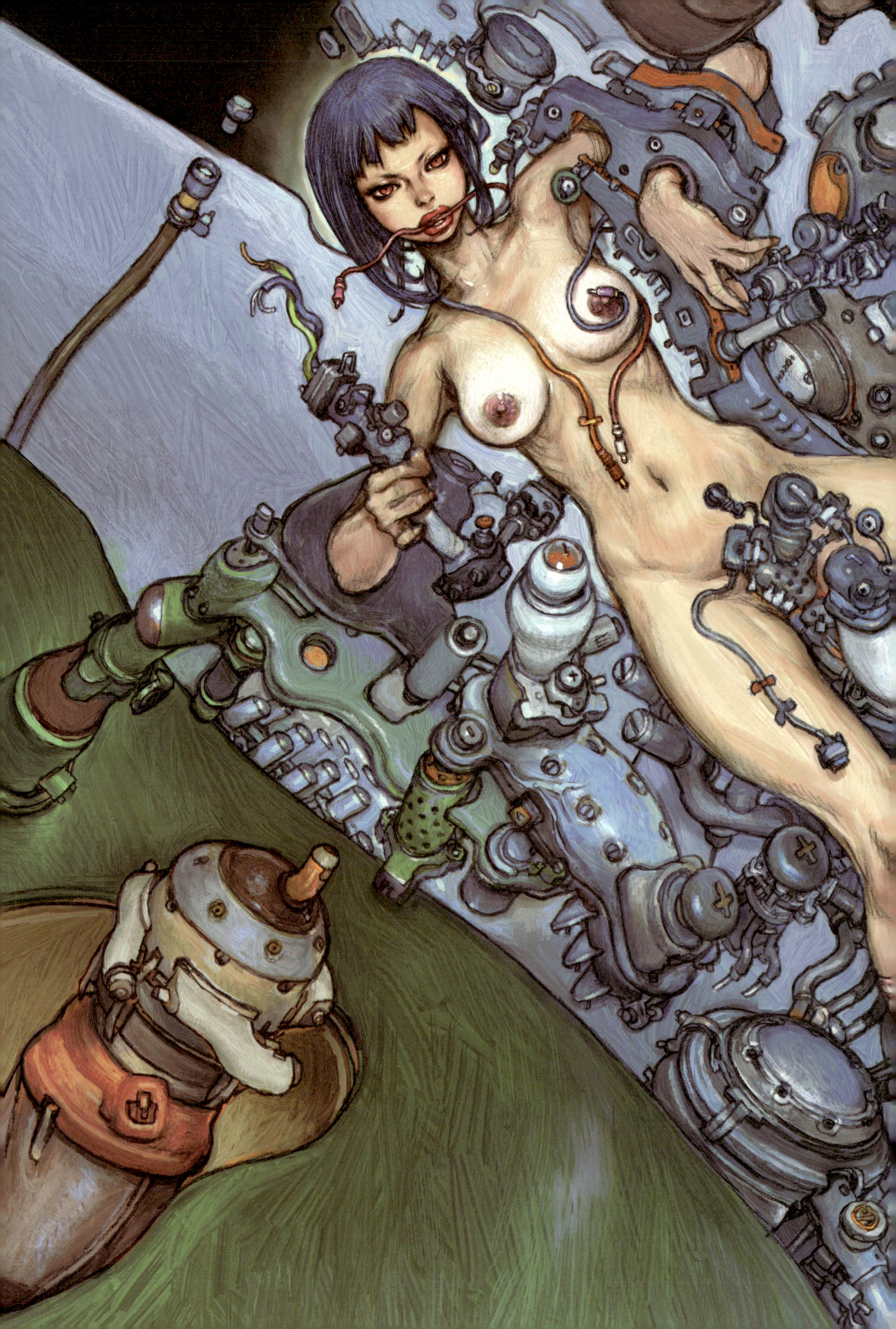

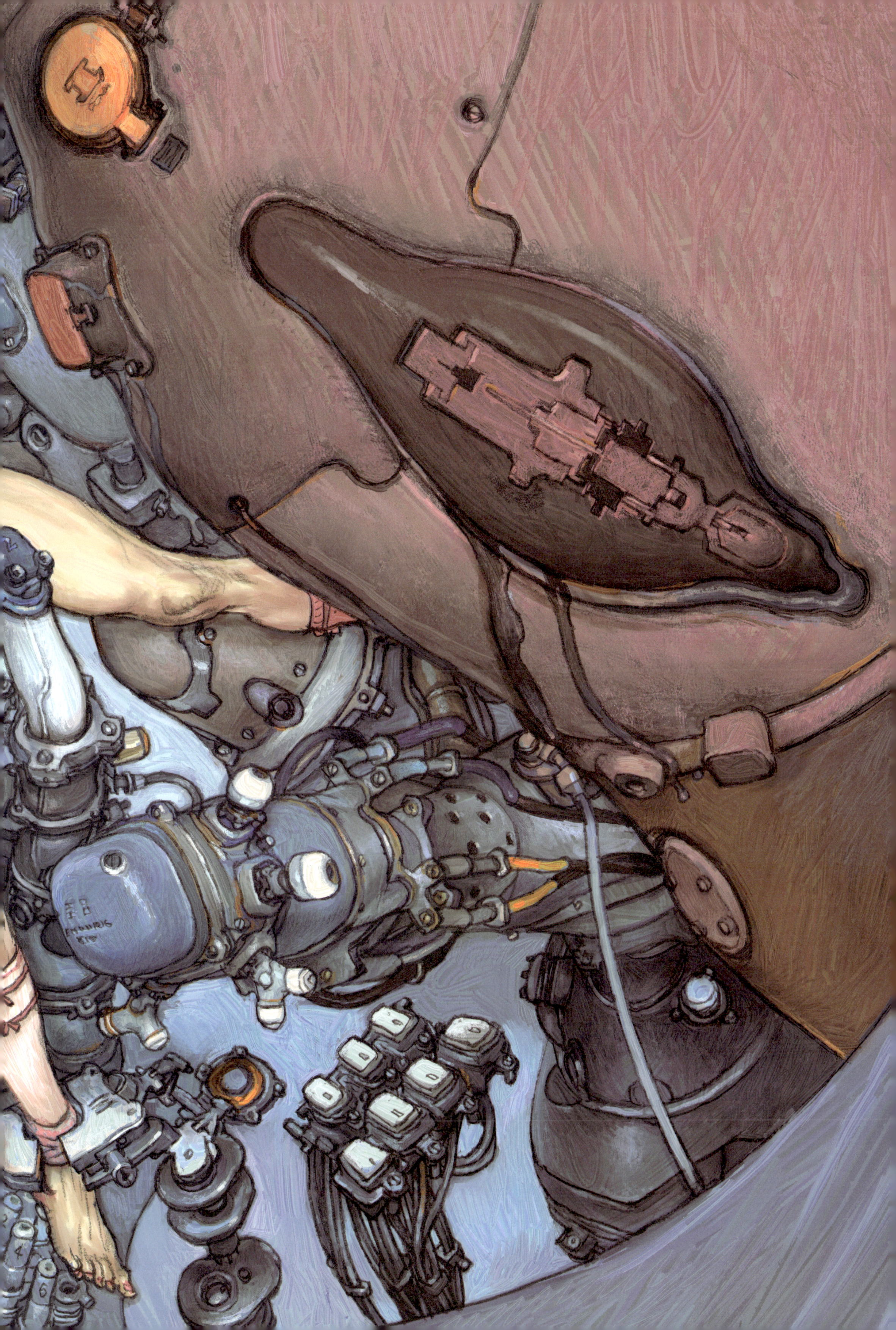

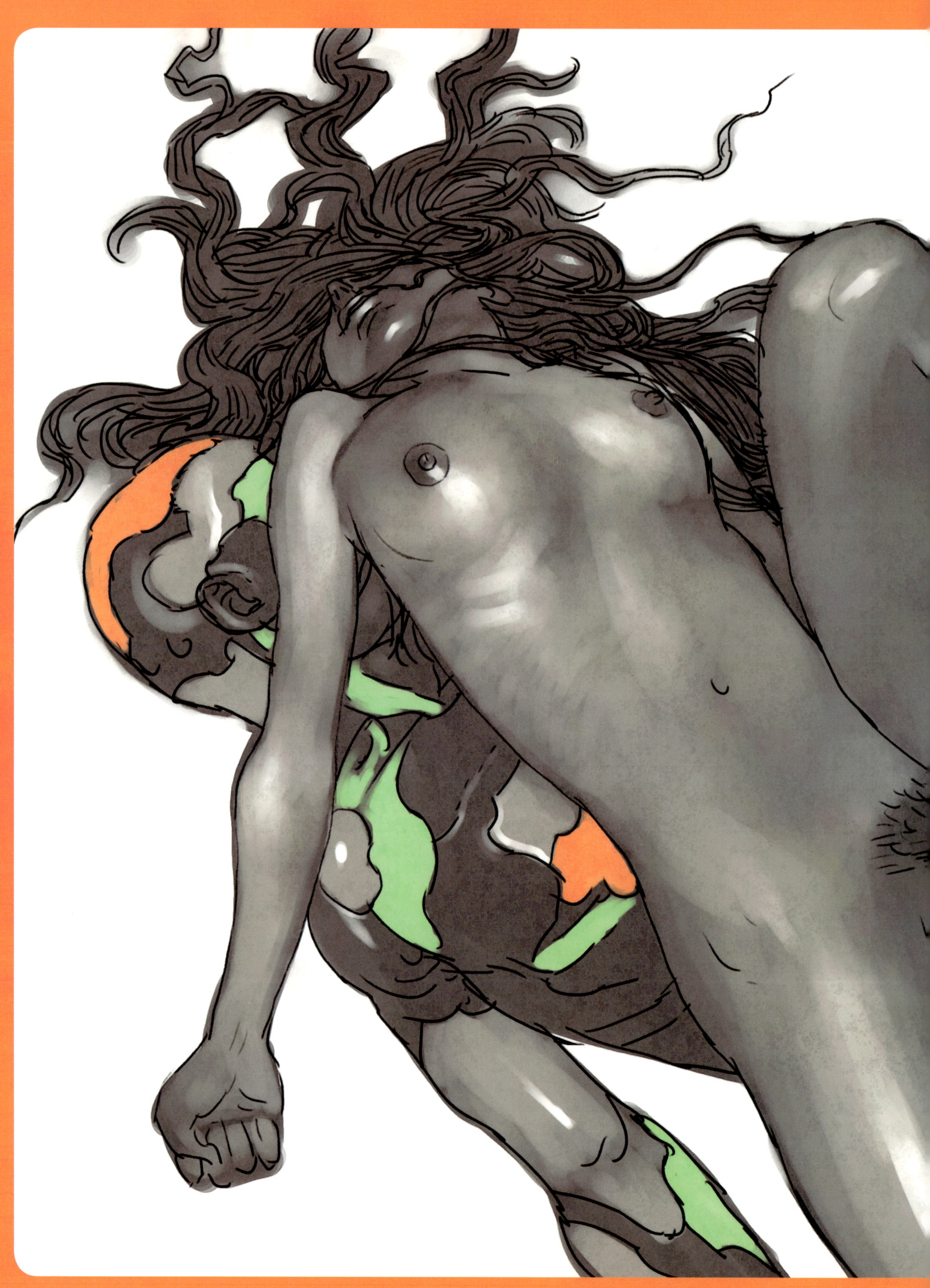

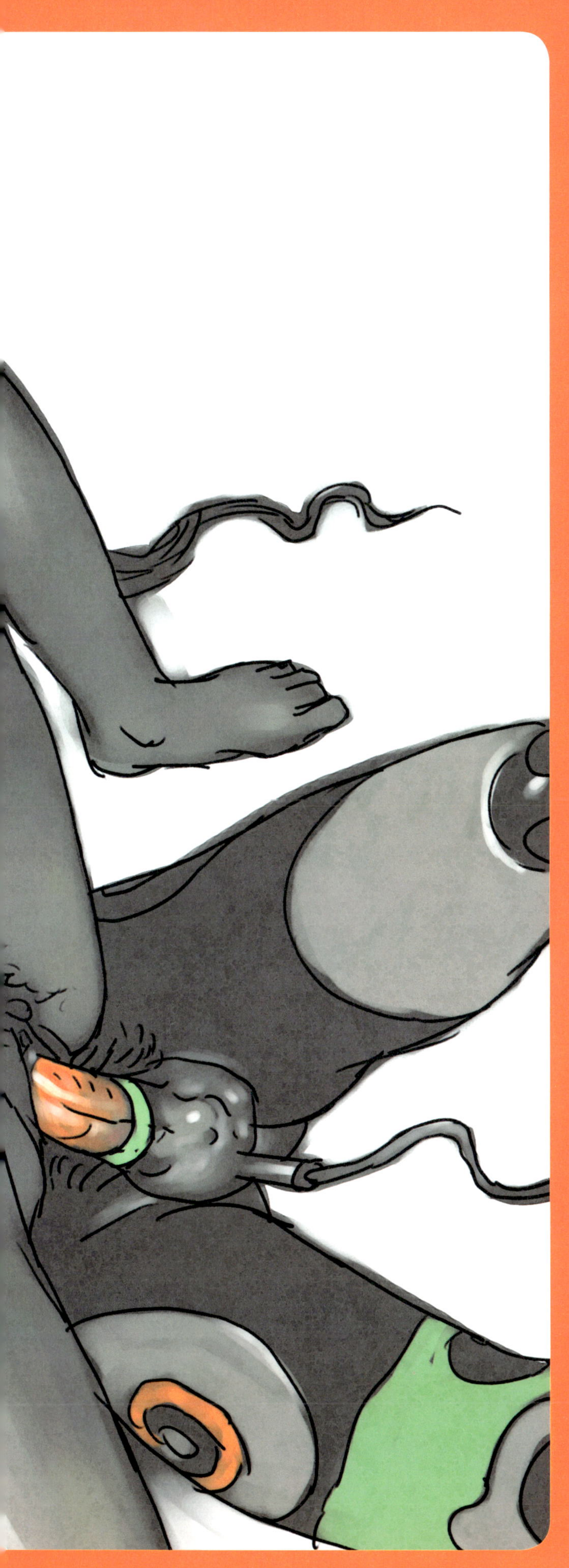

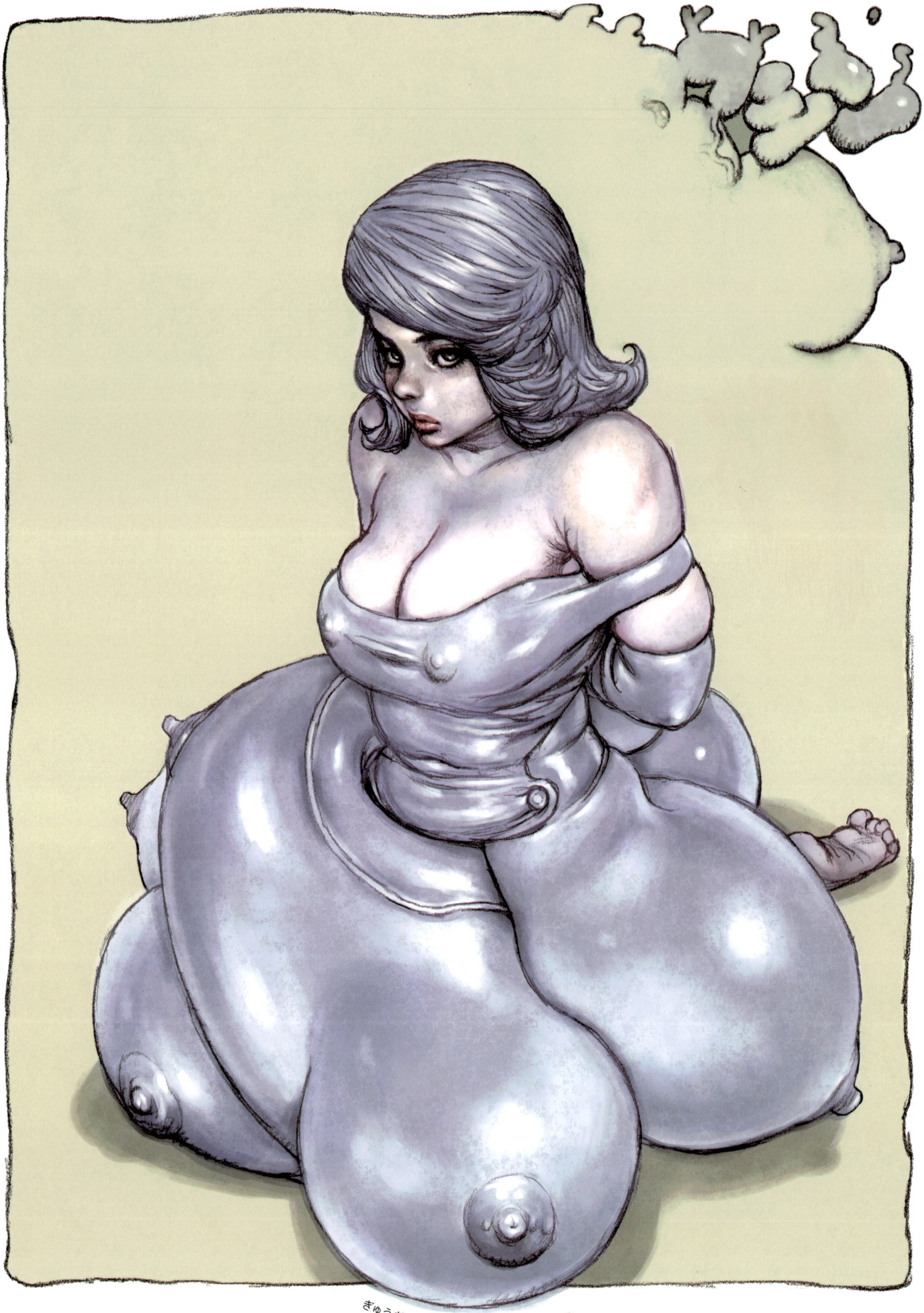

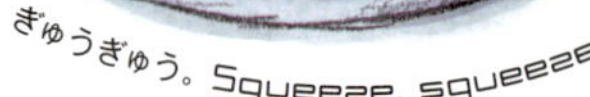
ぎゅうぎゅう。Squeeze, squeeze.

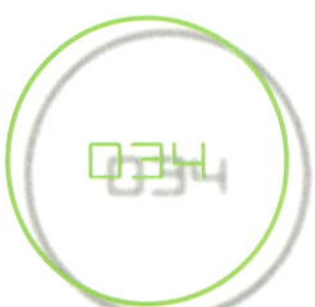

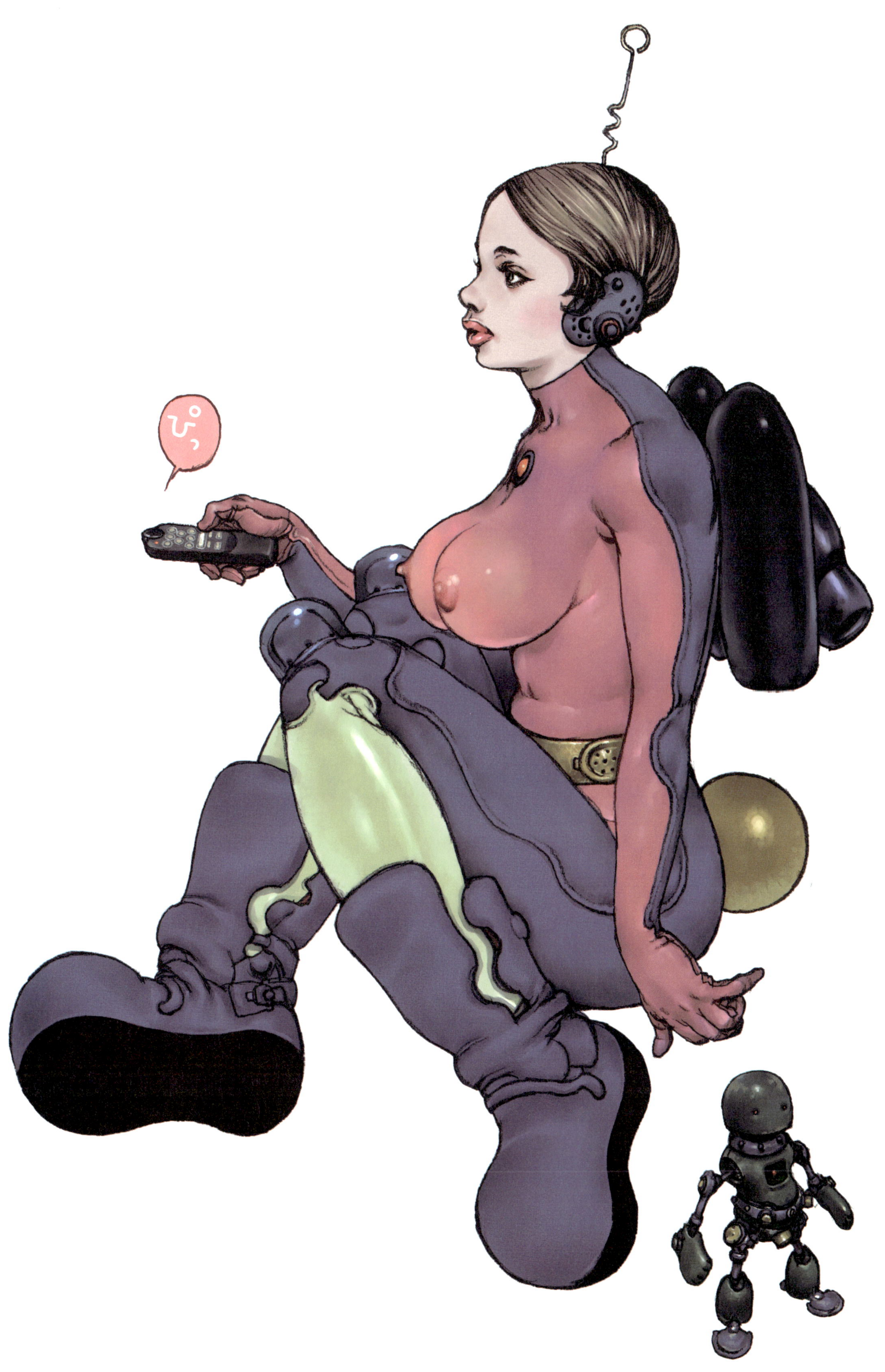
ぴっ

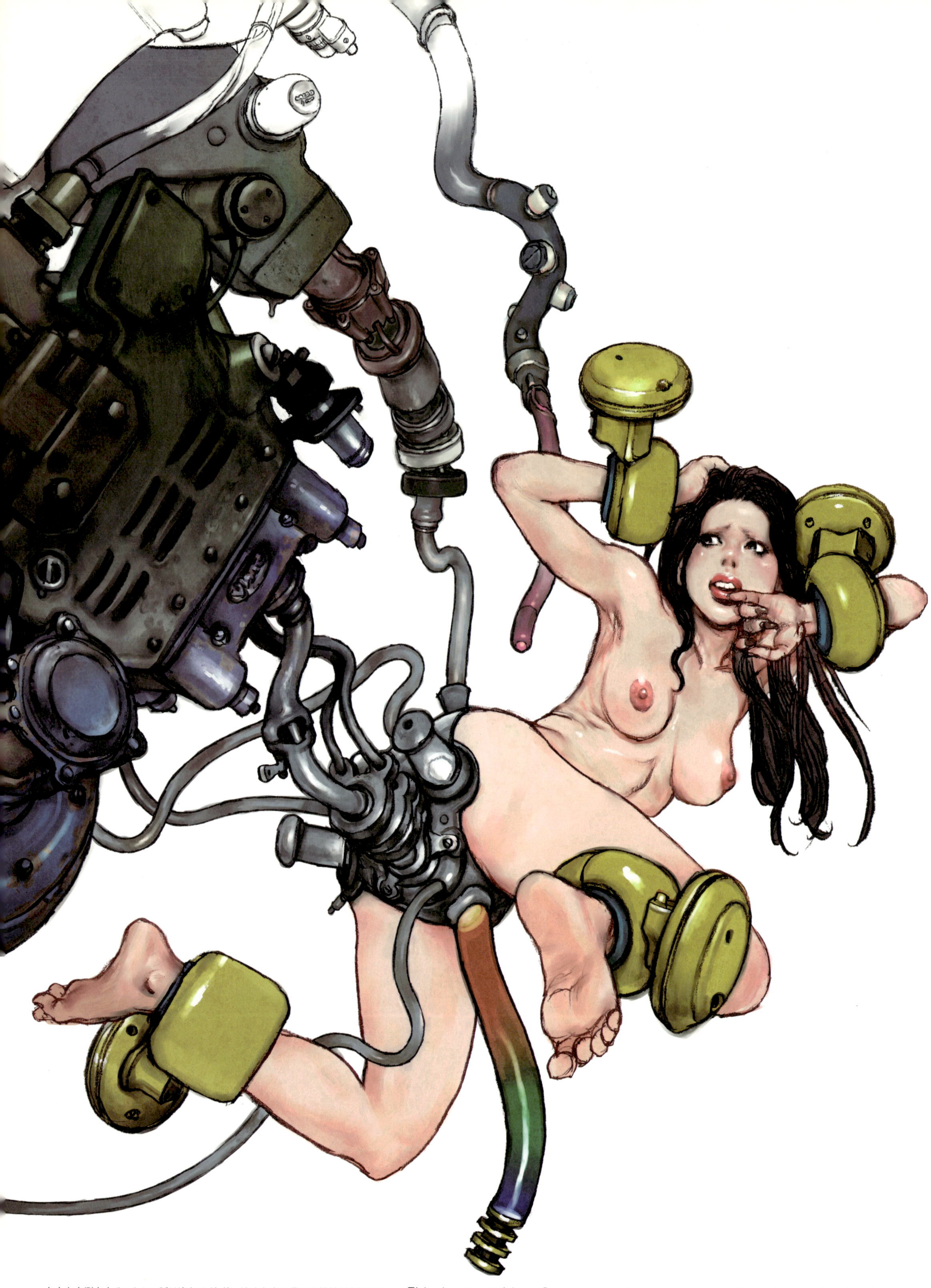

なんかを測定するマシン。話は逸れるが、使い込まれた工業用の機械が大好きだ！たまらない！
鋳造された筐体のガワが、べったりペンキで塗装されてて、経年劣化でペンキが剥げたところから地金が鈍く光ってたり、錆びてたりすると最高。なんかエロい。

This is a machine for measuring something. This is a bit off the subject, but I really like industrial machines that have been used a lot! They really turn me on! The main body is made from a mold and has been covered with thick paint and after years of use the paint has chipped off to show the dull bare metal beneath, and such machines are best if they are rusted. Somehow it seems erotic to me.

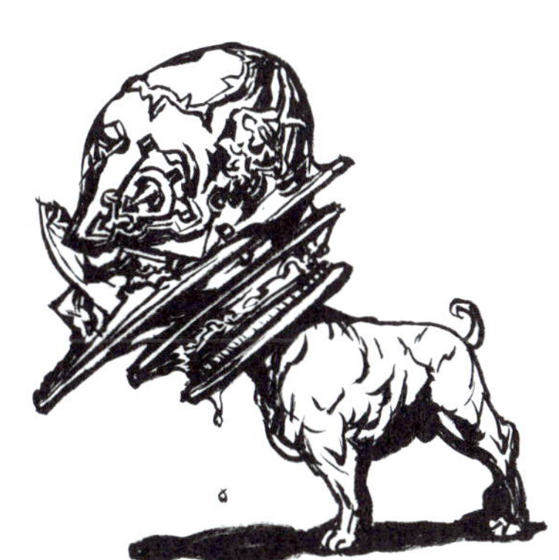

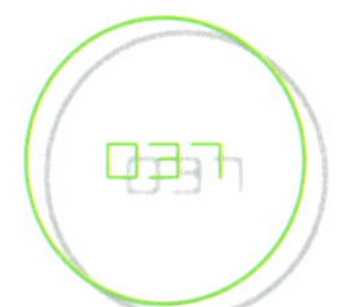

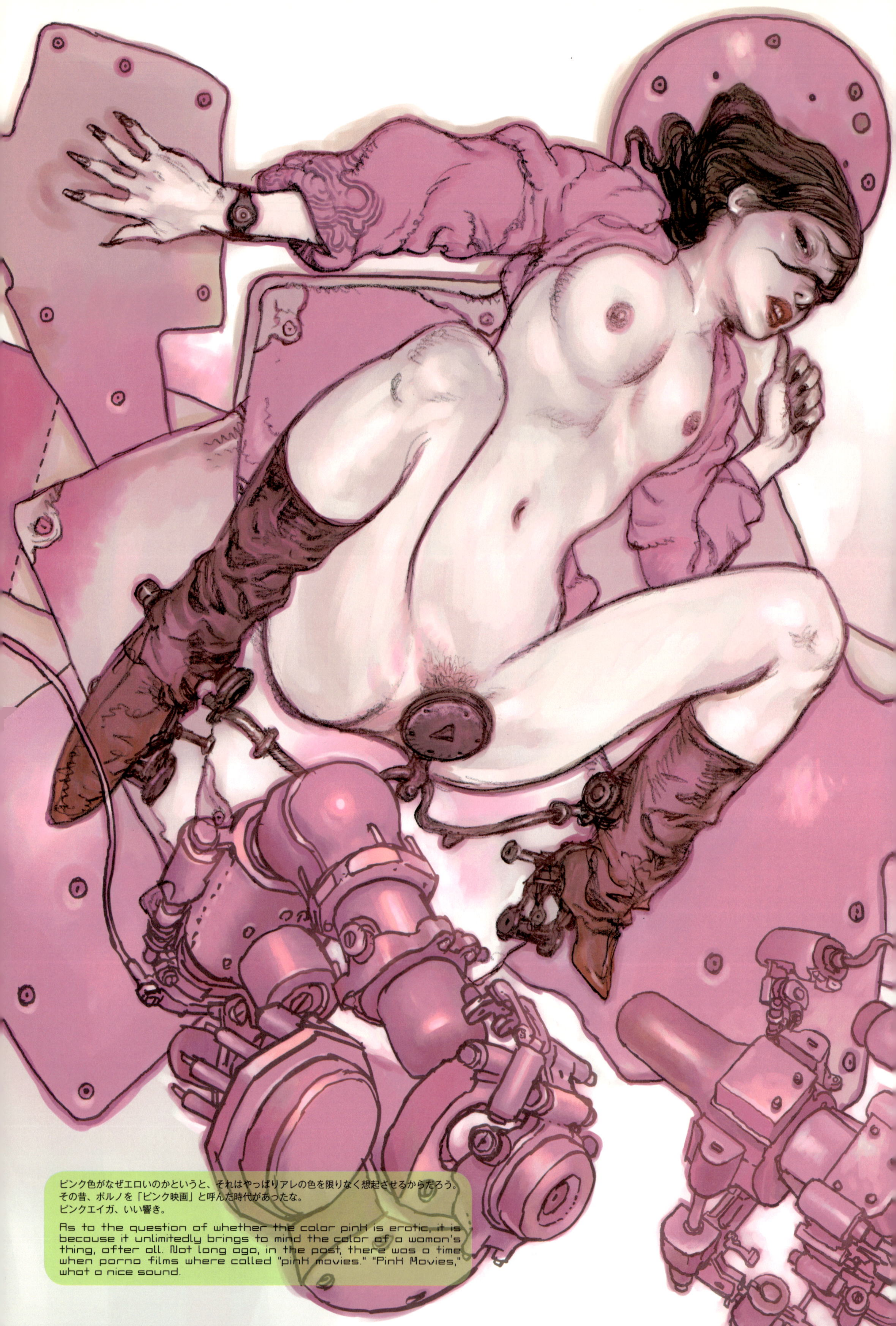

ピンク色がなぜエロいのかというと、それはやっぱりアレの色を限りなく想起させるからだろう。
その昔、ポルノを「ピンク映画」と呼んだ時代があったな。
ピンクエイガ、いい響き。

As to the question of whether the color pink is erotic, it is becouse it unlimitedly brings to mind the color of a woman's thing, after all. Not long ago, in the past, there was a time when porno films where called "pink movies." "Pink Movies," what a nice sound.

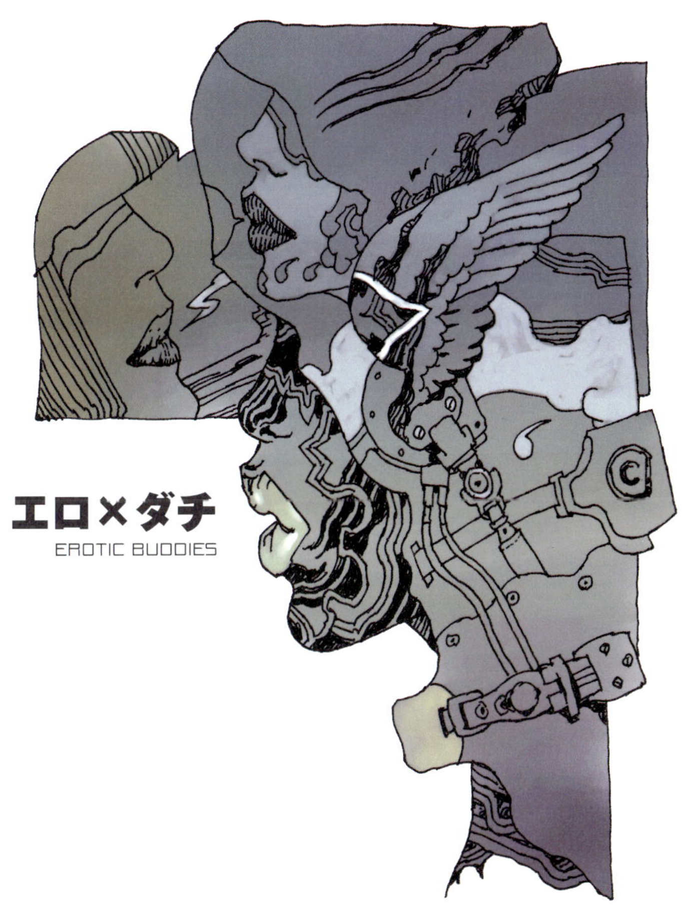

エロ×ダチ

EROTIC BUDDIES

エロ×ガキ コラージュ (pp.40-49)
河村康輔（コラージュ・アーチスト）
Erotic Kids
Collages by Kosuke Kawamura in collaboration with Katsuya Terada [pp40-49]
Kosuke Kawamura [Collage Arist]

エロ×ガキ コラージュ（pp.50-55）
寺田 克也
Erotic Kids
Collages by Katsuya Terada [pp.50-55]

エロ×ダチ (pp.56-57)
空山基（ピンナップ・マスター）
Erotic Buddies [pp.56-57]
Graffiti by Katsuya Terada on works by Hajime Sorayama
Hajime Sorayama [Master of Pinup Art]

エロ×ダチ (pp.58-59)
うしじまいい肉（グラビアアイドル・プロデューサー／服飾ブランド「PredatorRat」プロデューサー）
Erotic Buddies [pp.58-59]
Graffiti by Katsuya Terada on Ushijima Iiniku's portrait
Iiniku Ushijima [Photogravure idol producer|clothing and accessory brand "PredatorRat"producer]

* We wish to express our gratitude to Hajime Sorayama, Iiniku Ushijima, and Kosuke Kawamura for their kind cooperation

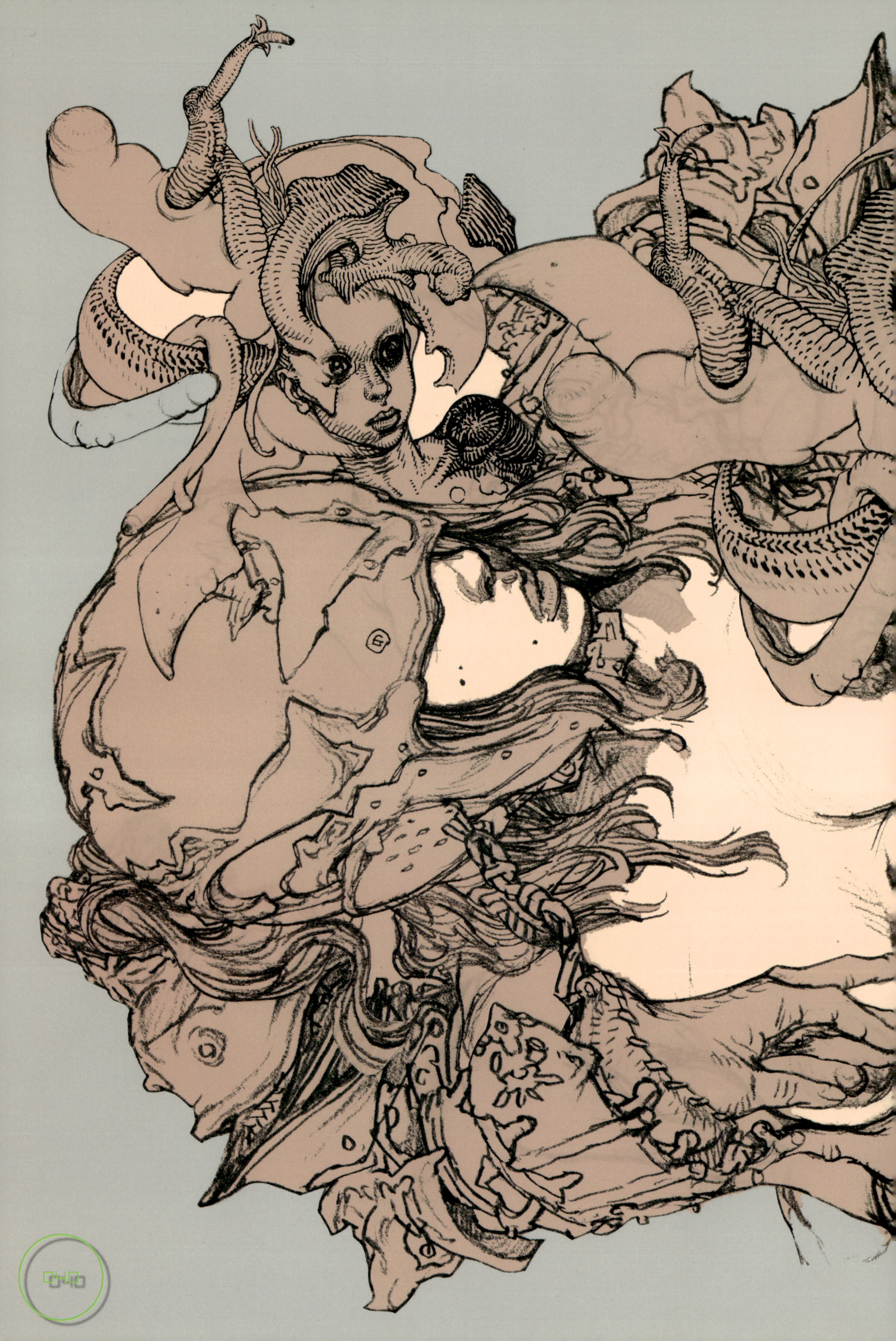

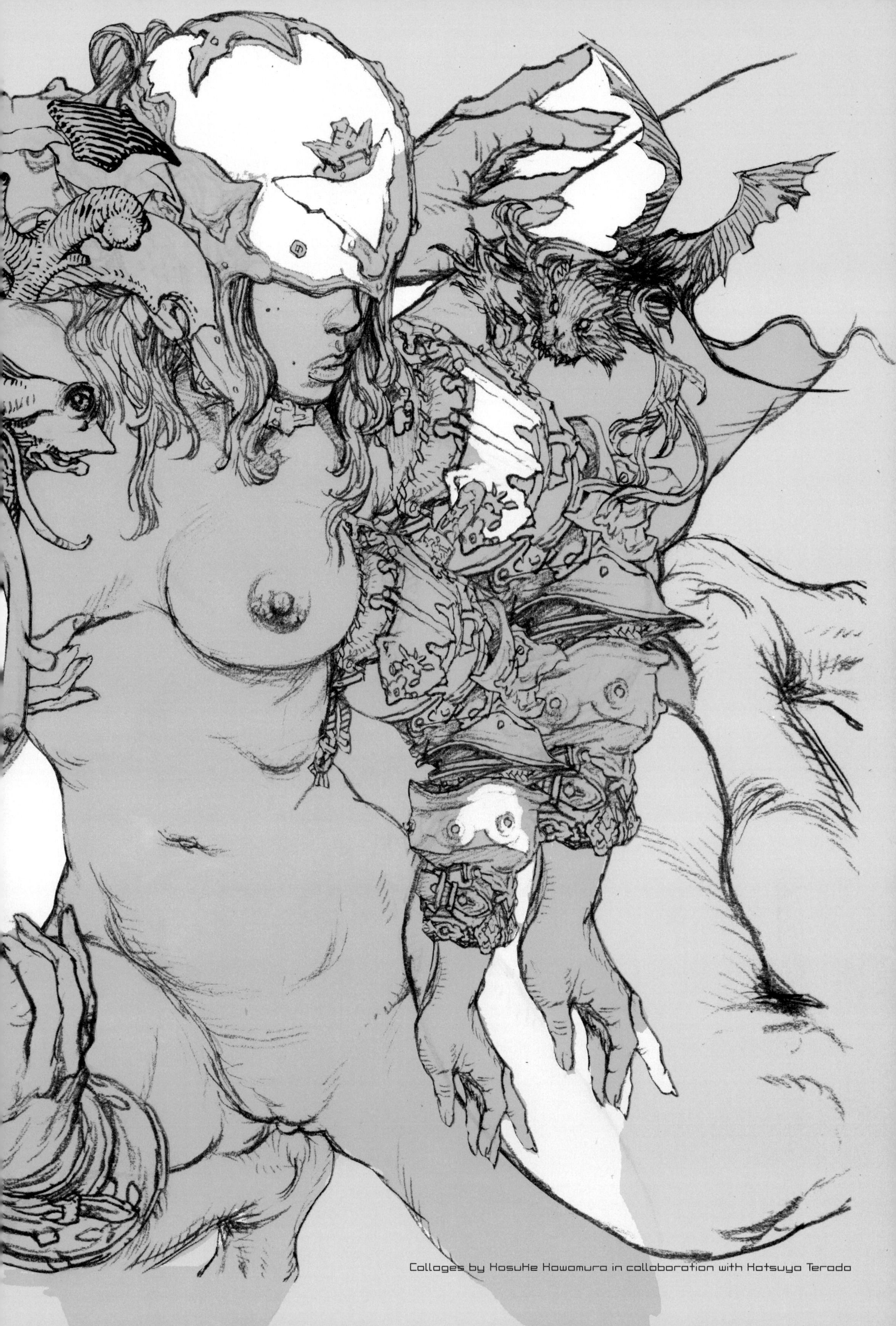

Collages by Kosuke Kawamura in collaboration with Katsuya Terada

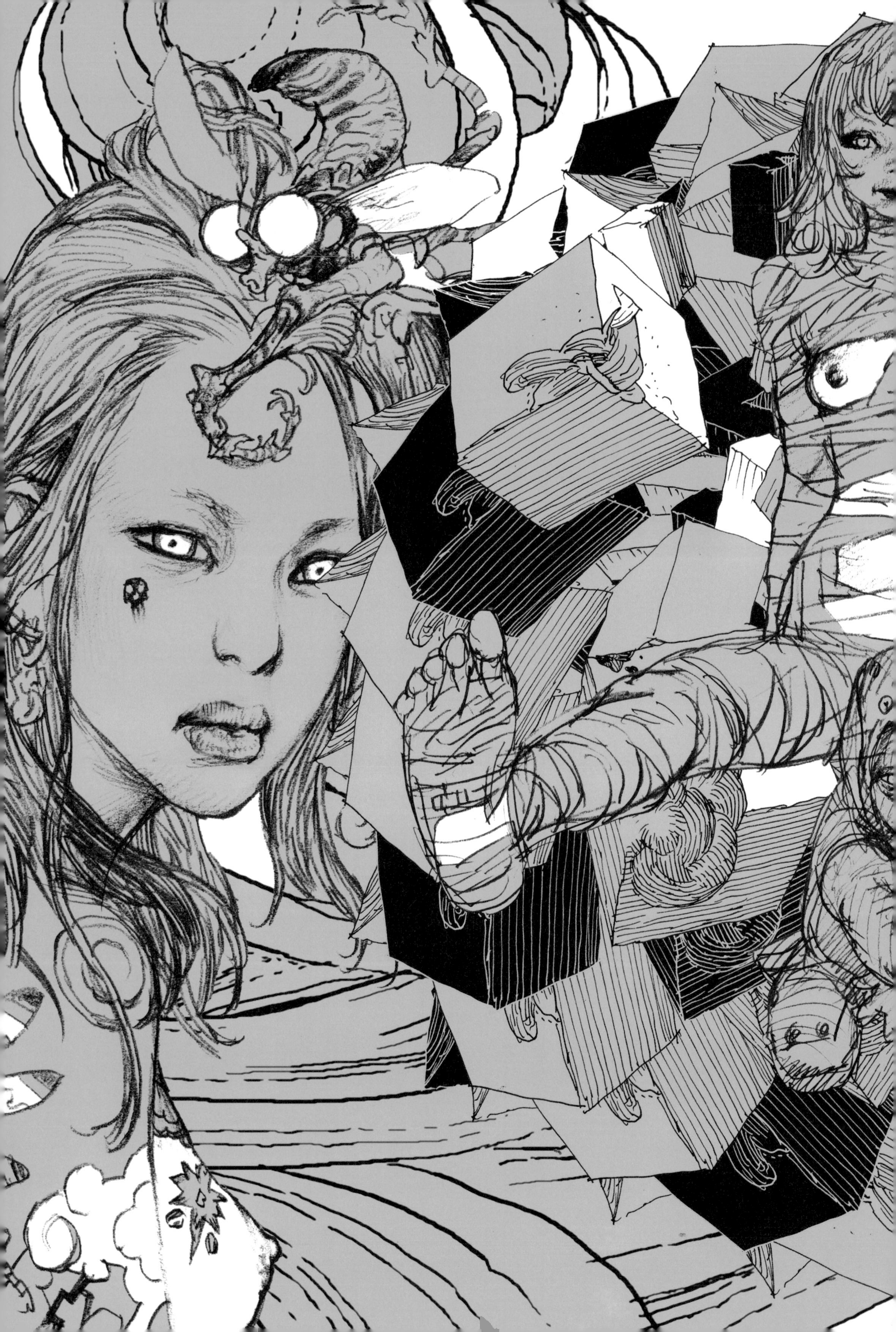

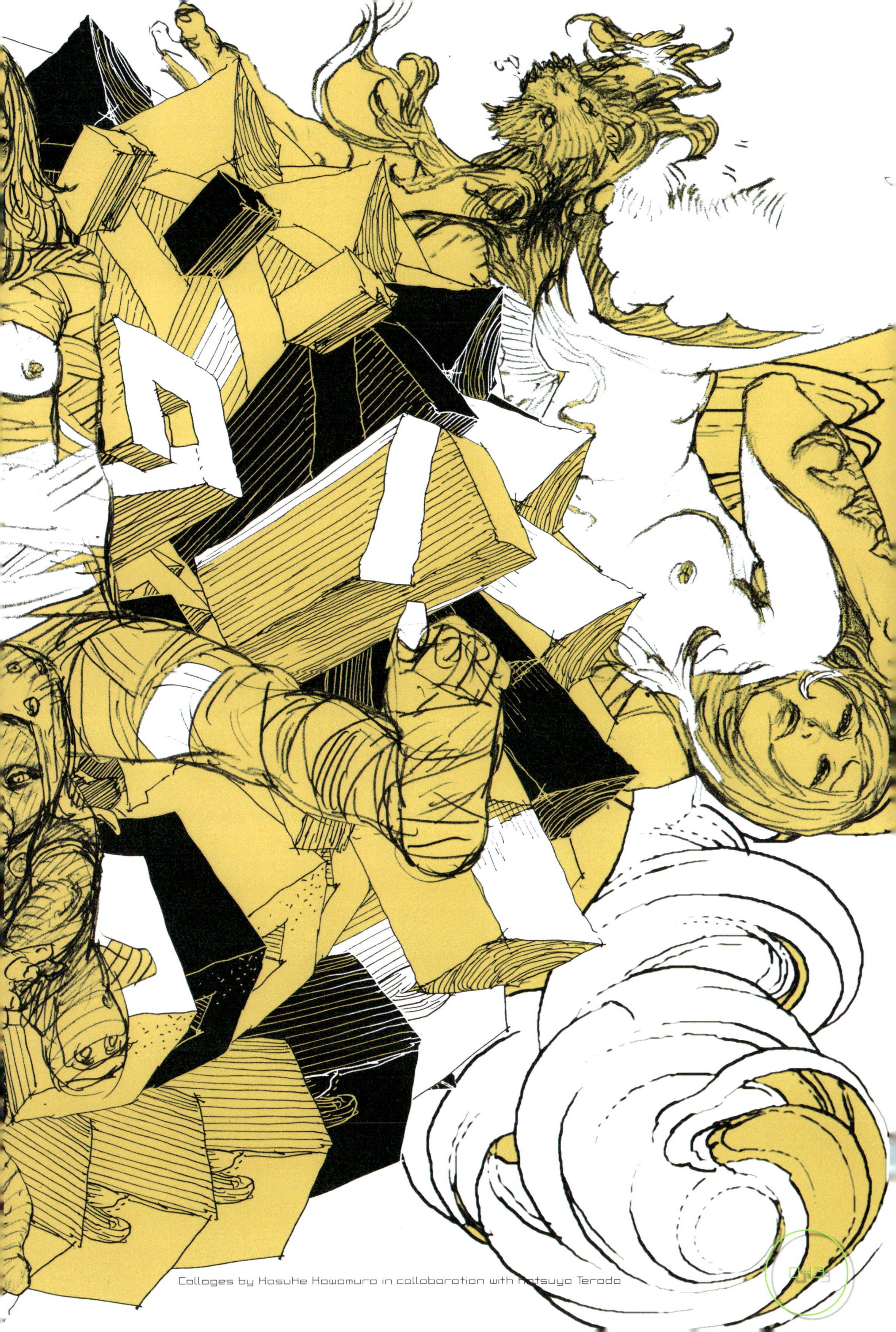

Collages by Kosuke Kawamura in collaboration with Katsuya Terada

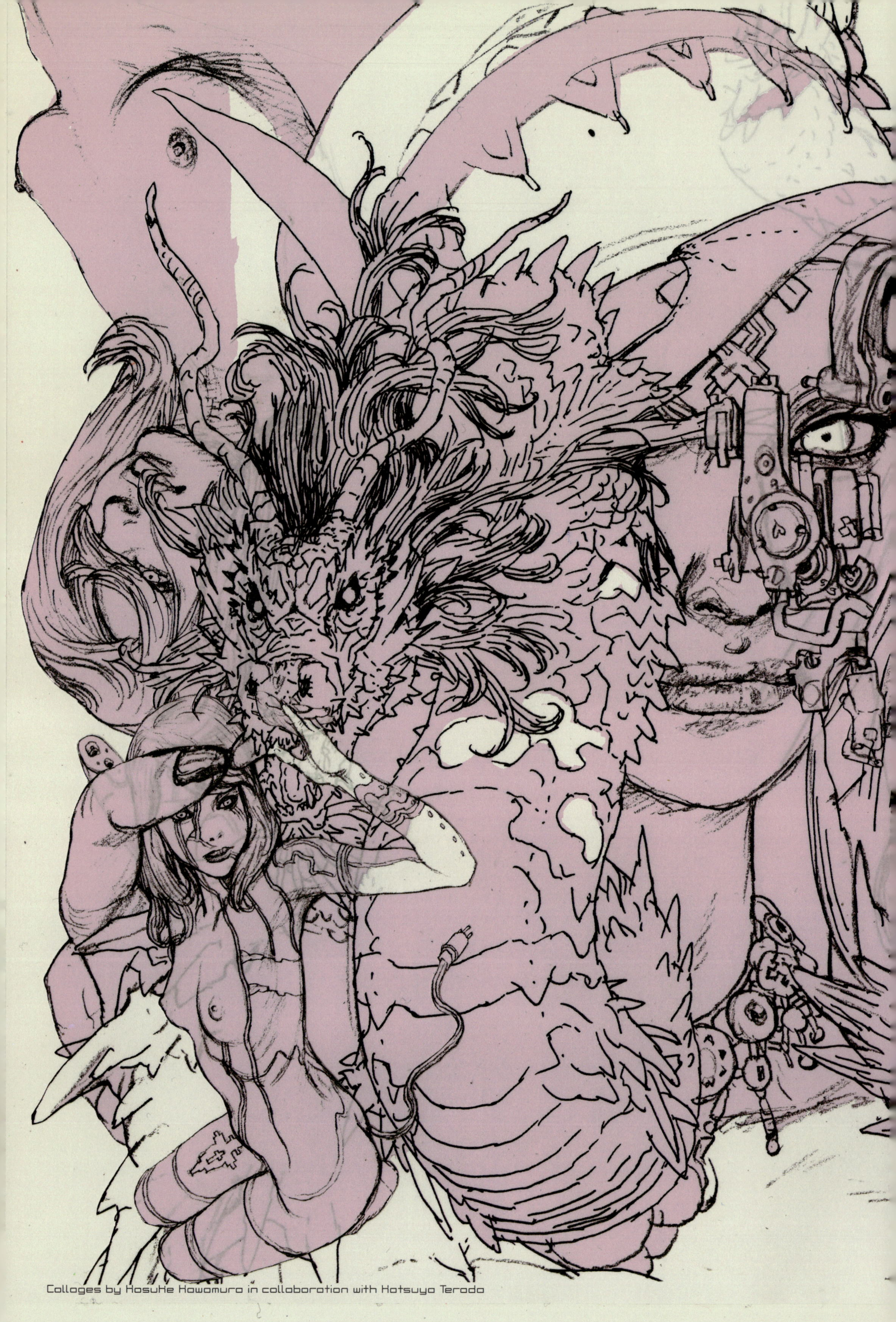

Collages by Kosuke Kawamura in collaboration with Katsuya Terada

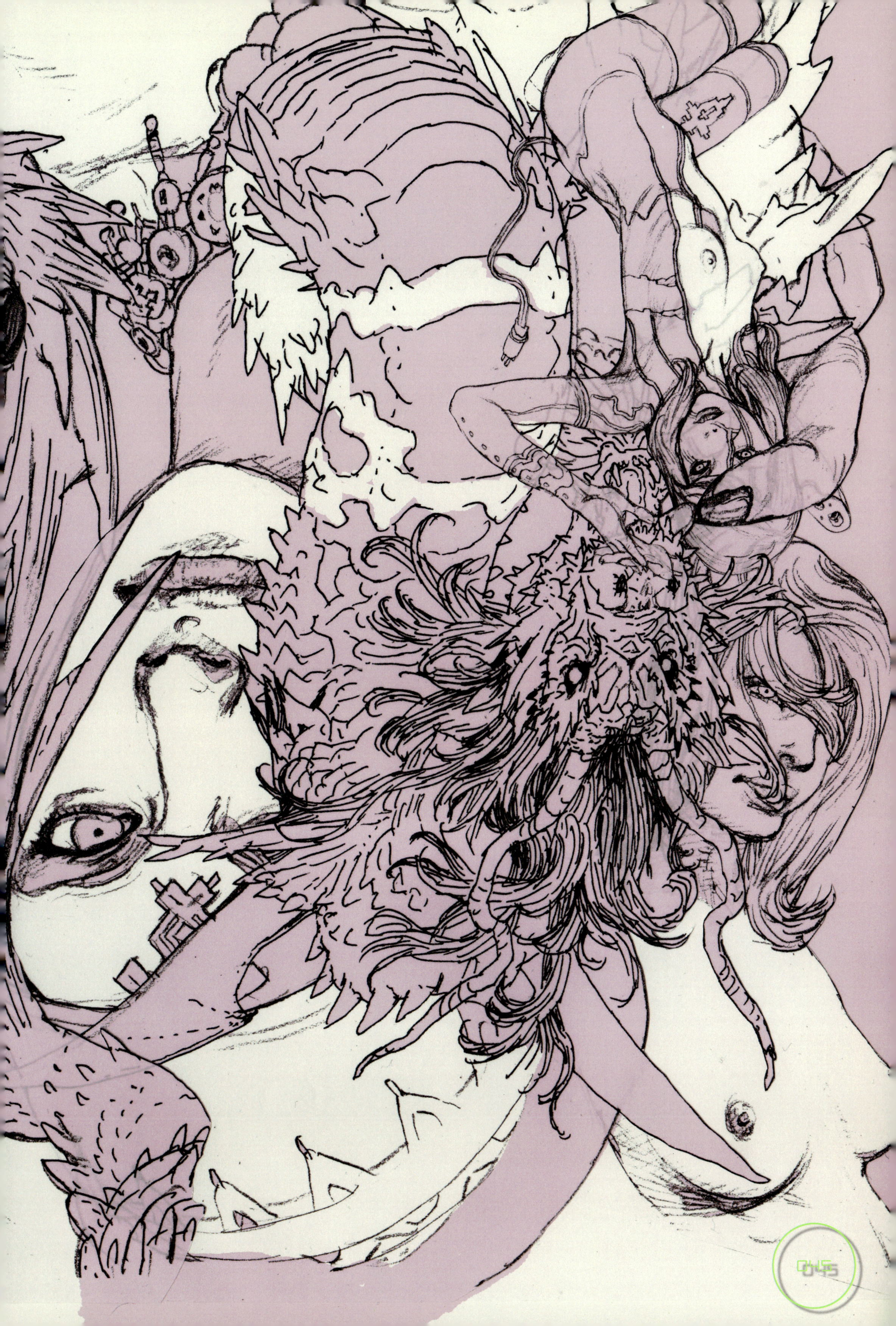

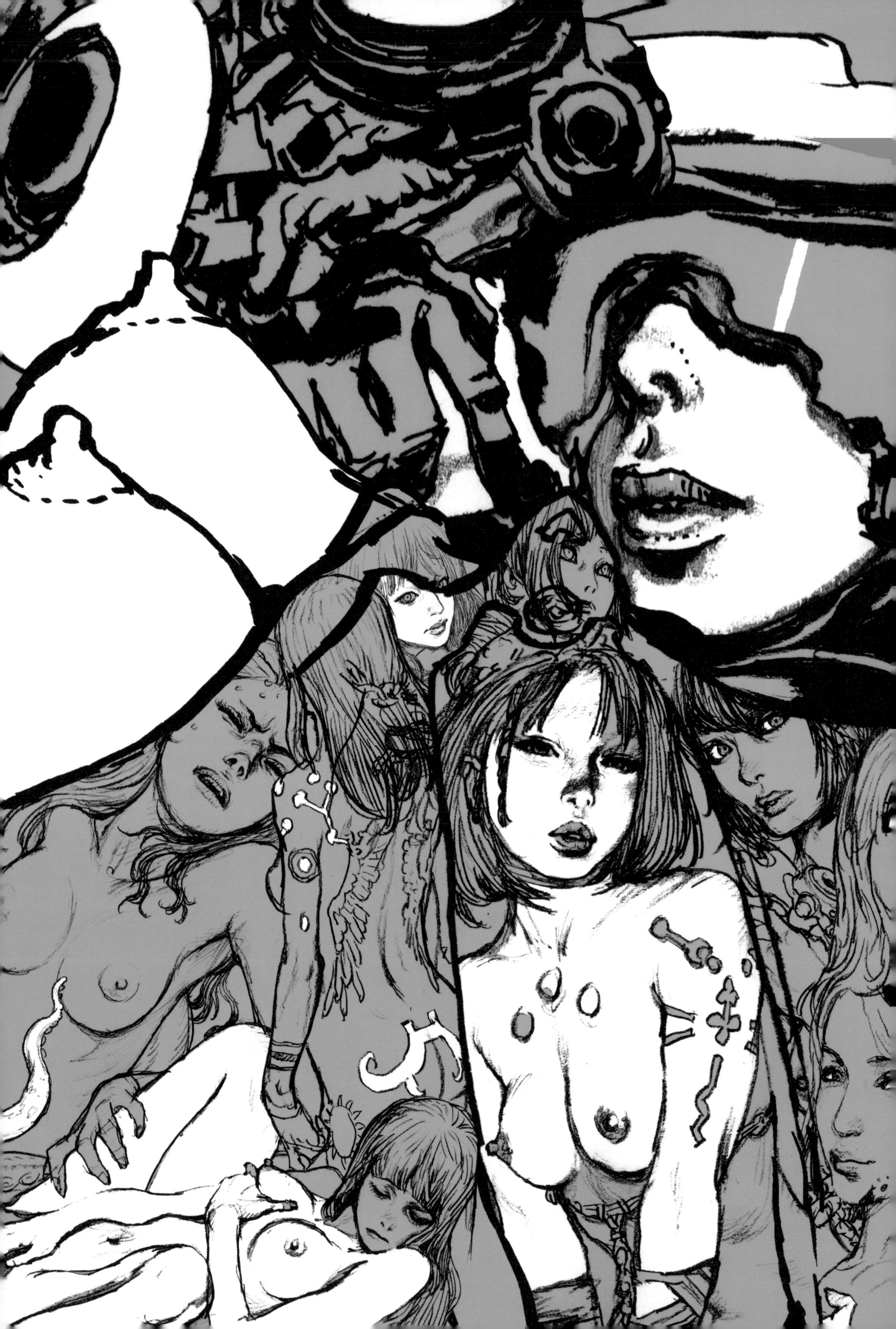

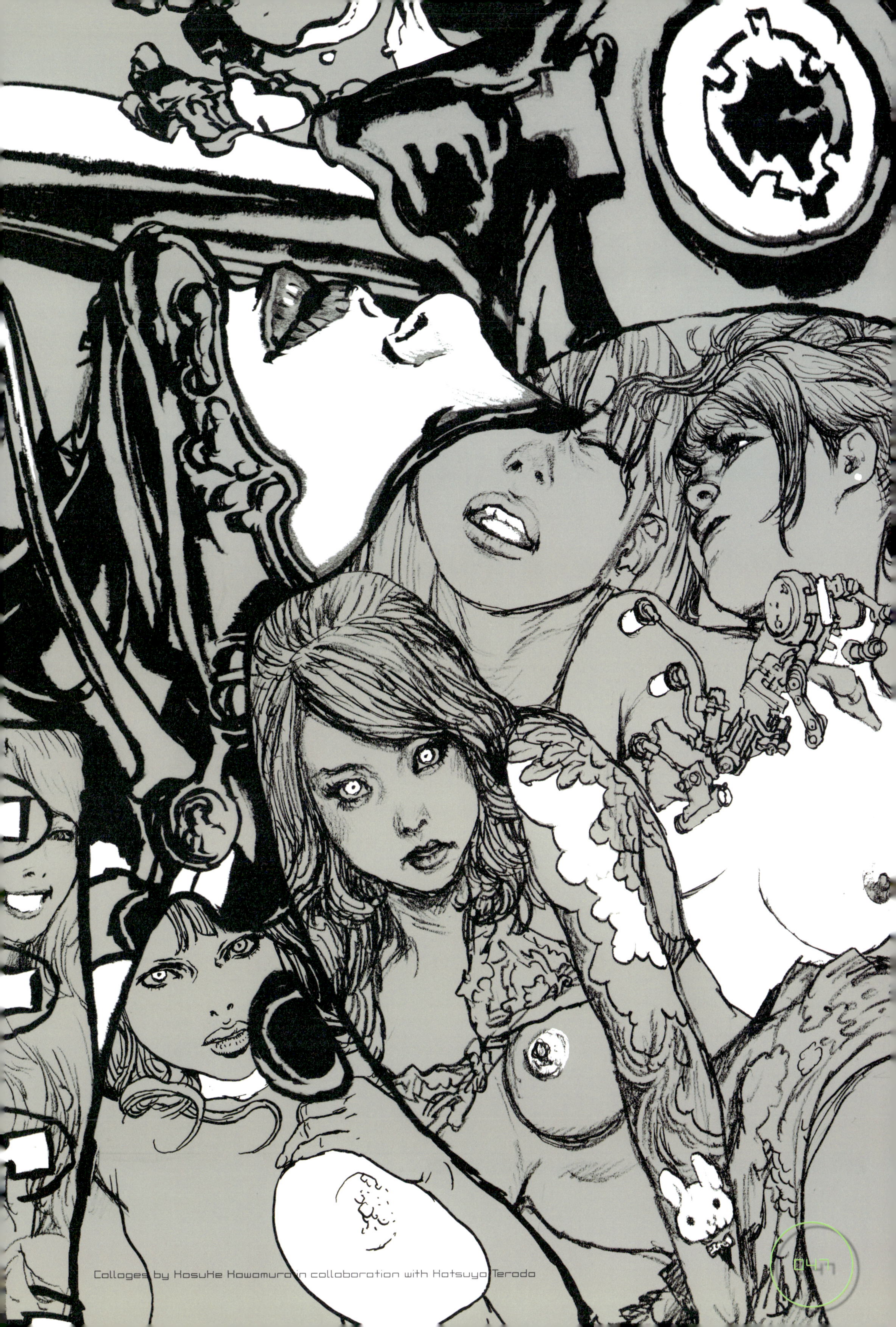

Collages by Kosuke Kawamura in collaboration with Katsuya Terada

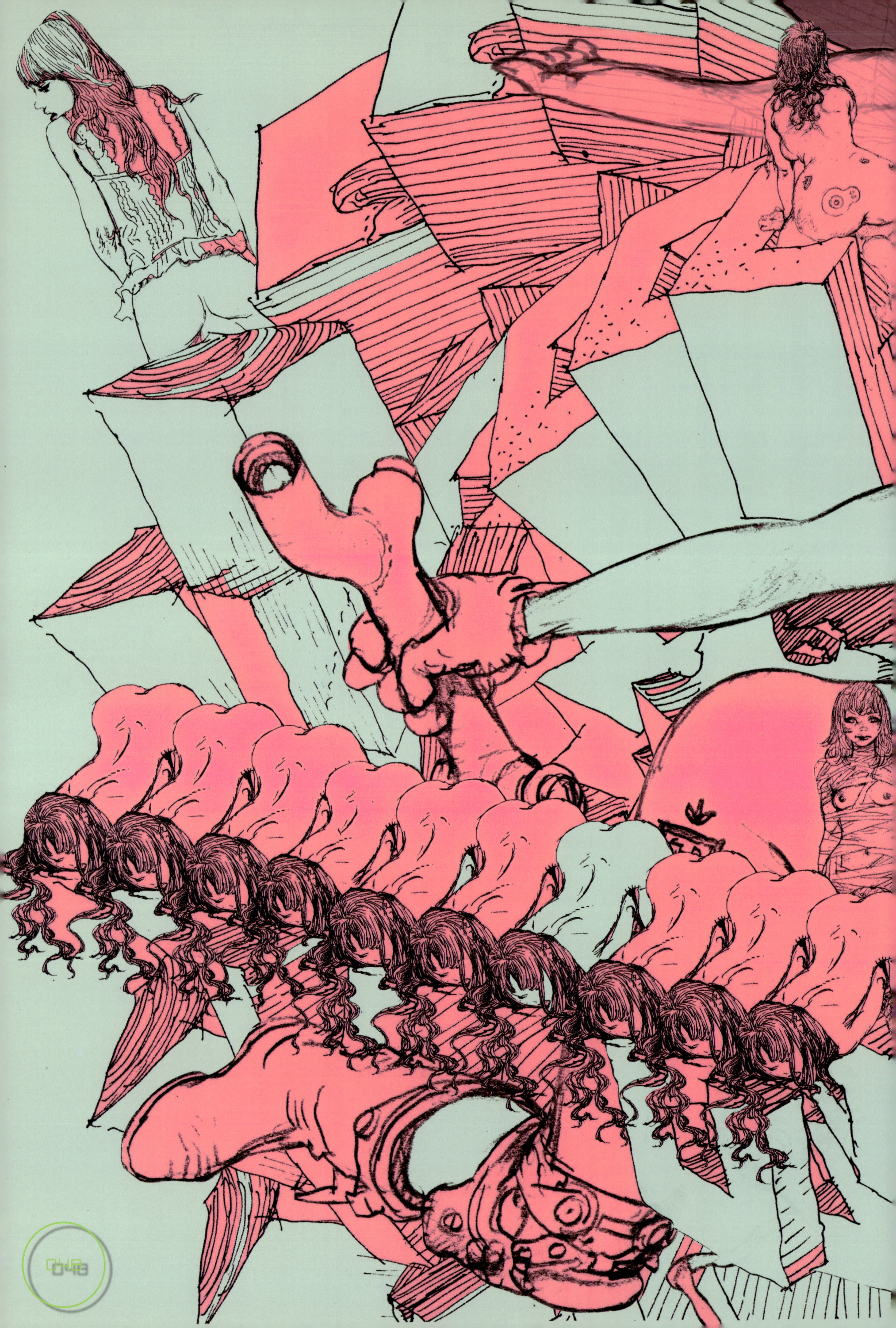

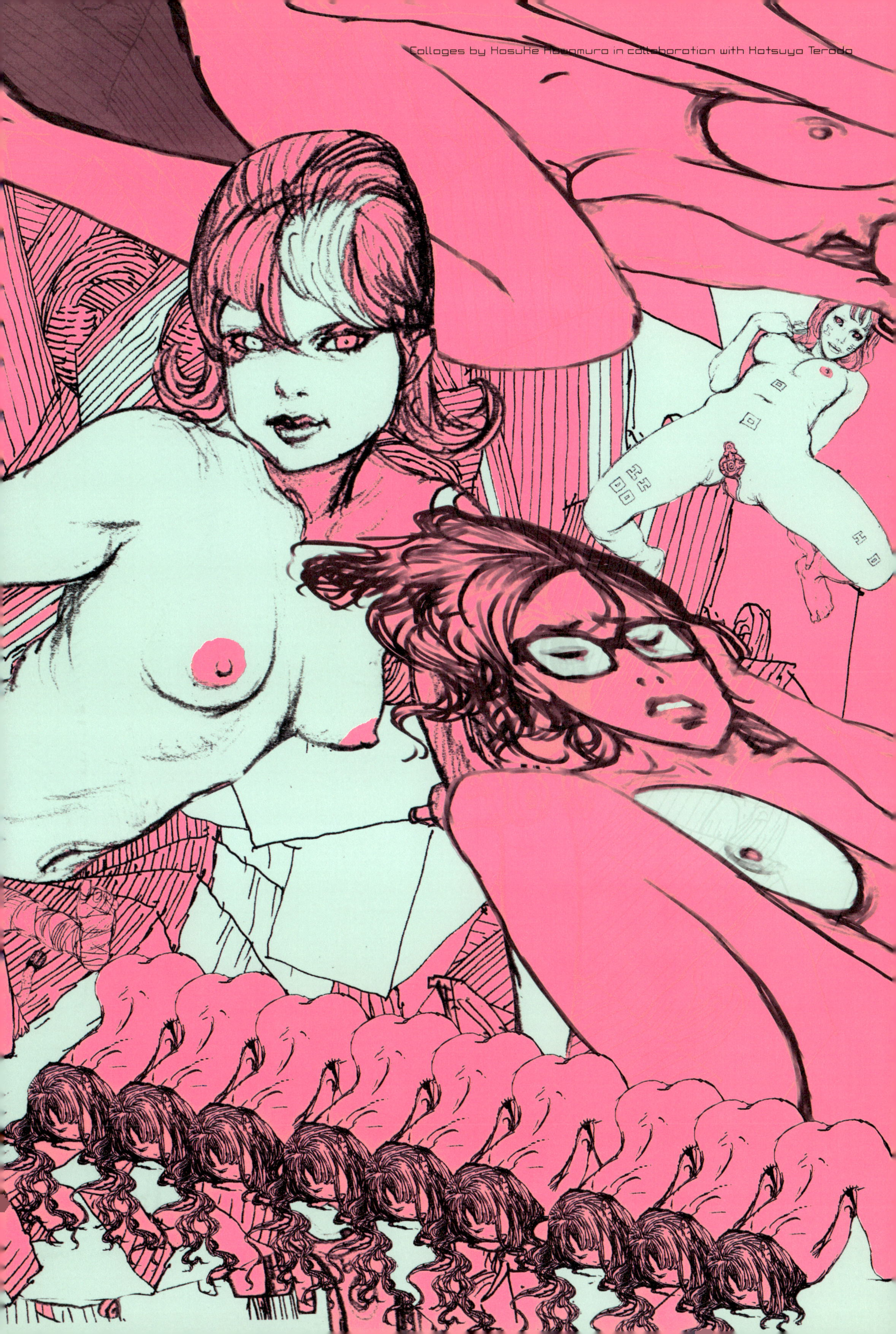

Collages by Kosuke Kawamura in collaboration with Katsuya Terada

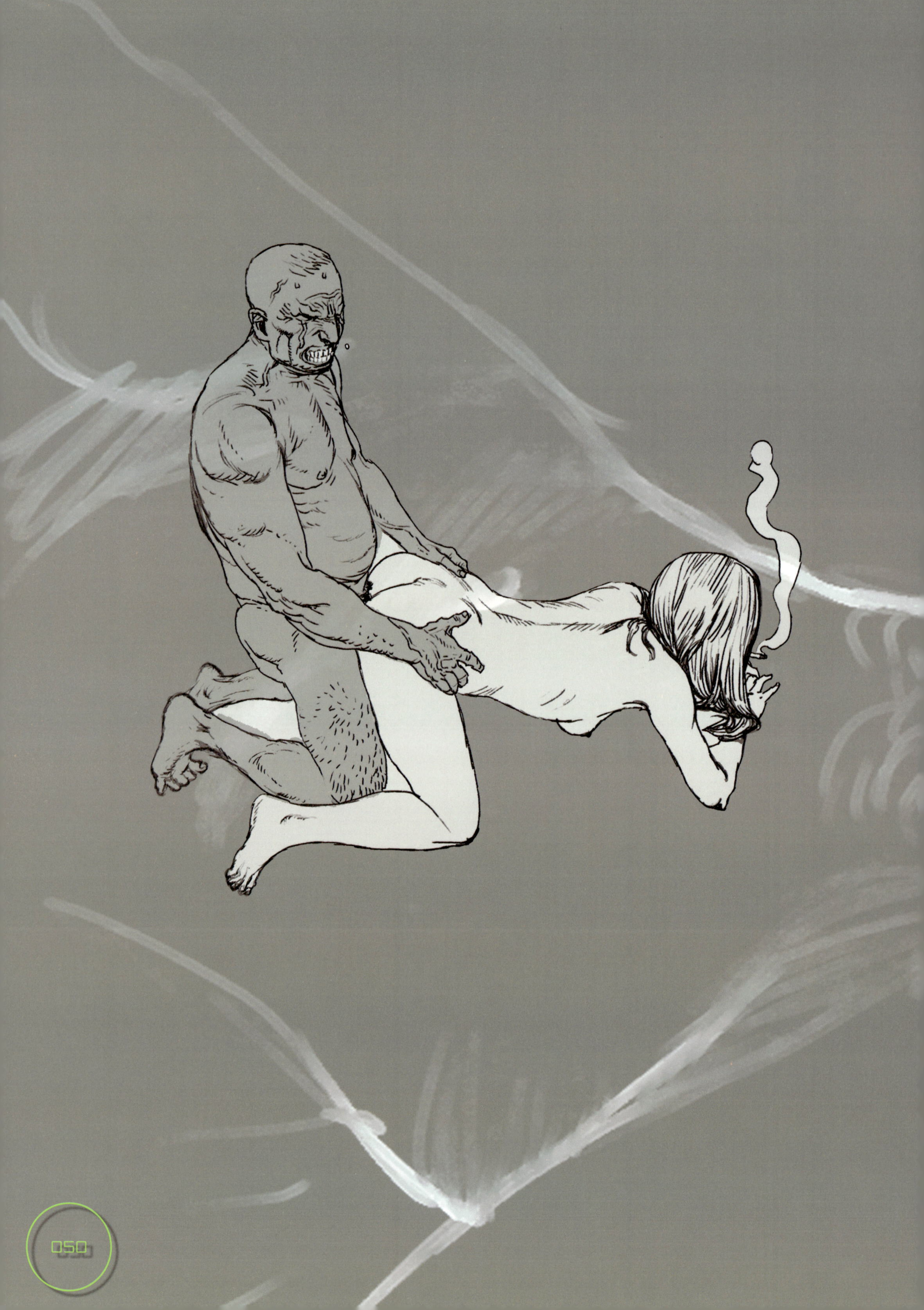

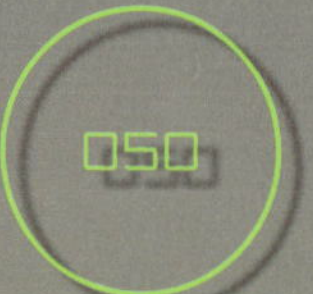

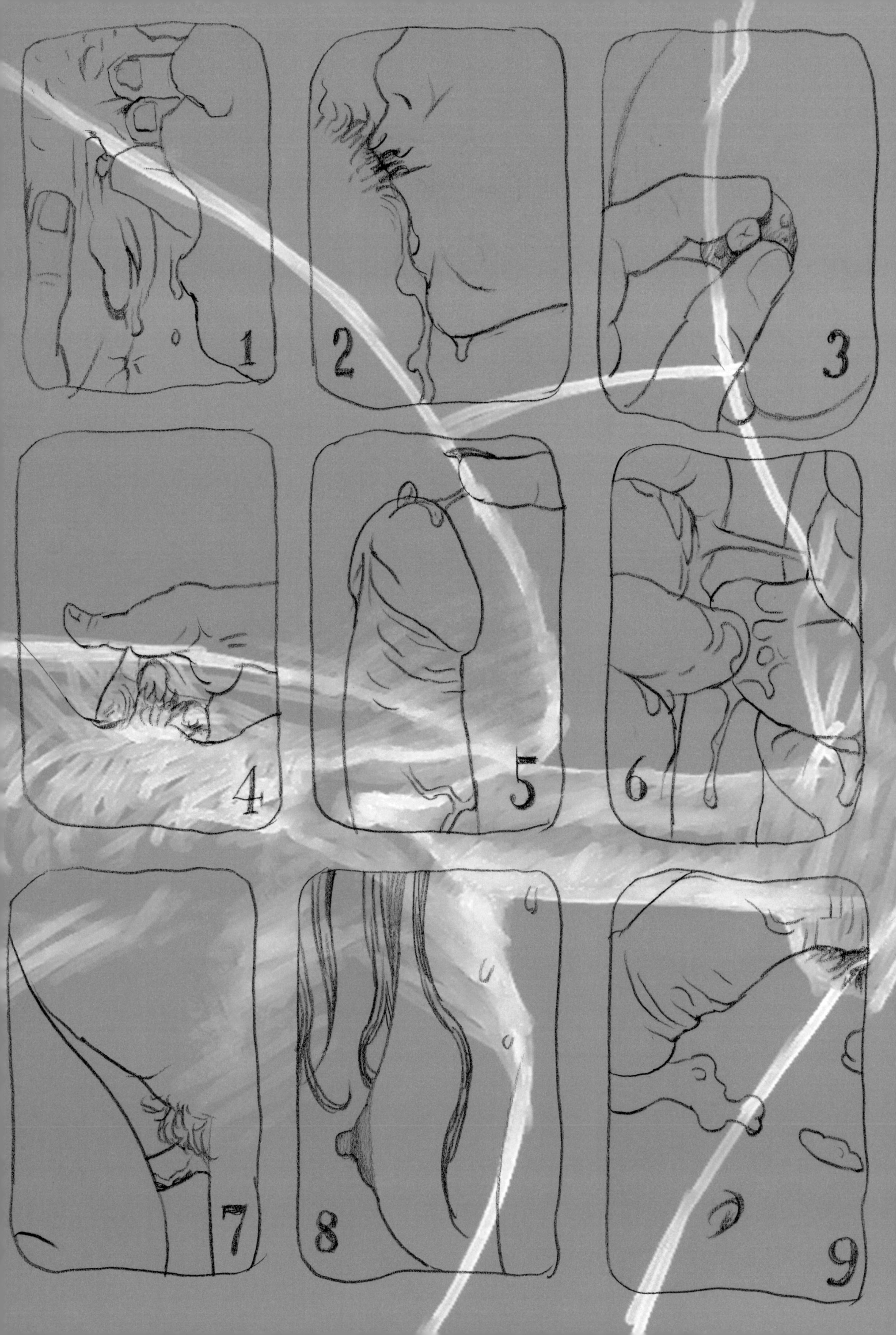
1
2
3
4
5
6
7
8
9

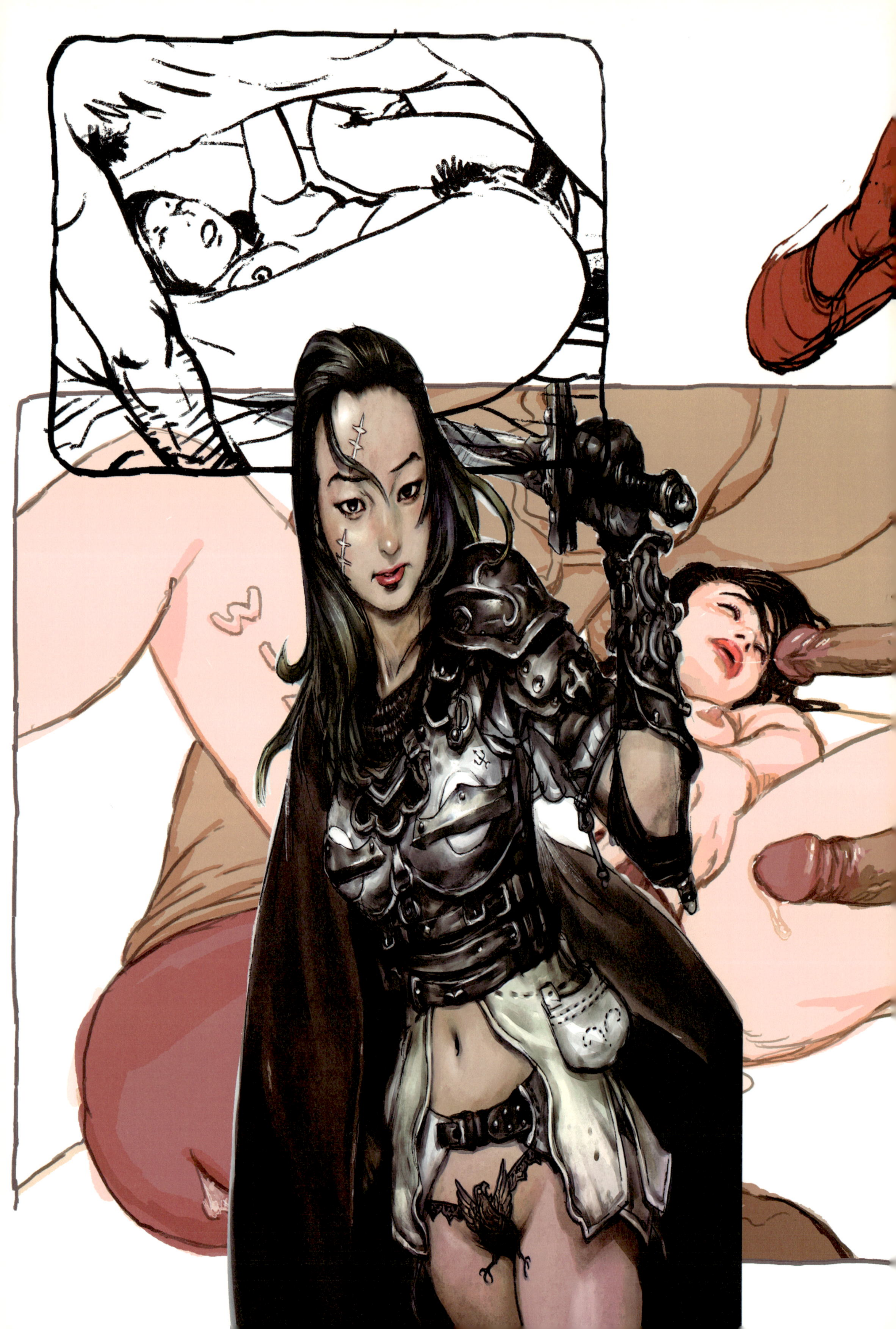

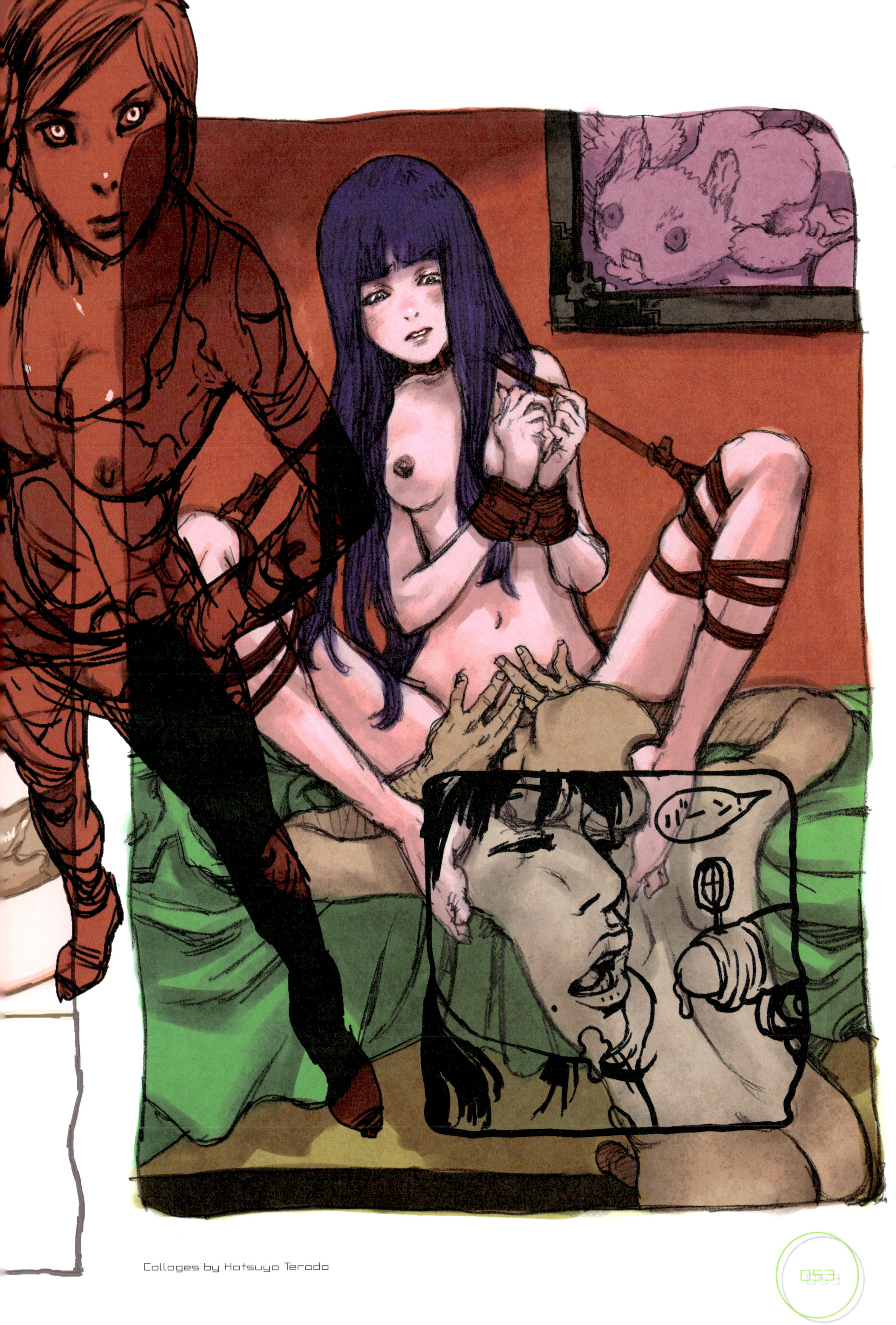
バーン

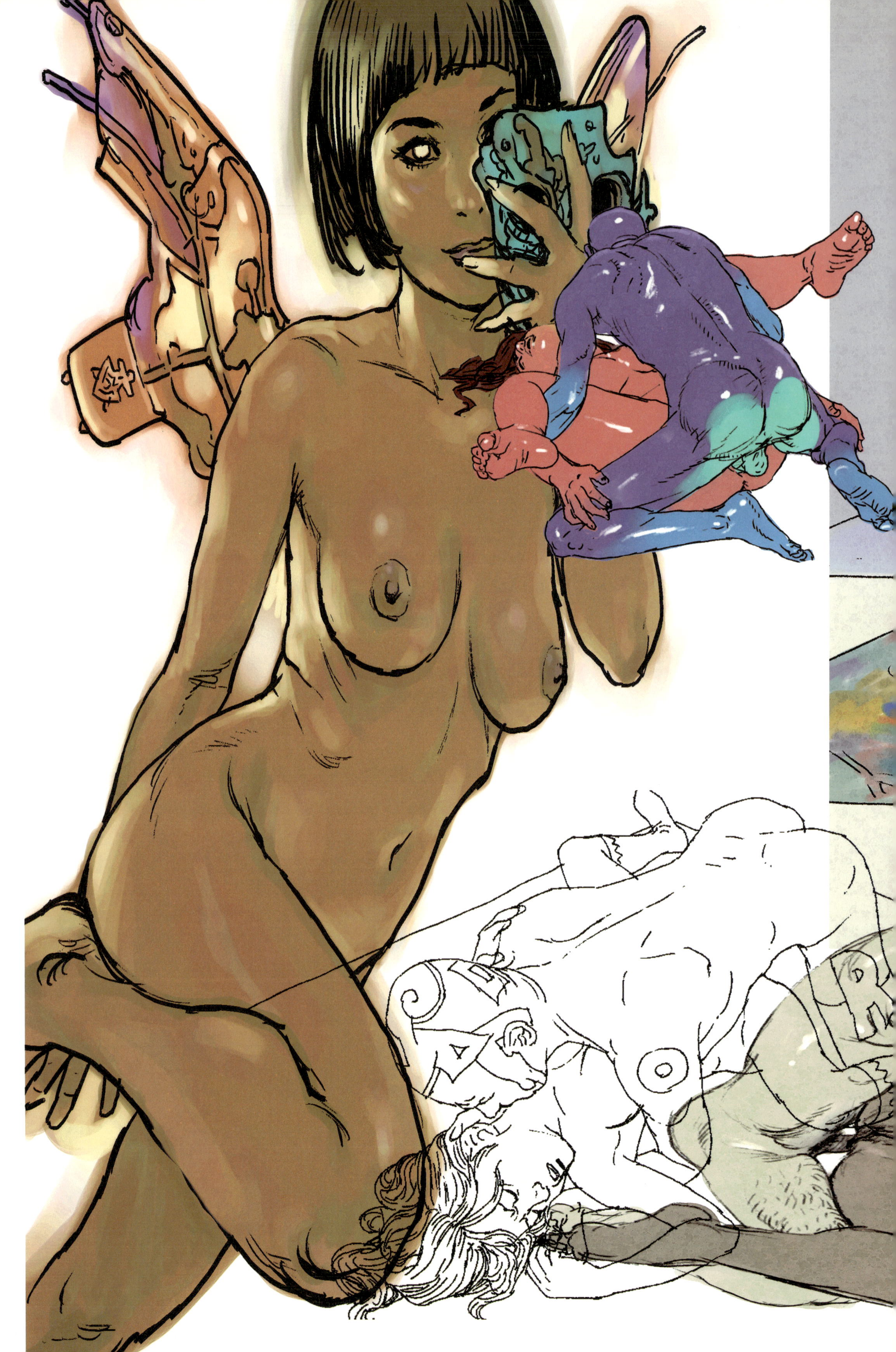

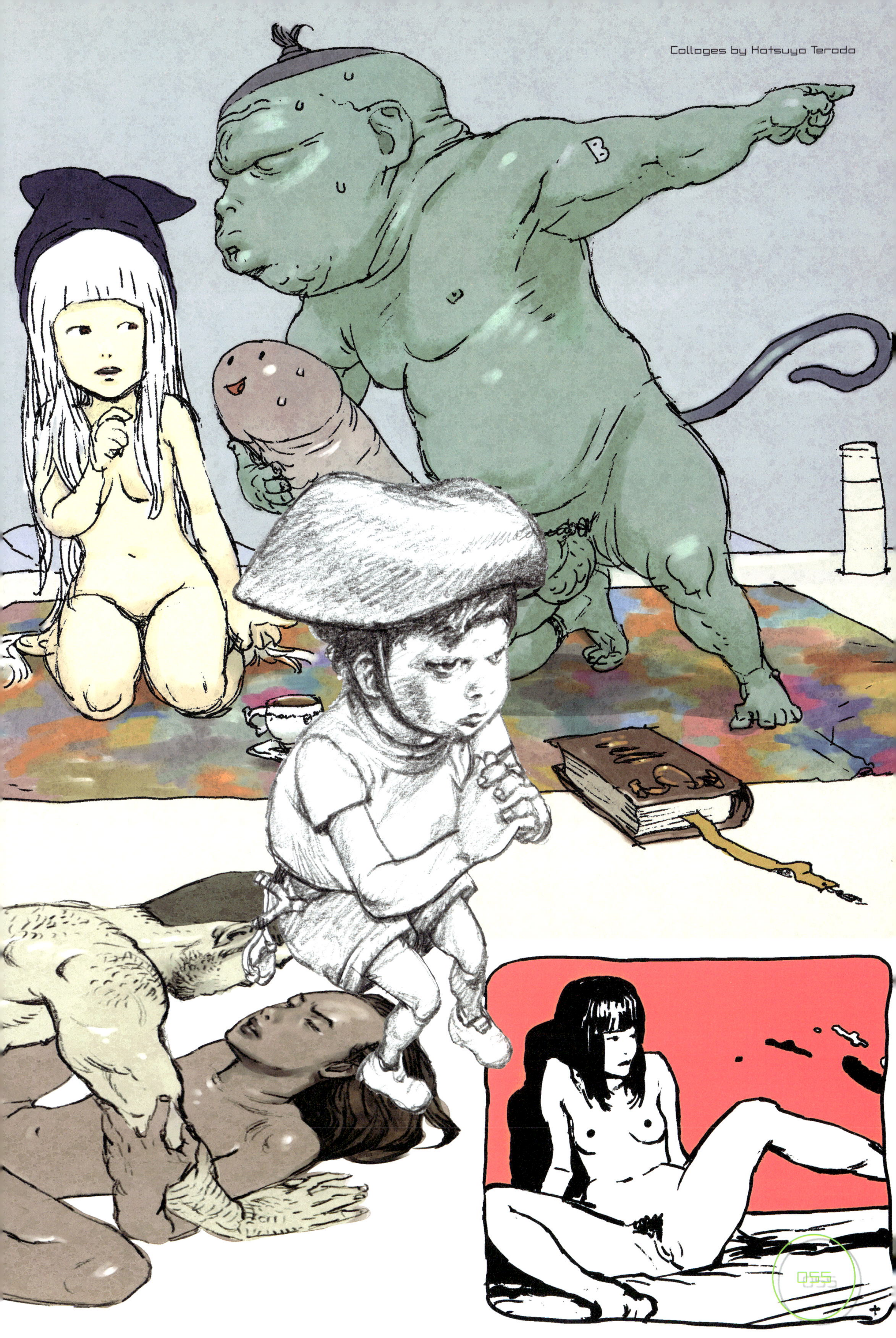
Collages by Katsuya Terada

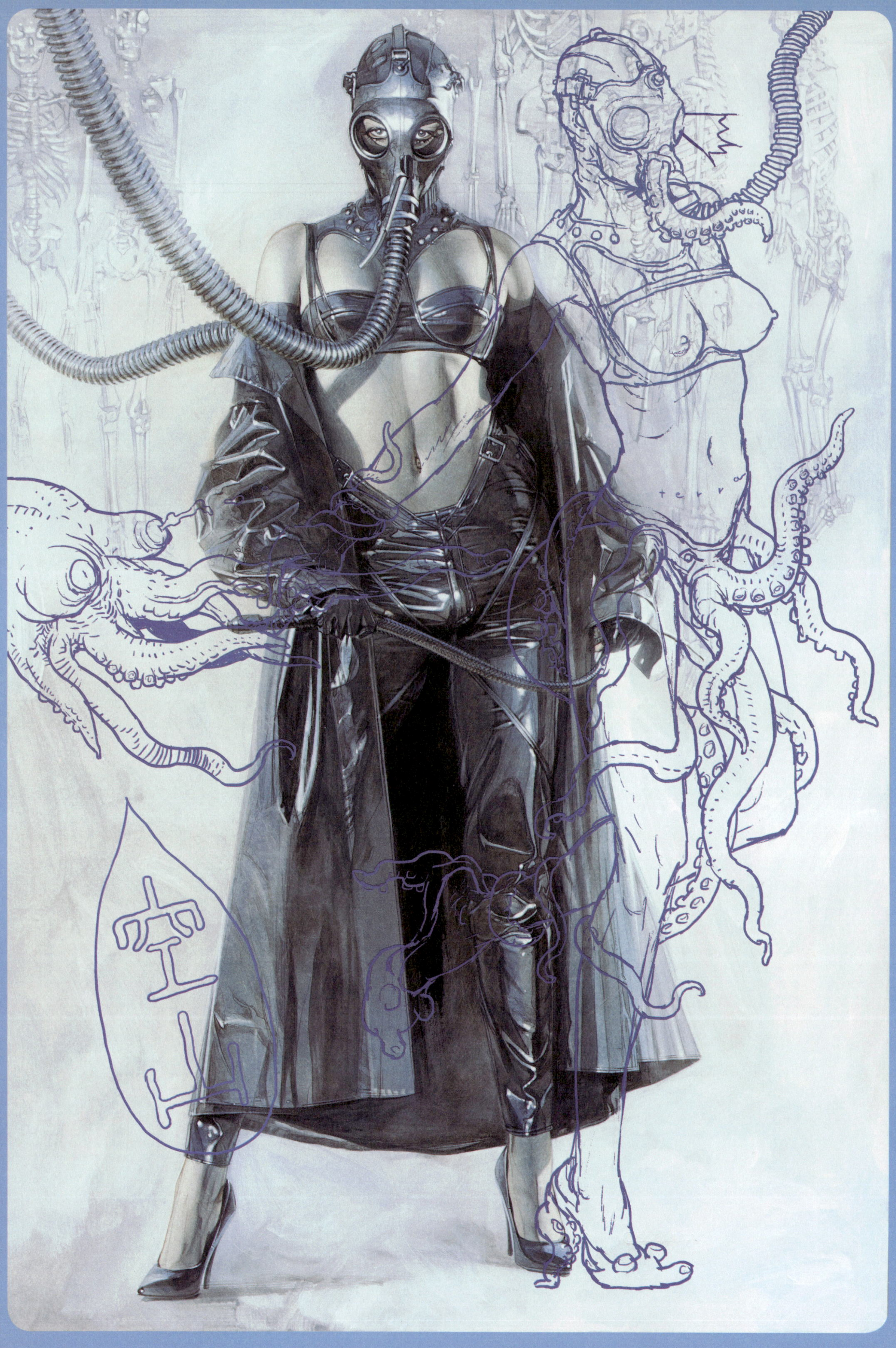

Graffiti by Katsuya Terada on works by Hajime Sorayama

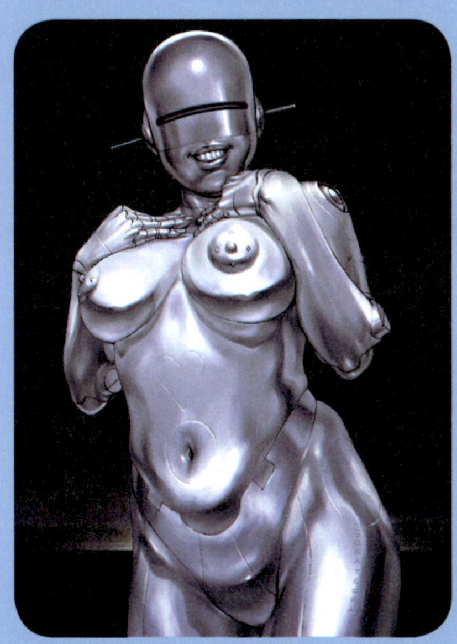

空山さんが描かないであろう太めのセクシーロボットをトリビュートで描いた！

エロ×ダチ
空山基（ピンナップ・マスター）

イラスト・まんが界の大スターが、世間様からうしろ指さされる＜エロ＞の領域に堂々と御旗をたてて参戦してもらえるのはすごく心強い。この手のジャンル（私の作品は他人からいつも「この手の絵」といわれます（汗））で孤軍奮闘してきた絵描きとしては、才能あふれるアーチストがどんどん〈エロ〉のジャンルを活性化させ革新して世界を驚かせて欲しいですね。仲間が増えれば私も新しい刺戟をもらえるし、それが次の創作のエネルギーになるのです。

Erotic Buddies
Hajime Sorayama [Master of Pinup Art]

It is extremely encouraging to me for a superstar of the illustration and manga world to raise his flag and unstintingly join in the battle in the realm of 'eroticism' that makes people talk behind one's back. I have continued to fight a lonely battle in this type of genre [people are always speaking of my pictures as 'this type of genre'[sweat]]. So much so that I do hope that artists with burgeoning talent, who will persist in vivify, innovating, and shocking the world through the 'erotic' genre. If associates in this field increase in number, it will both stimulate me and provide me with creative energy for my future work.

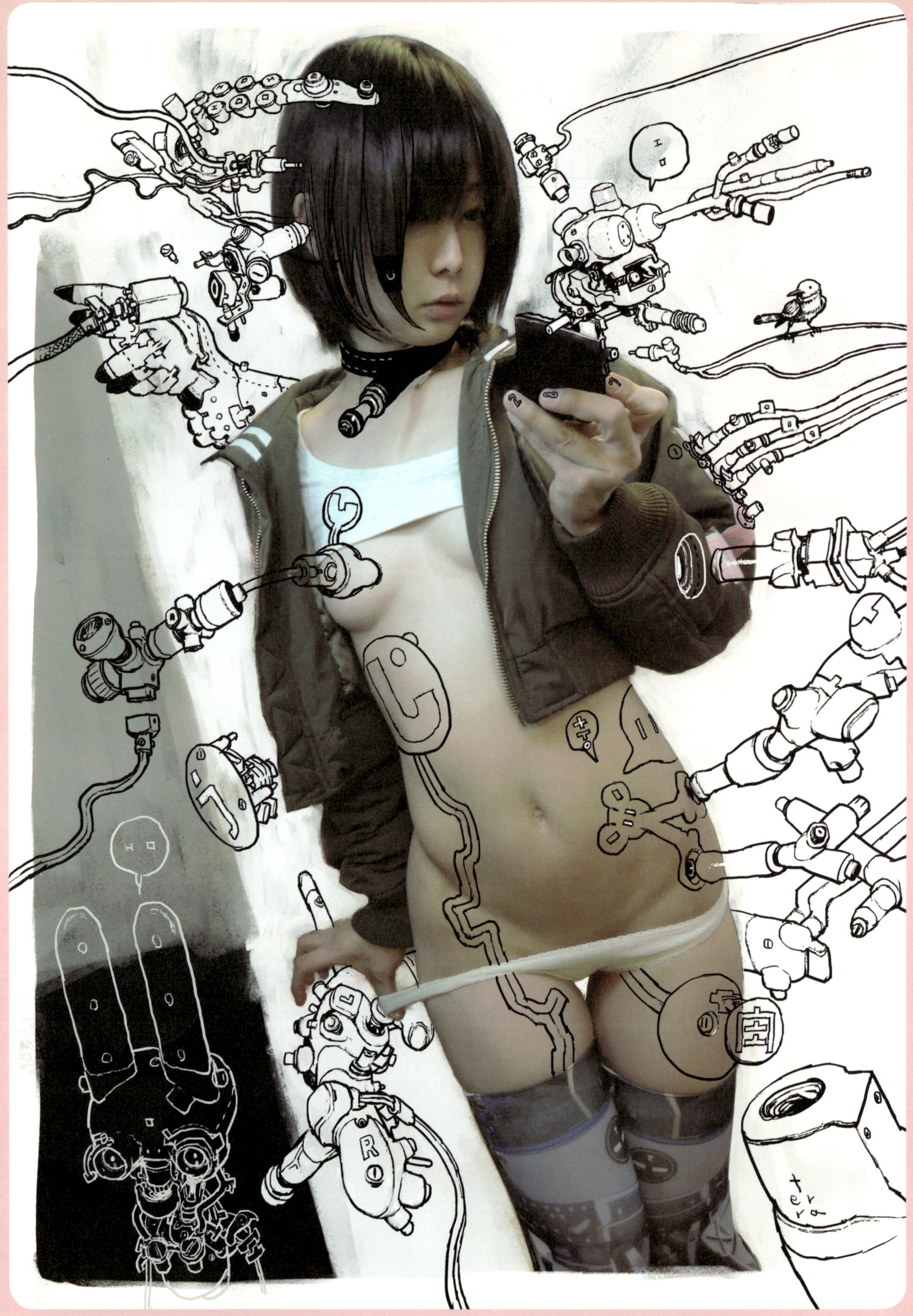

Graffiti by Katsuya Terada on Ushijima Iiniku's portrait

エロ×ダチ
うじじまいい肉
(グラビアアイドル・プロデューサー／服飾ブランド「PredatorRat」プロデューサー)

私は普段エロに関してPTAの人が怒ったりするような活動を行っていますが、寺田さんのように、単純にその絵が超かっこいいから裸の女のイラストだろうが、PTAが怒り出さないというのがやっぱり一番真っ当でかっこよくて憧れるなあ～と思いました。

Erotic Buddies
Iiniku Ushijima
[Photogravure idol producer / clothing and accessory brand "PredatorRat" producer]

I normally carry out erotic activities that anger PTA people. But I think that the reason that Terada's illustrations do not cause the PTA to get angry is because they are so simply and extremely cool, even though they depict naked women, and in the final analysis, that they are ultimately respectable and attractive.

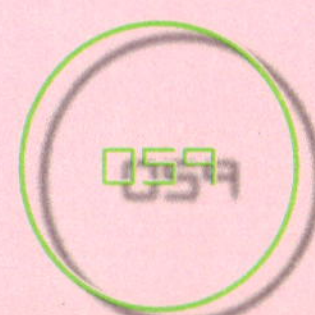

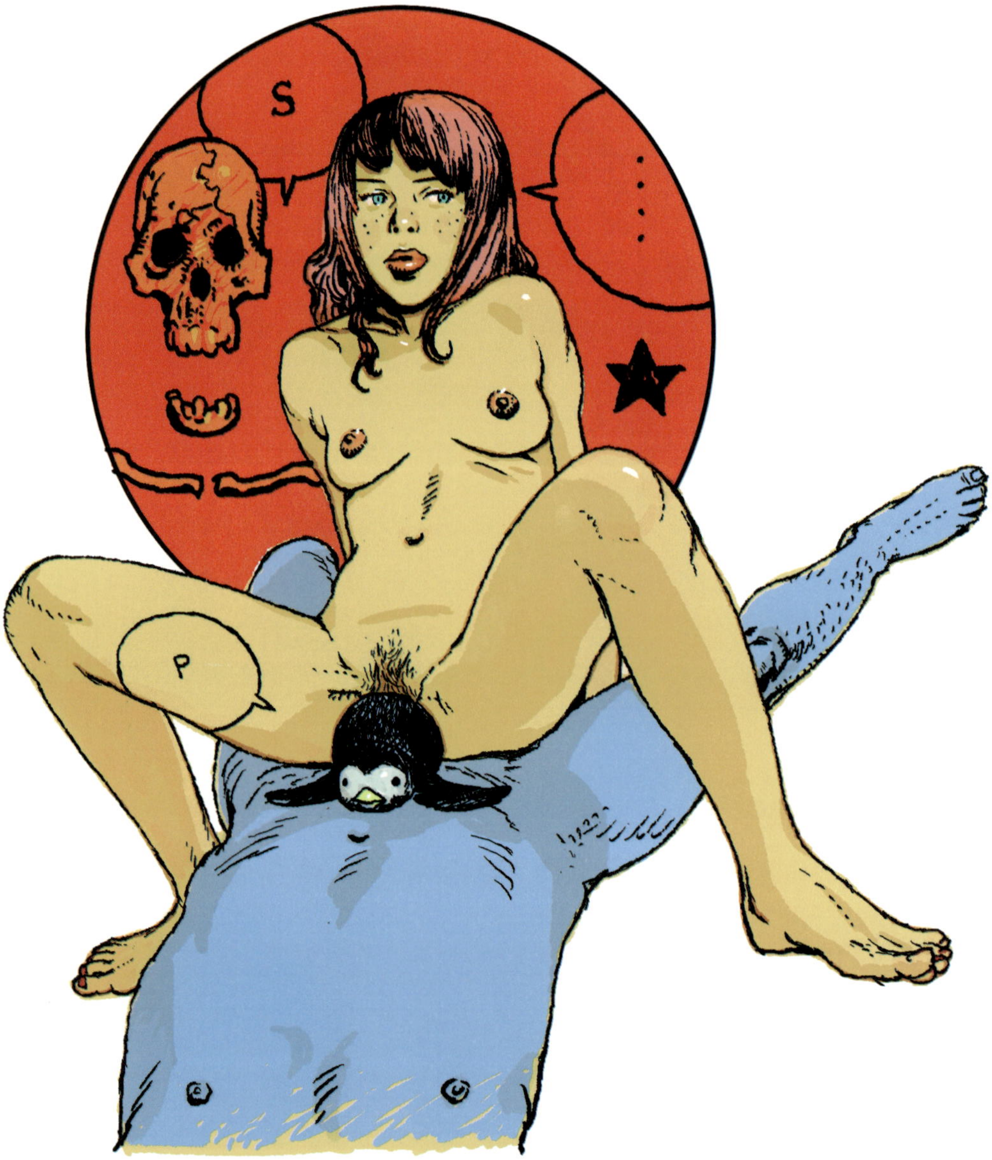

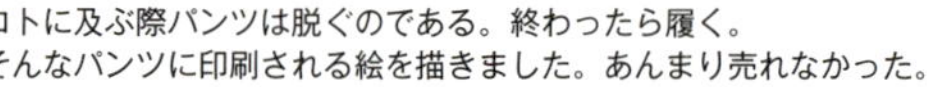

コトに及ぶ際パンツは脱ぐのである。終わったら履く。
そんなパンツに印刷される絵を描きました。あんまり売れなかった。

When getting it on, you take off your underpants. When you are finished, you put them back on. I painted this picture for printing on those underpants. But they didn't sell very well.

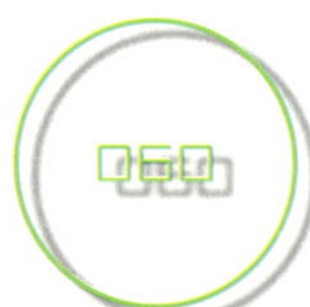

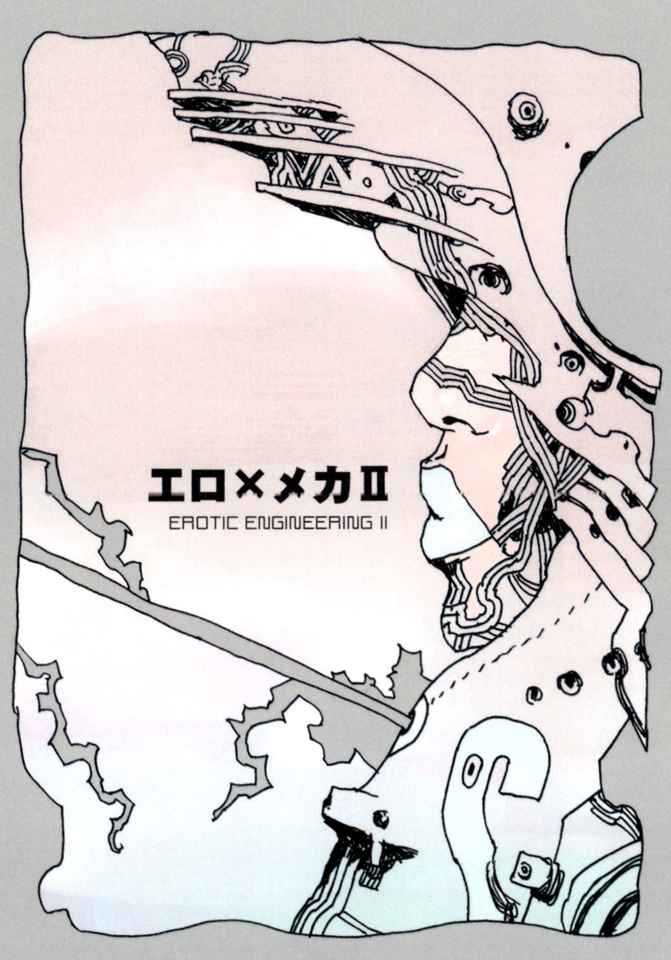
エロ×メカⅡ
EROTIC ENGINEERING II

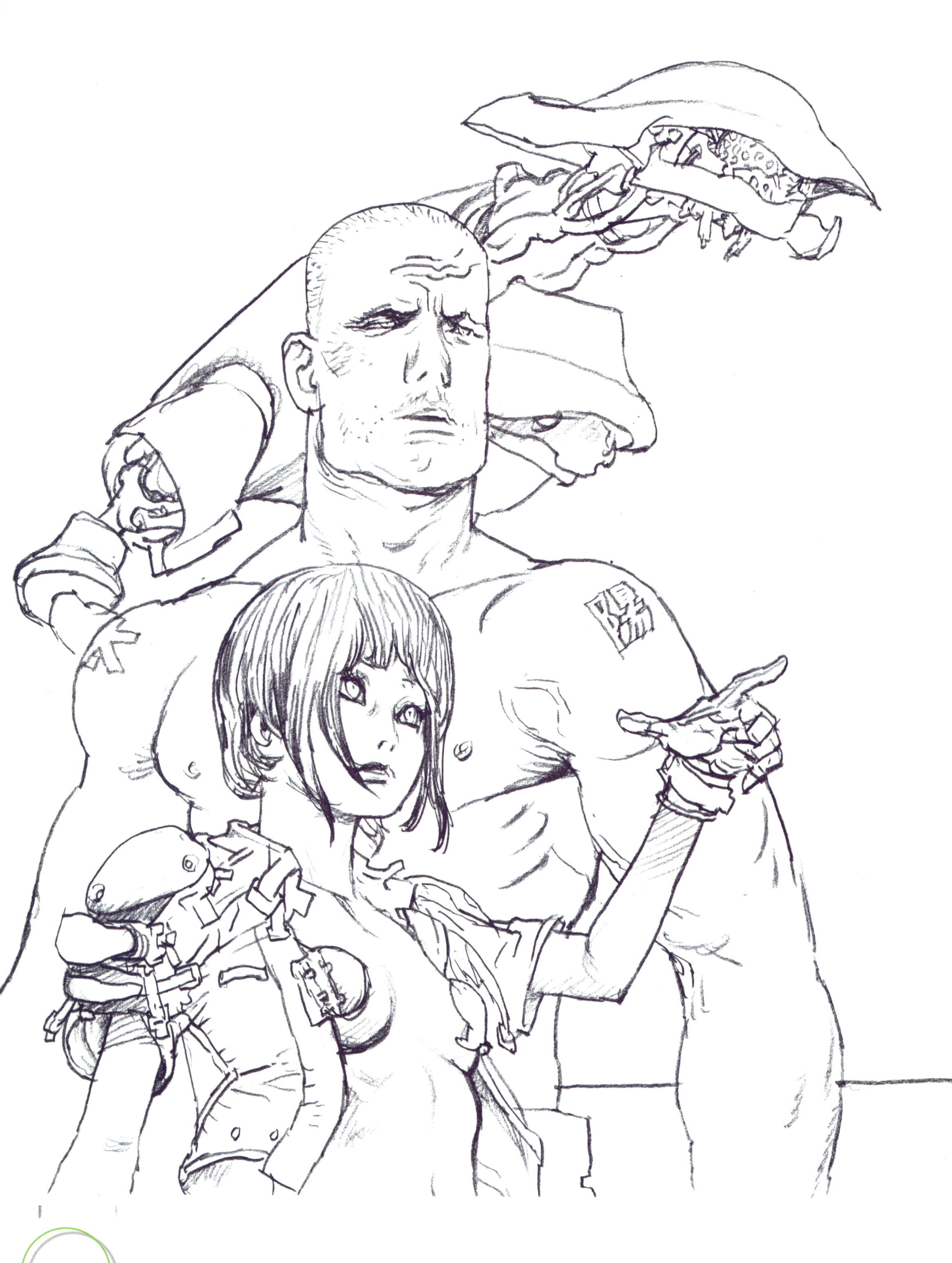
陽

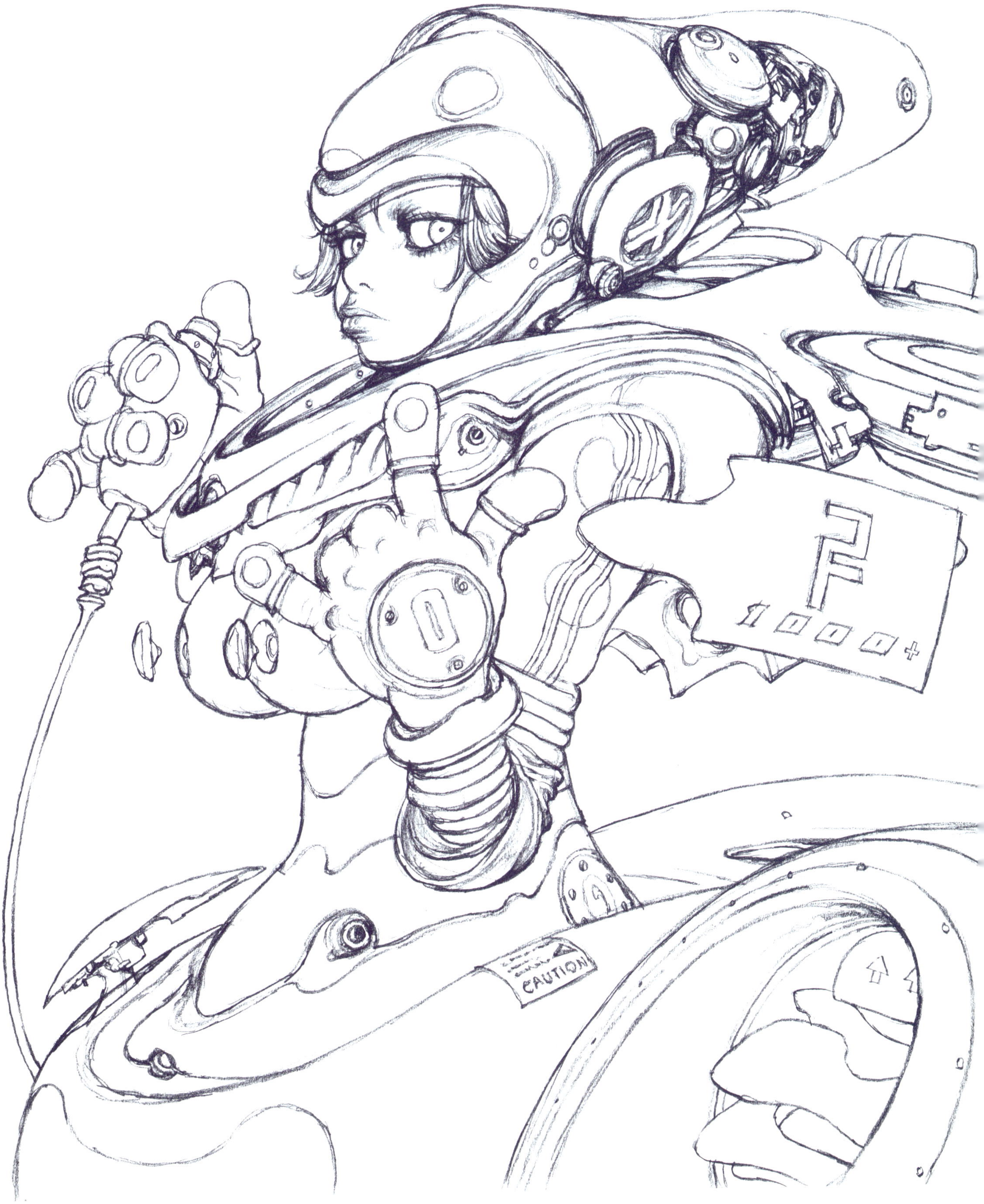

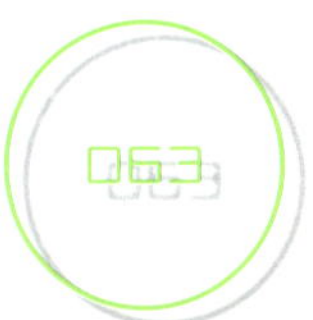

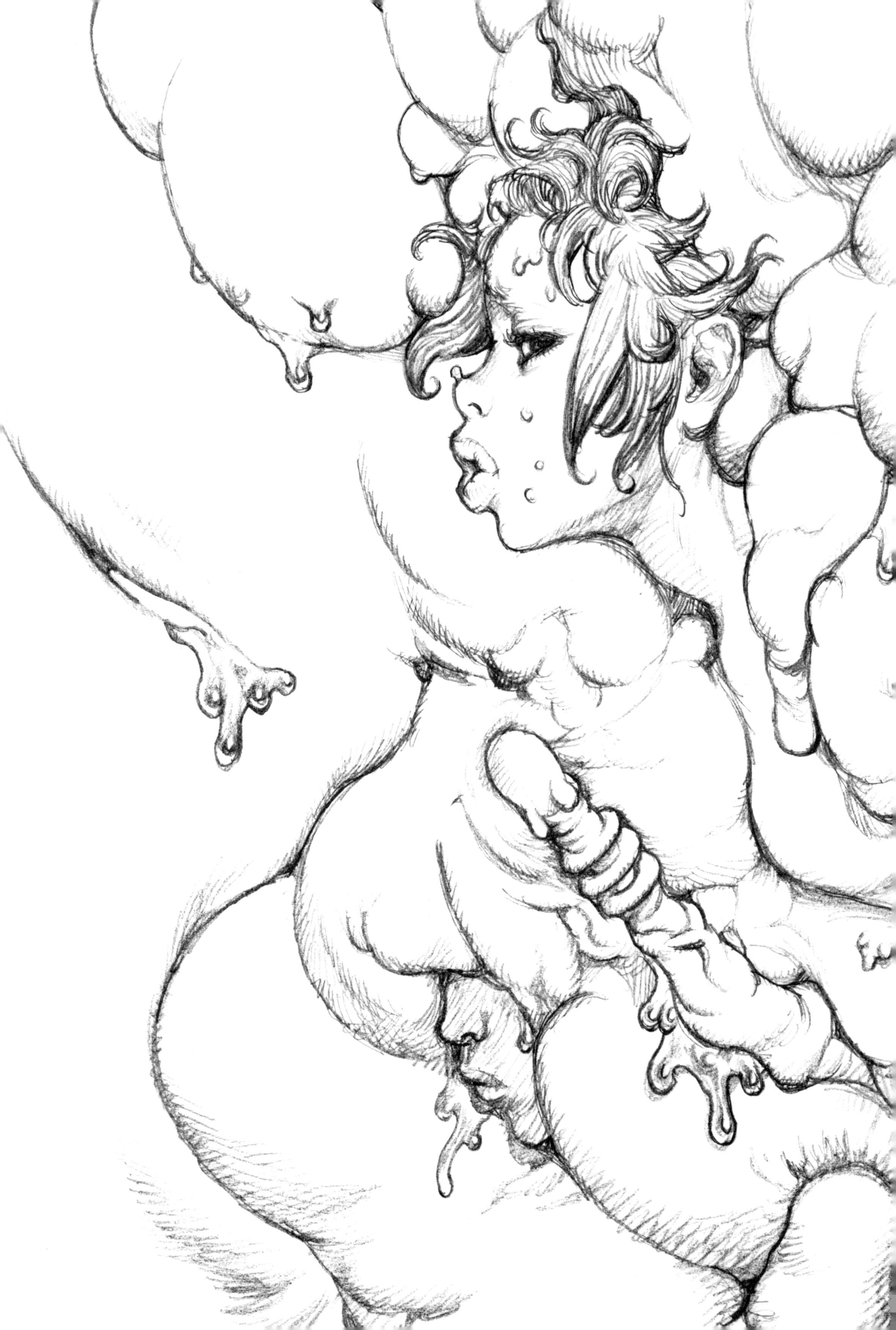

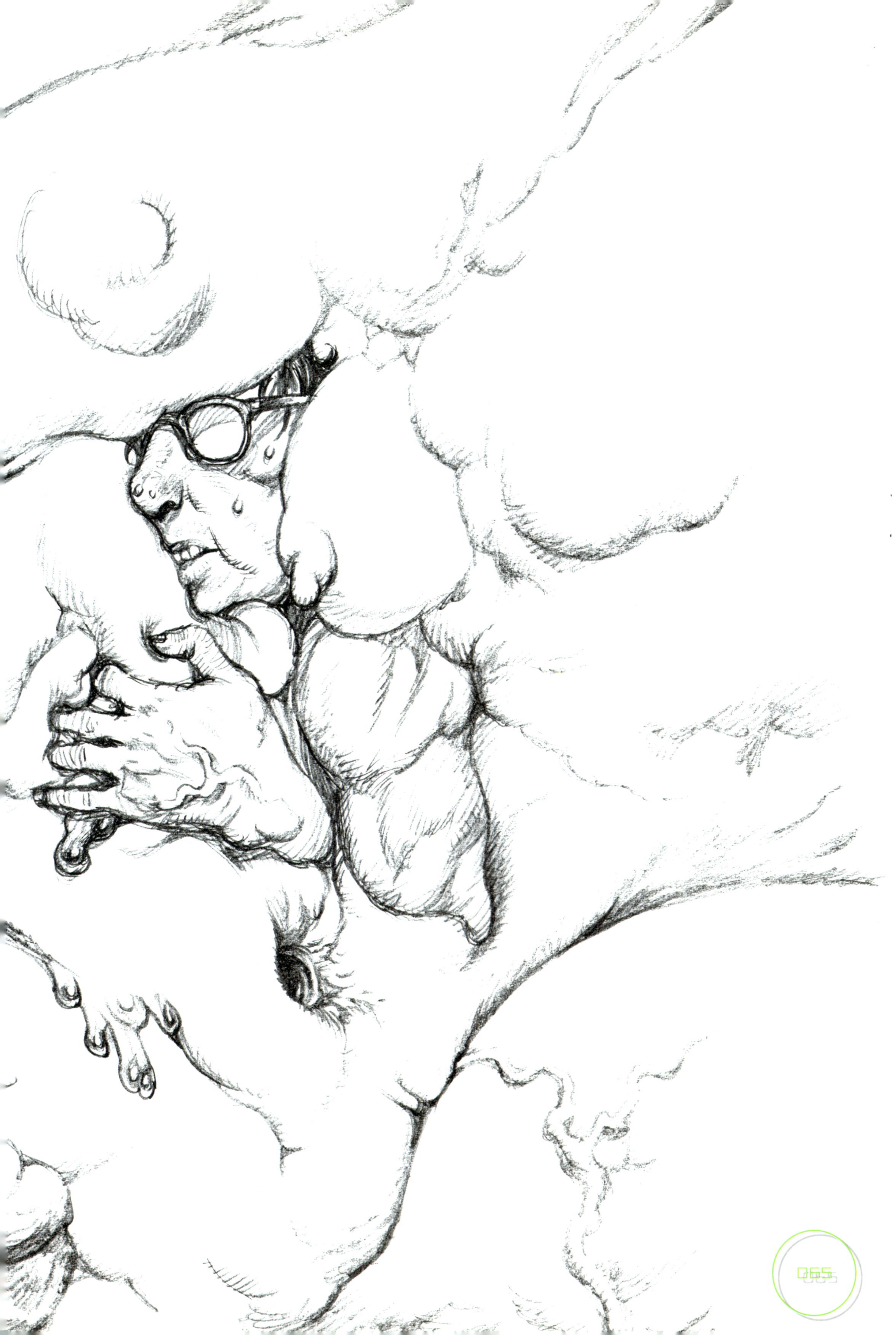

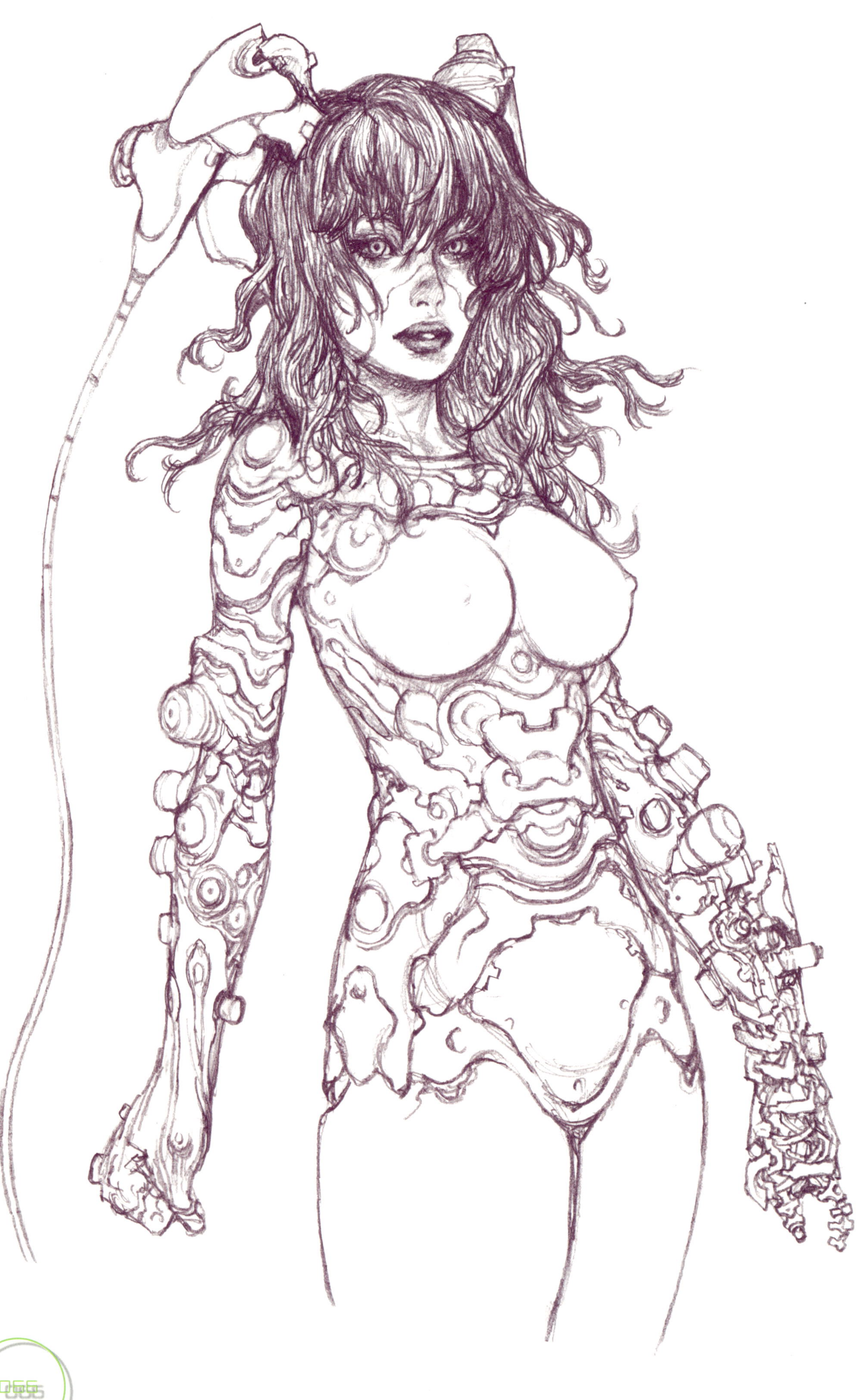

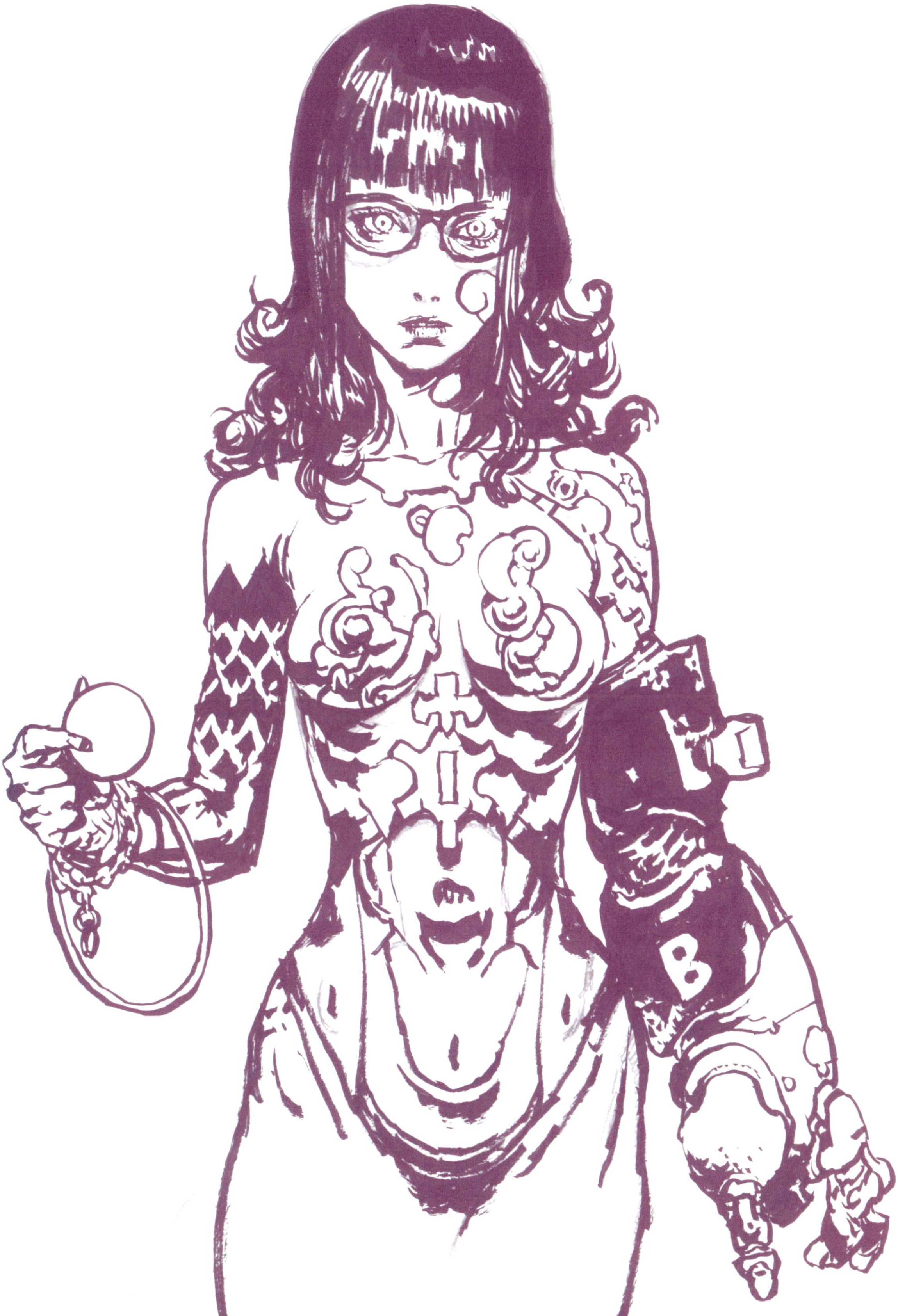

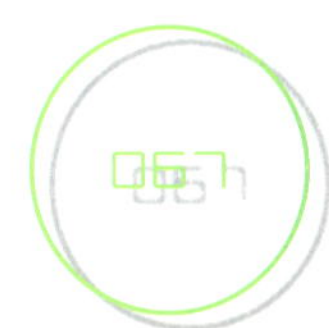

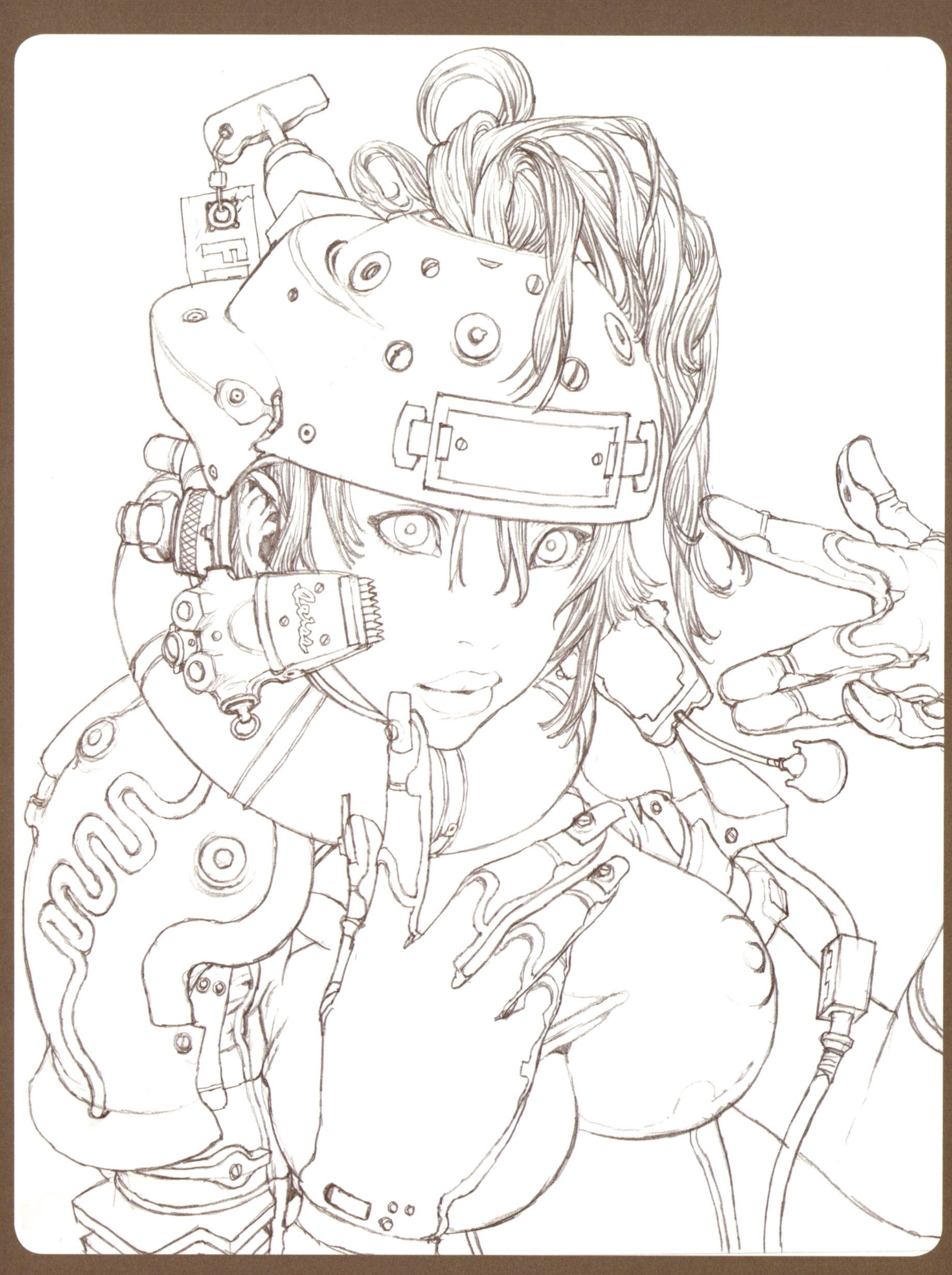

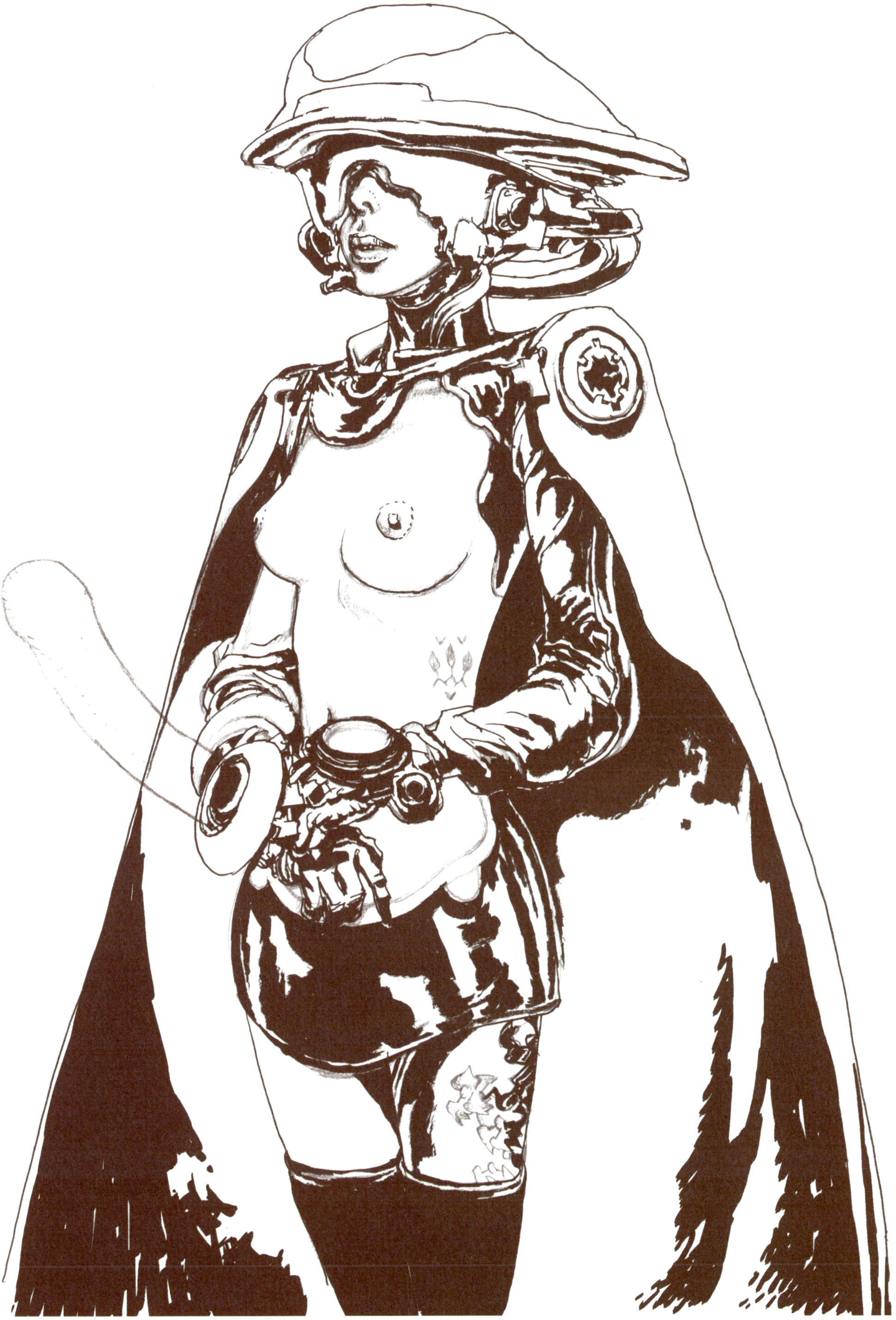

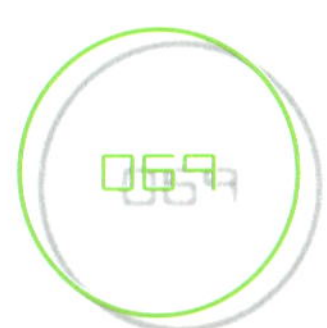

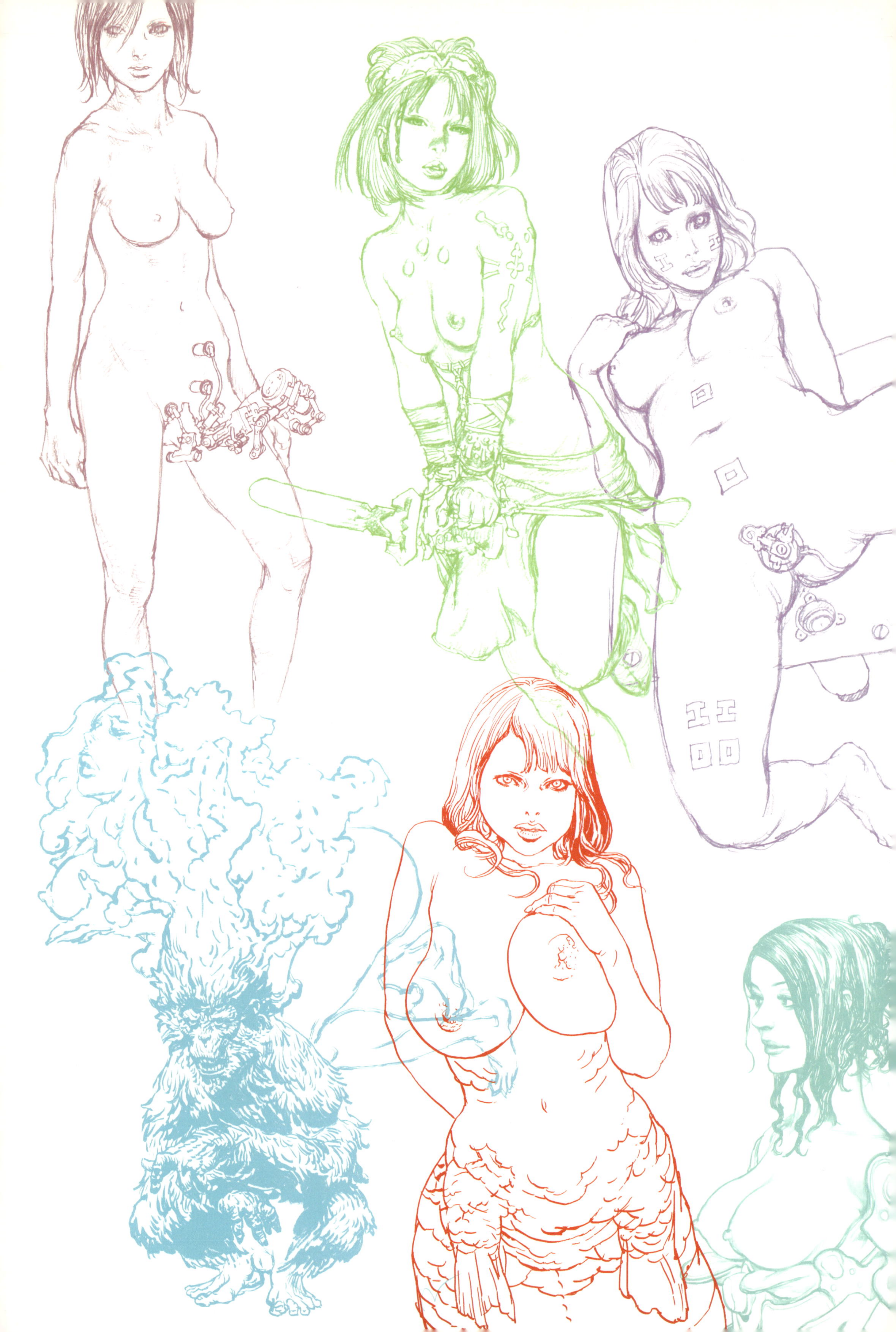

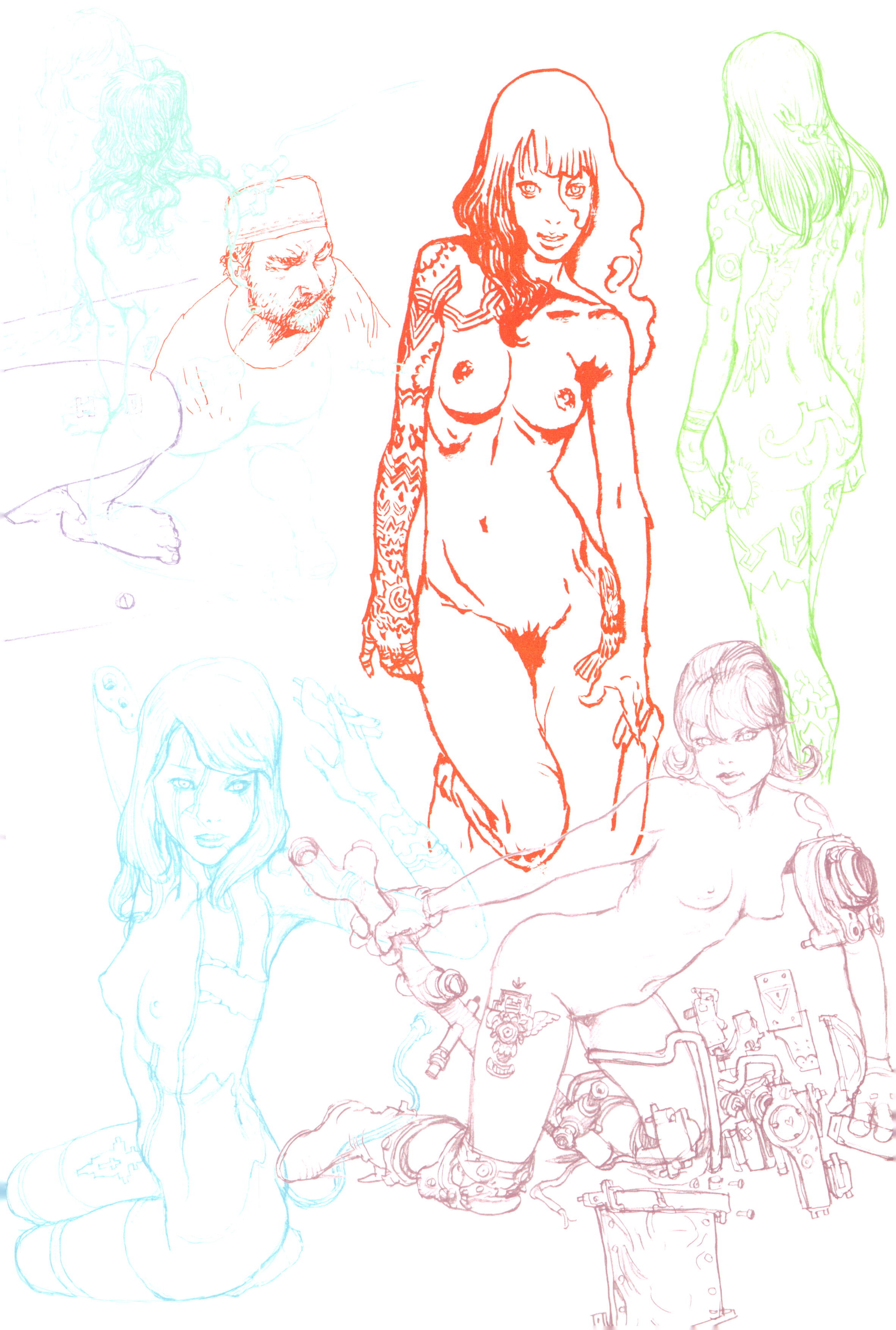

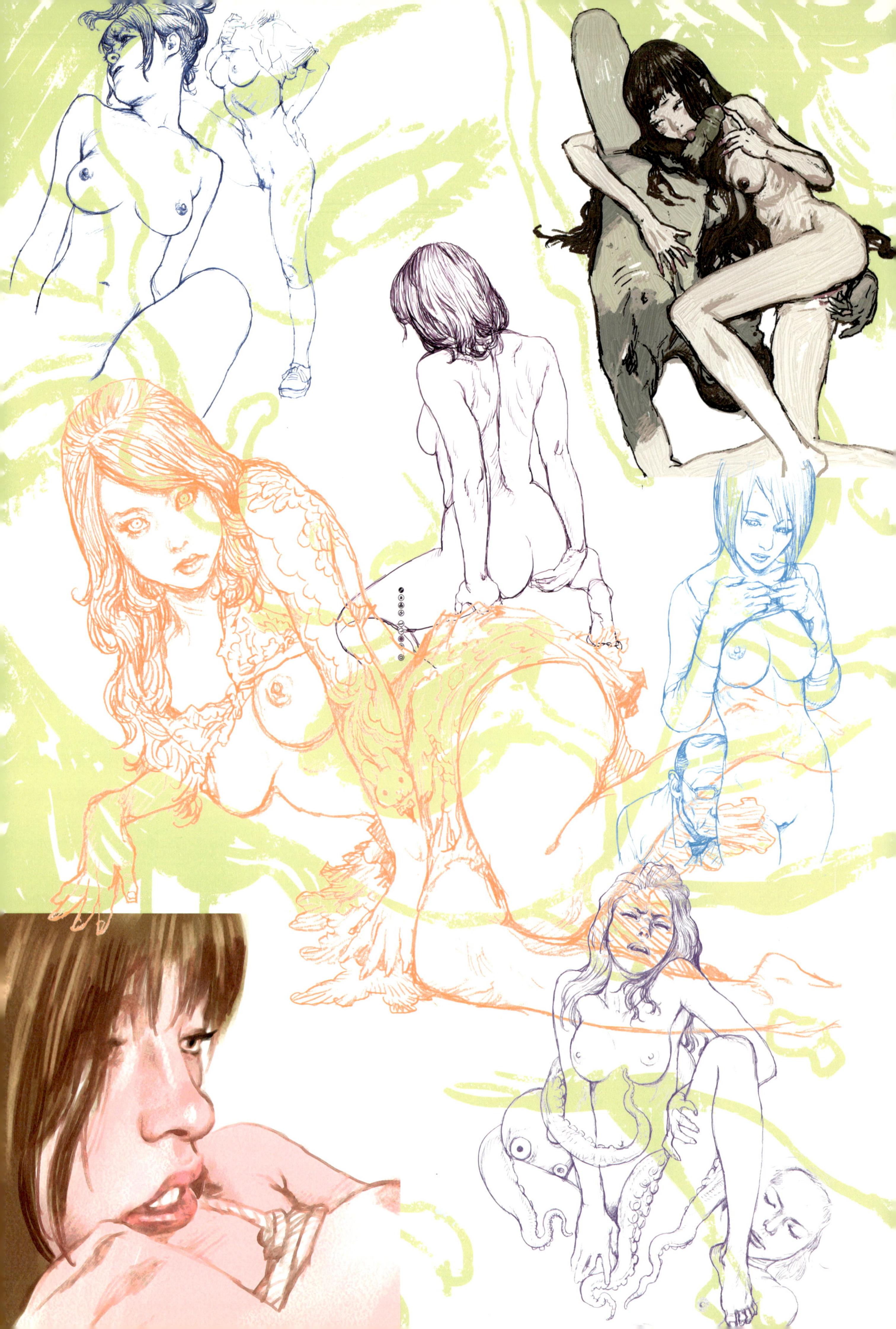

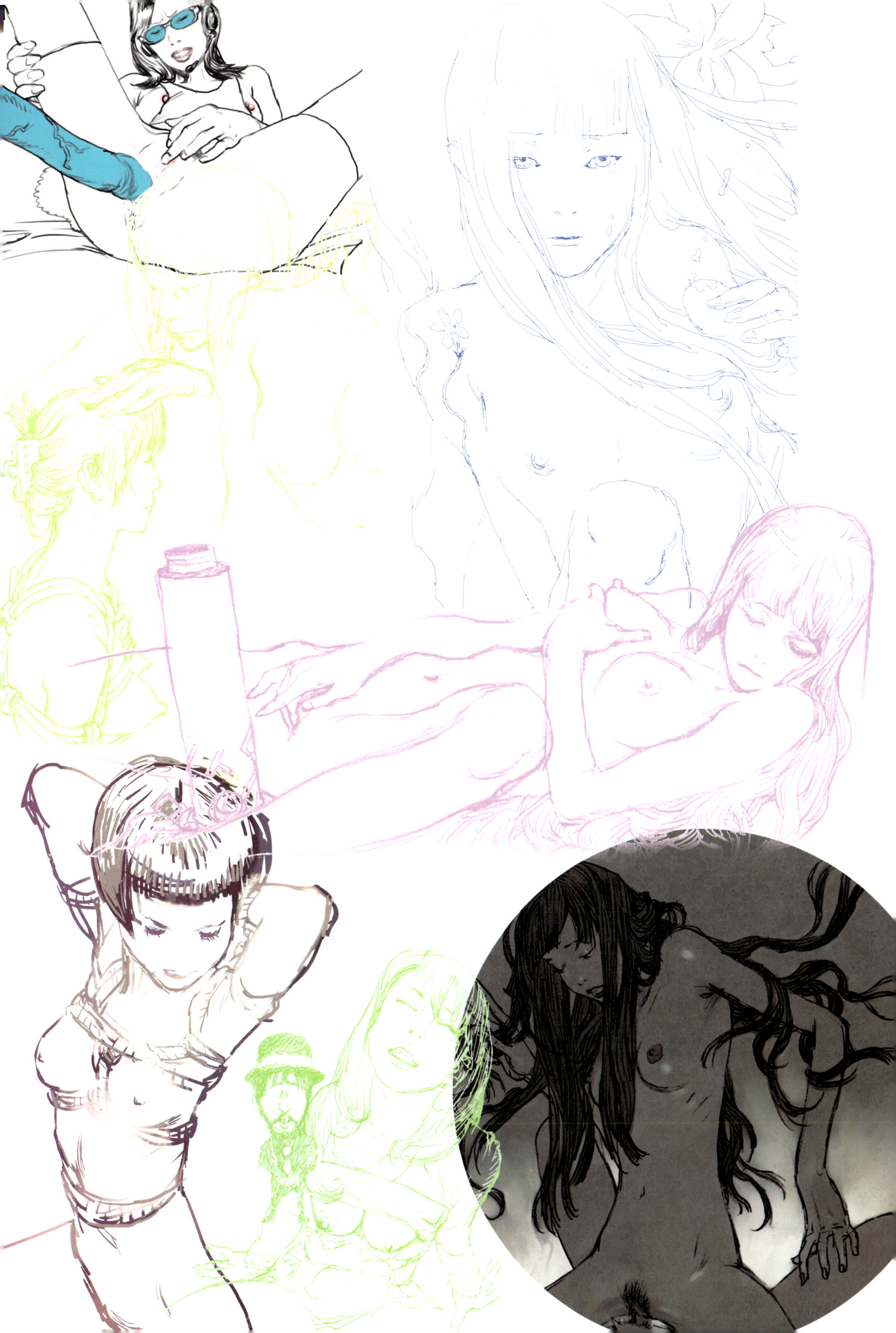

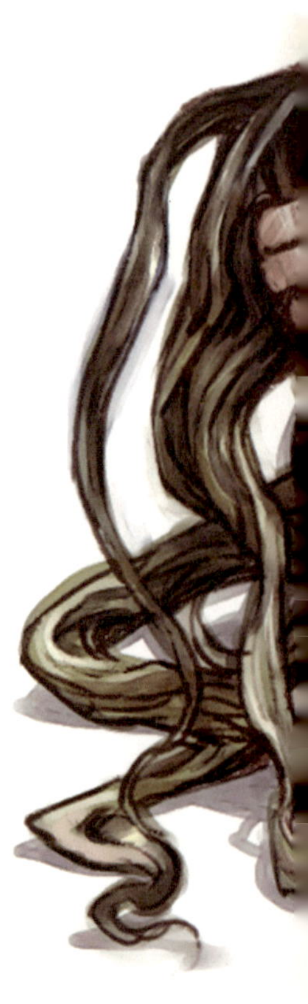

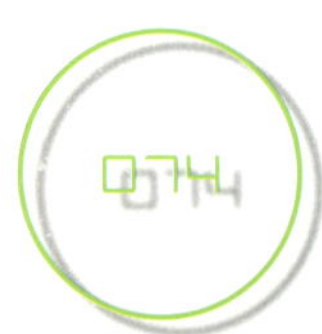

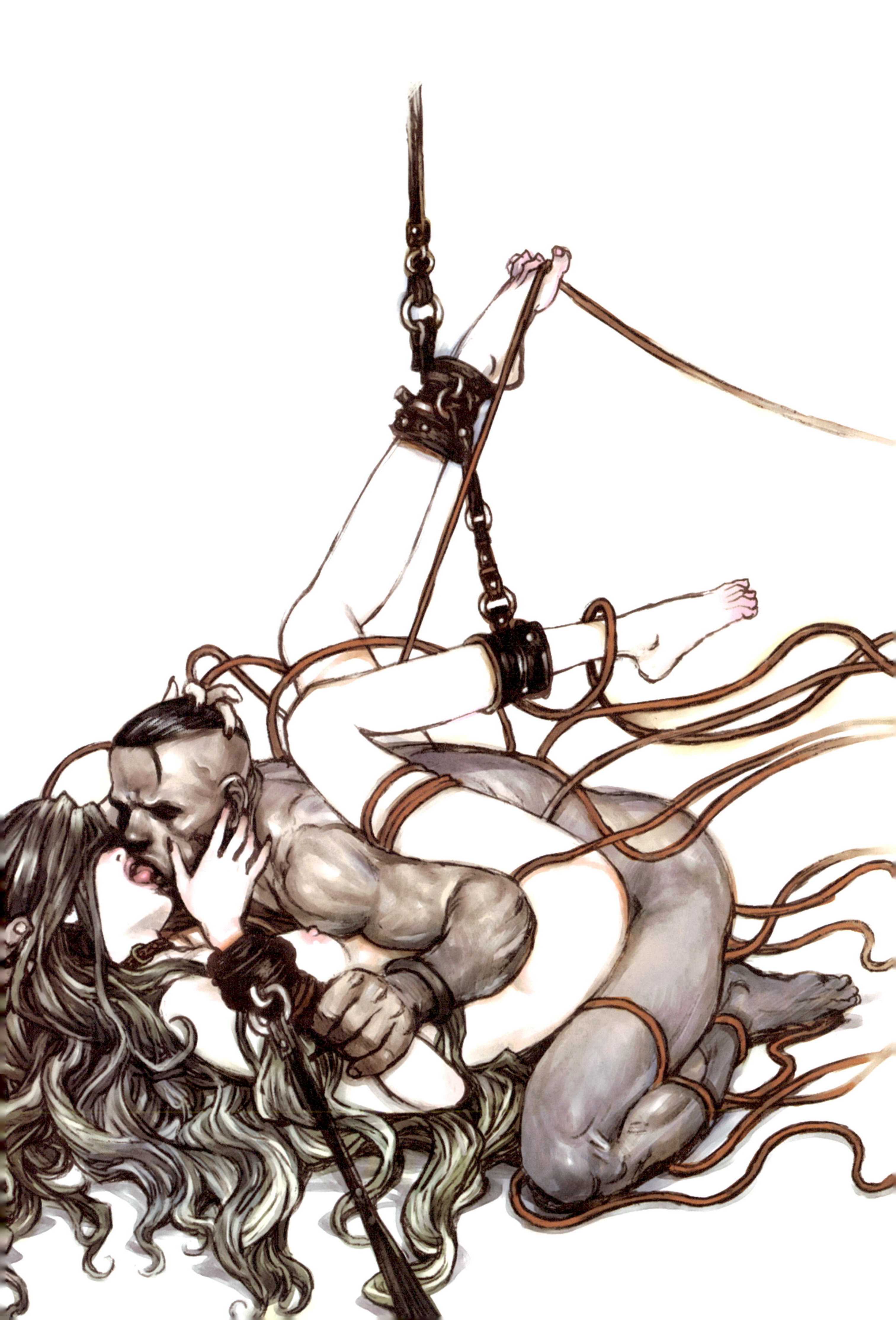

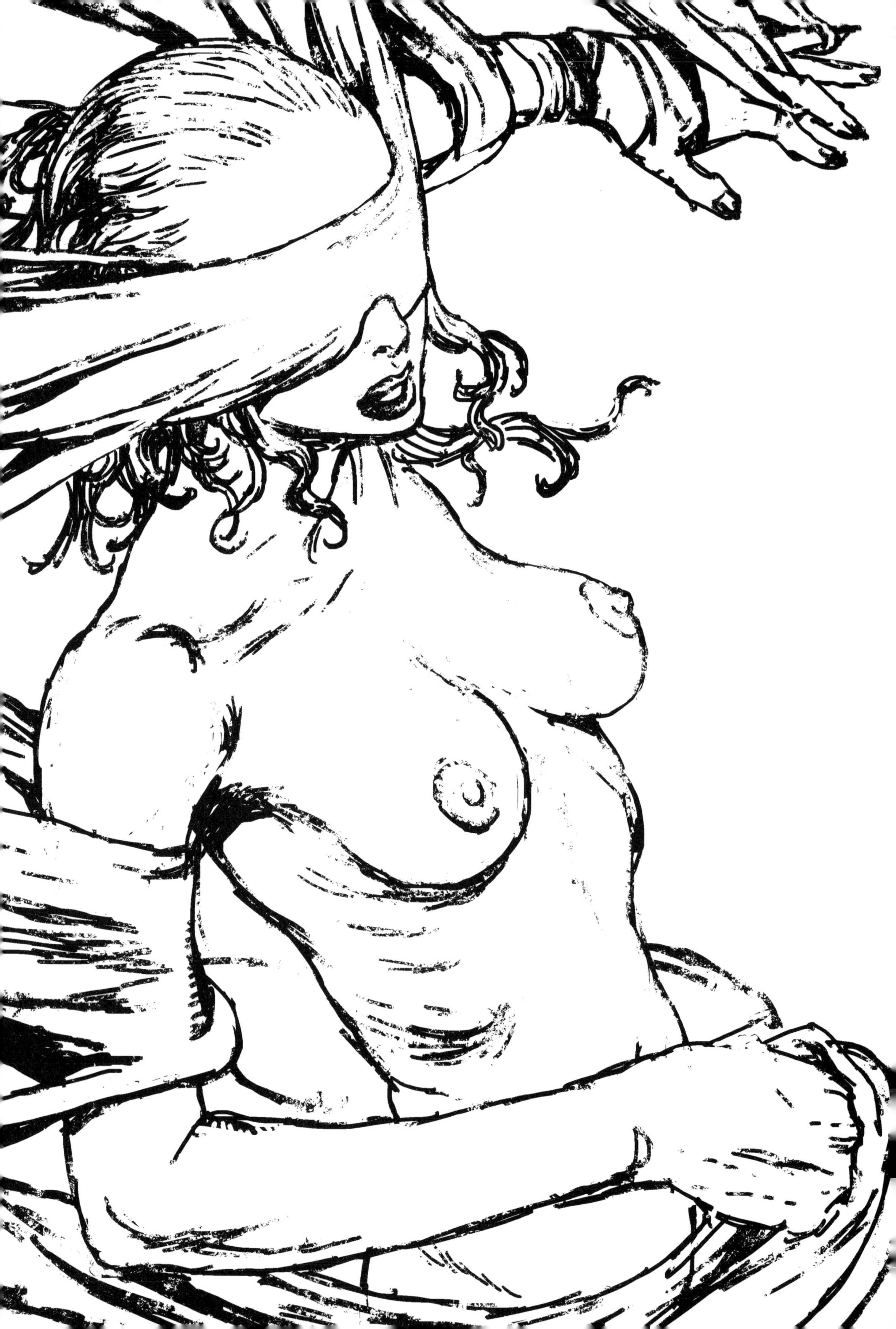

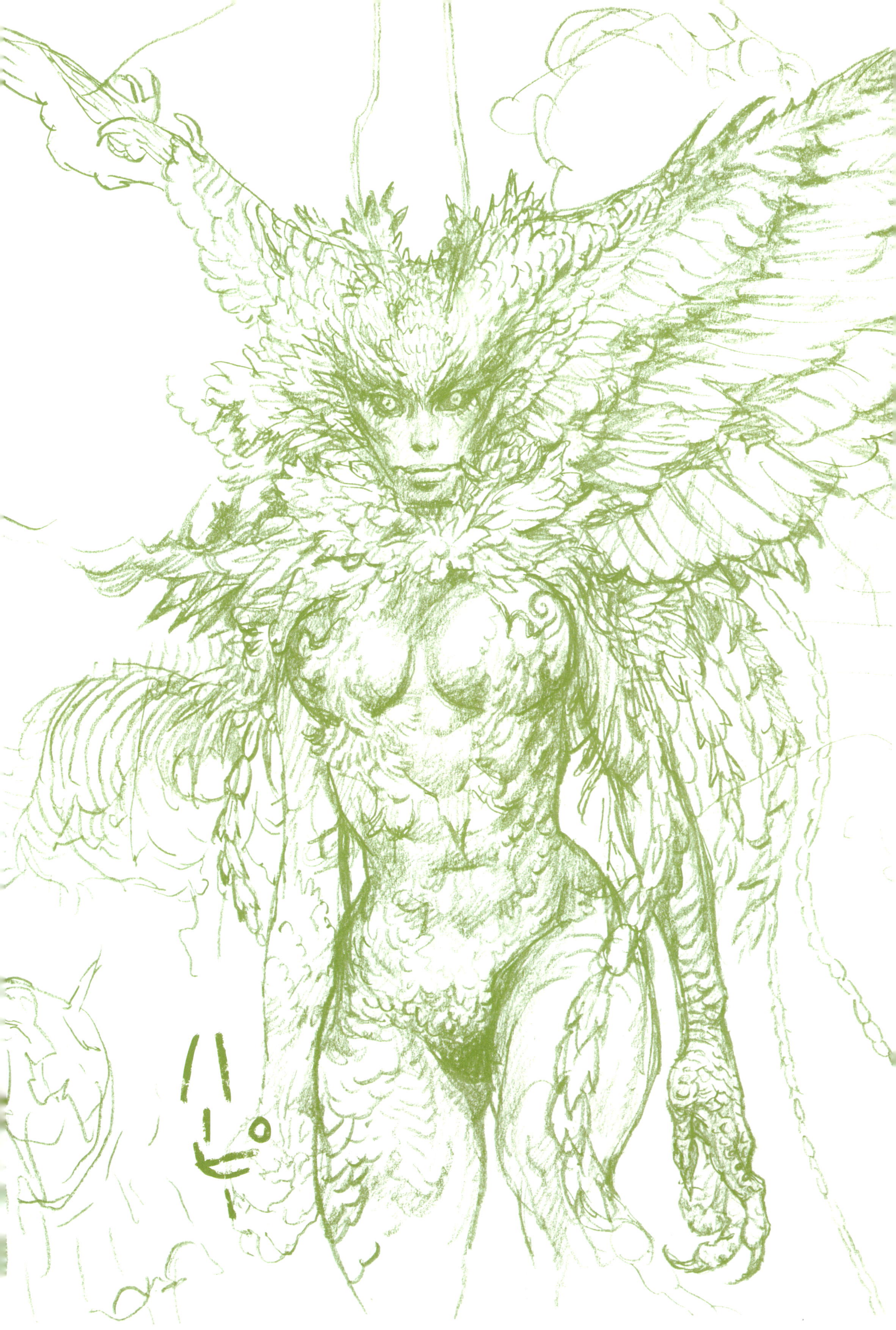

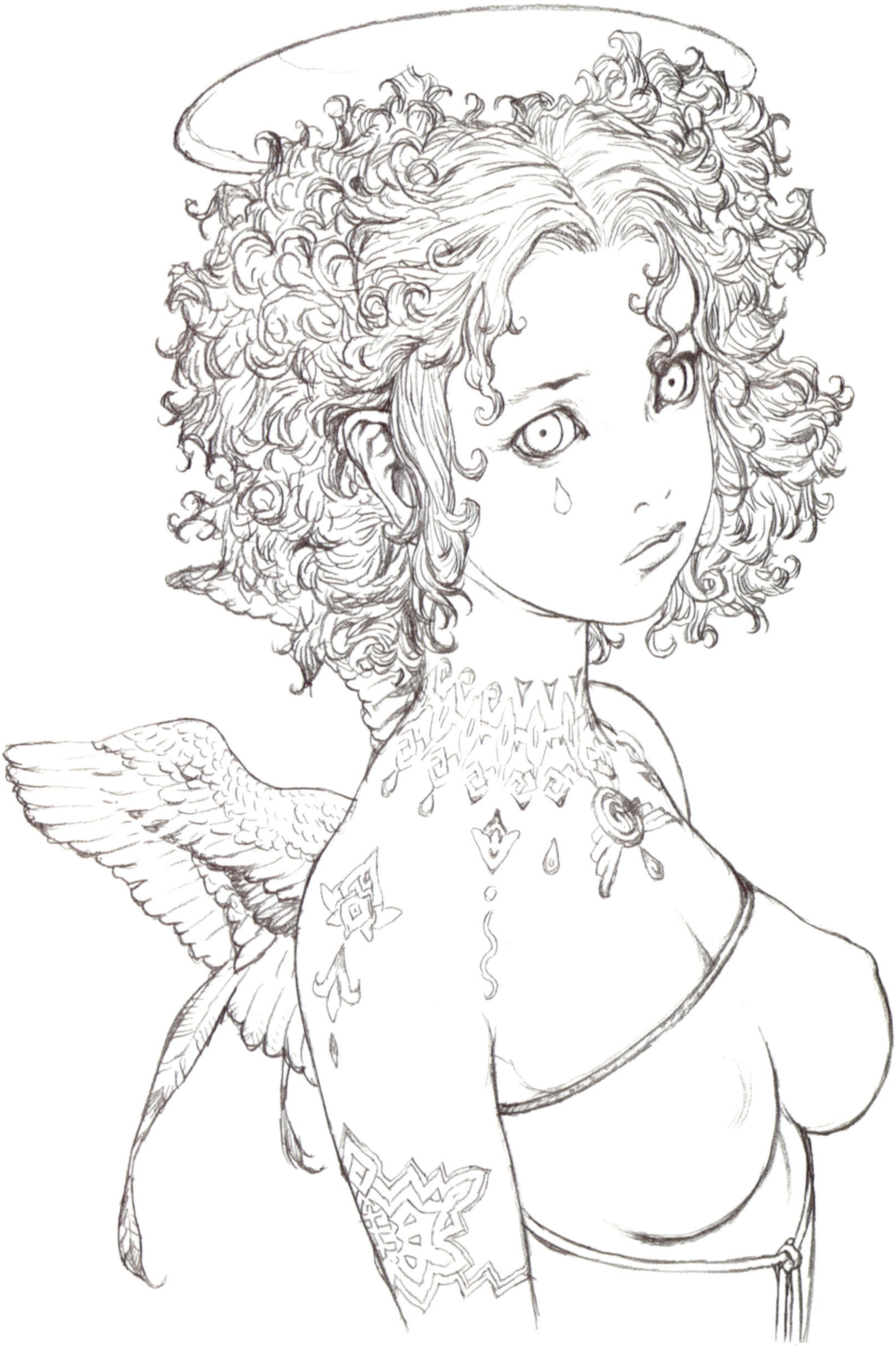

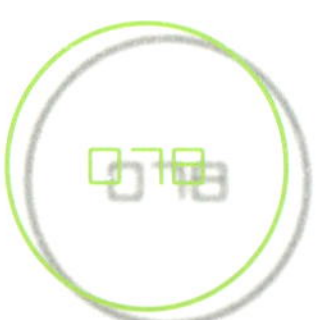

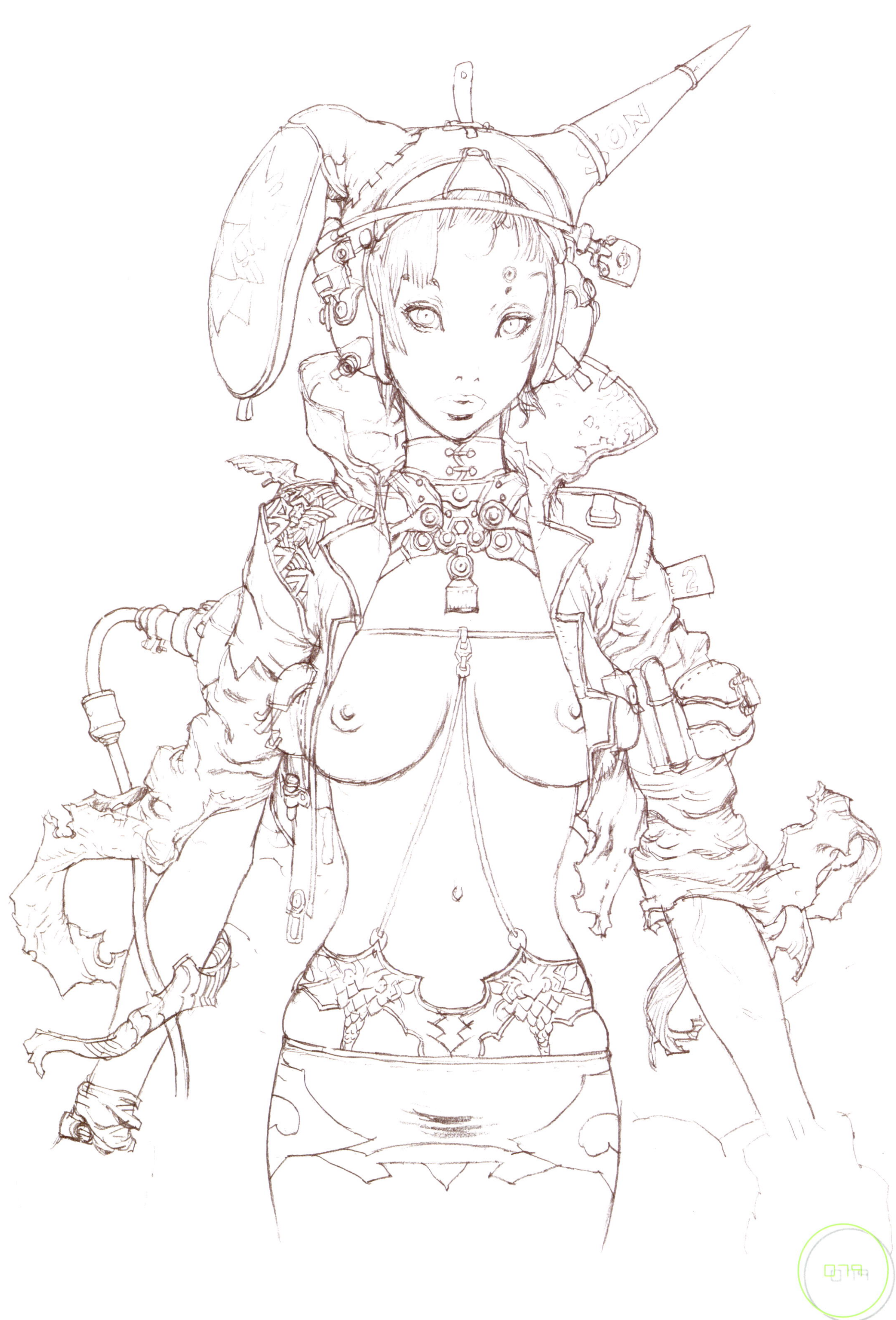

2

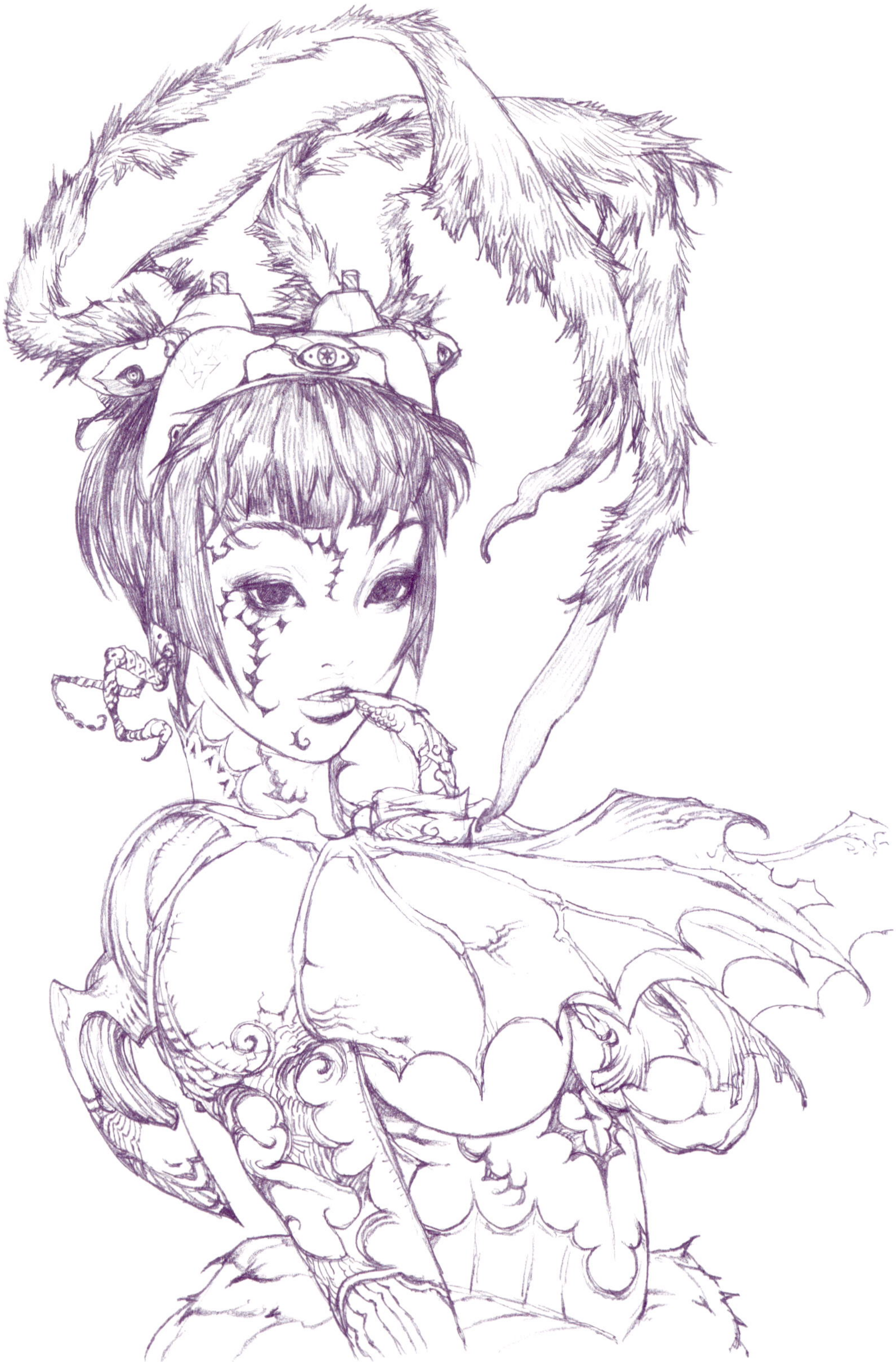

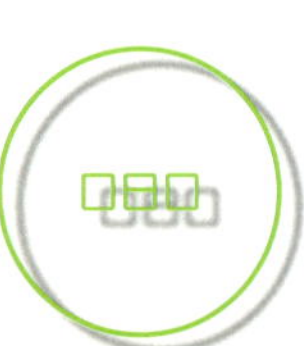

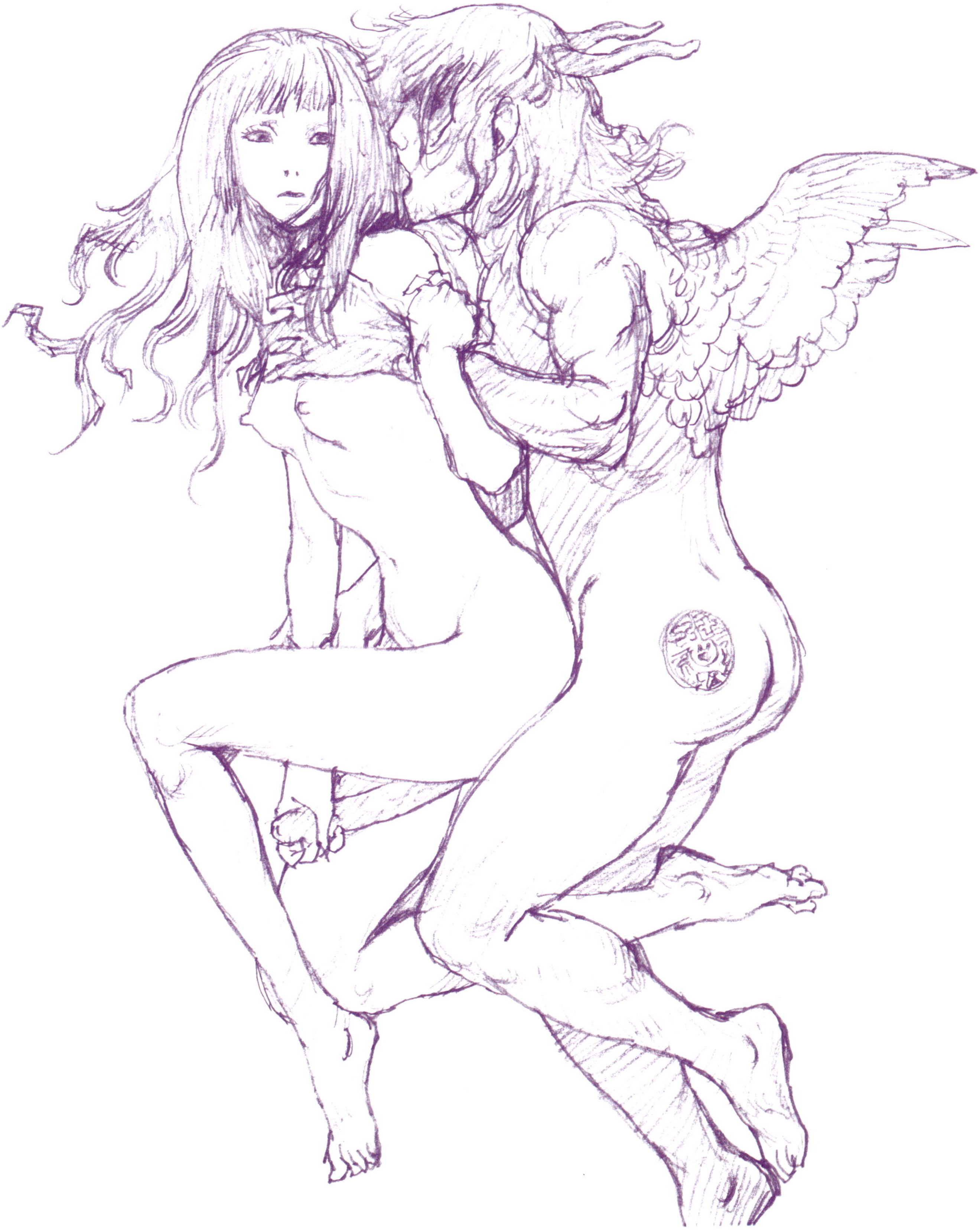

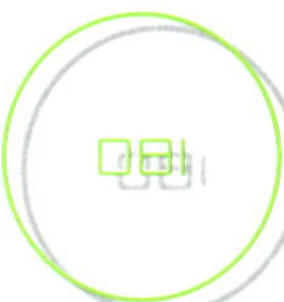

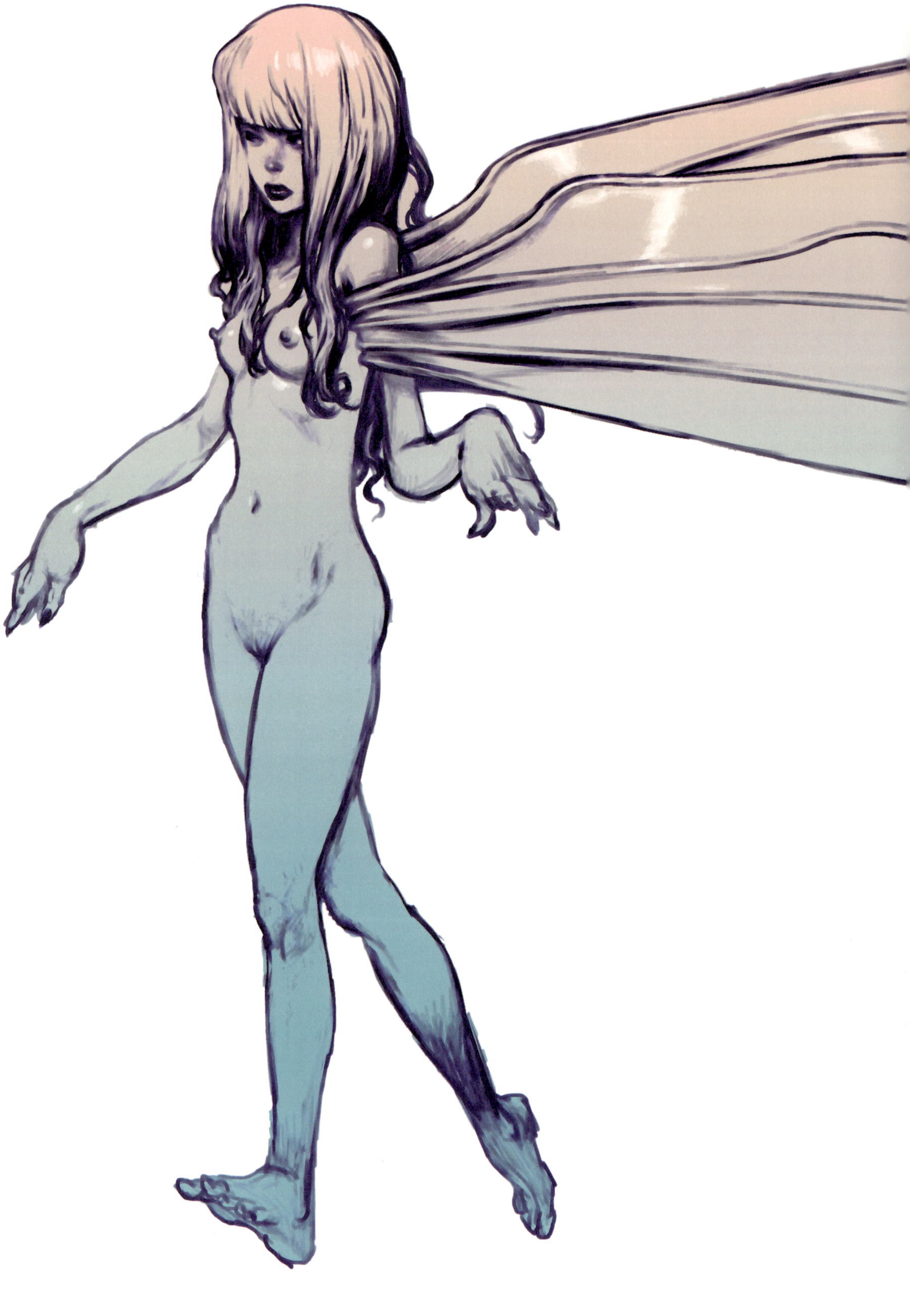

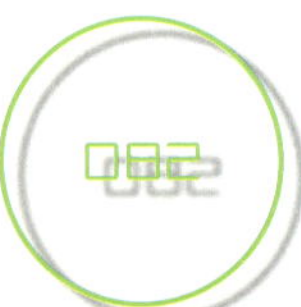

エロ×メカIII

EROTIC ENGINEERING III

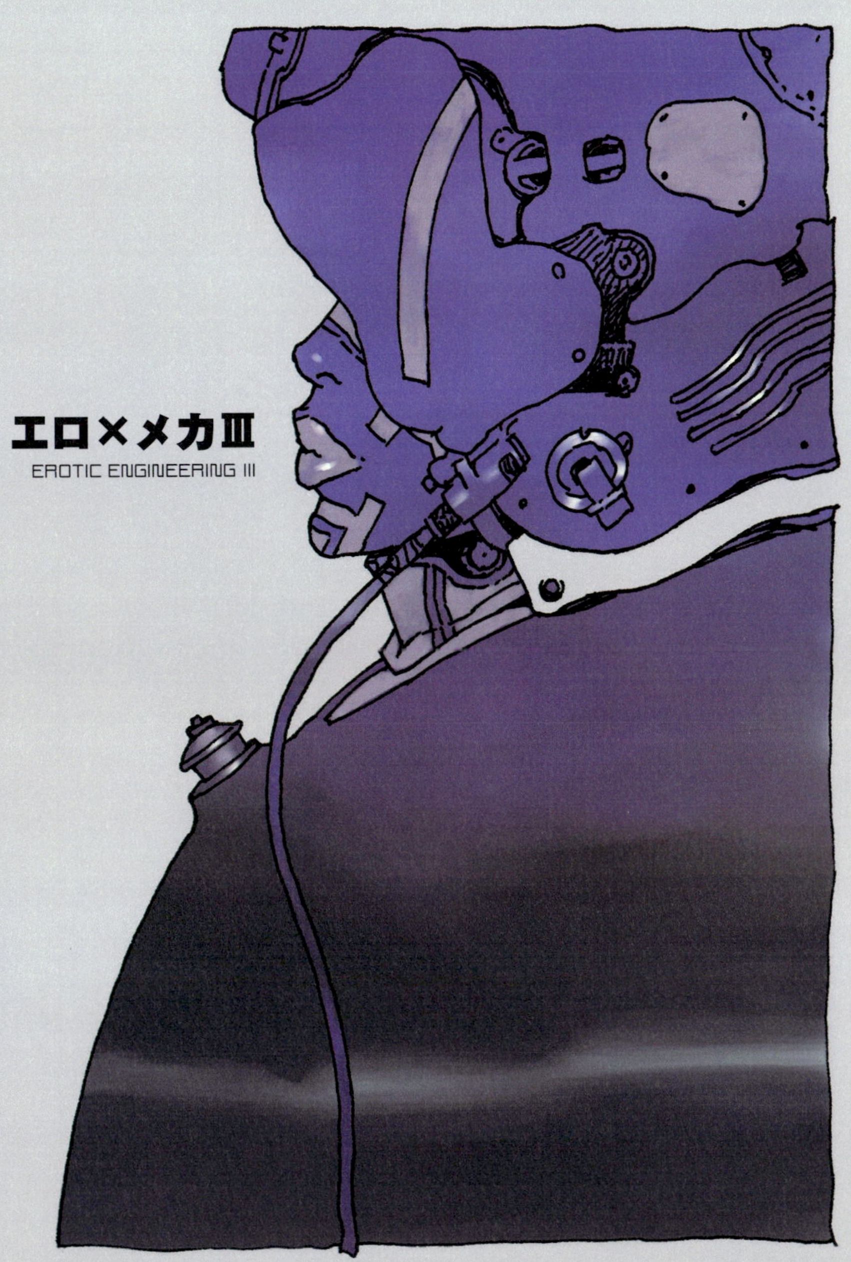

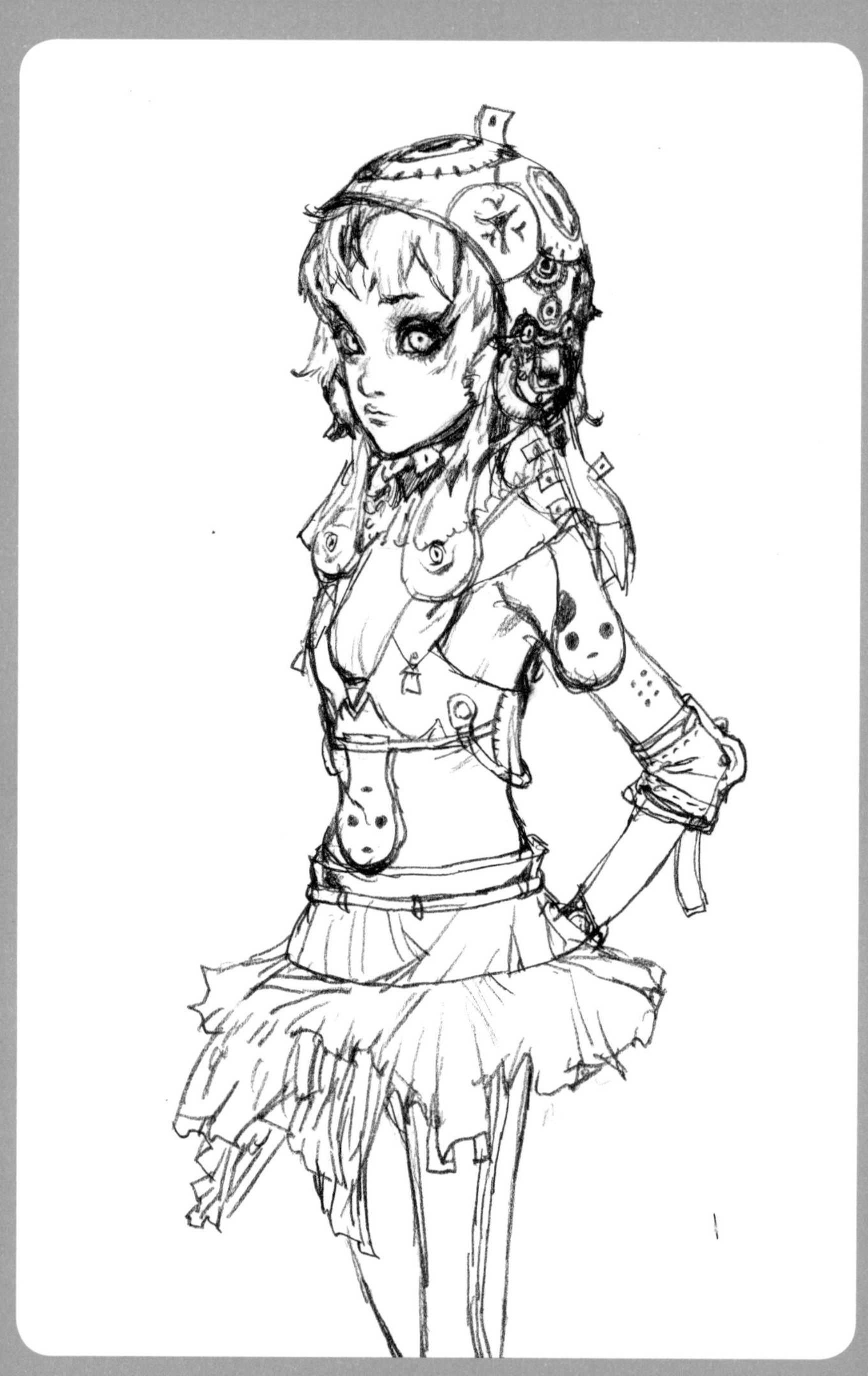

肉体と異物が融合した姿もエロかっこいい。
身近なところでは歯列矯正の器具を装着した姿とかもなかなかにいい。
究極的には翼を直接カラダに埋め込んでもらいたい。
全裸で羽ばたき天空高く舞い上がる姿に激しく勃起していきたいと思う。

Fusions of flesh and foreign objects are also cool and erotic. In the case of familiar situations, I find people with braces on their teeth pretty cool. Eventually, I want wings to be directly embedded in bodies. I want to get a violent hard-on when I see a totally naked body flap its wings and fly high up into the sky.

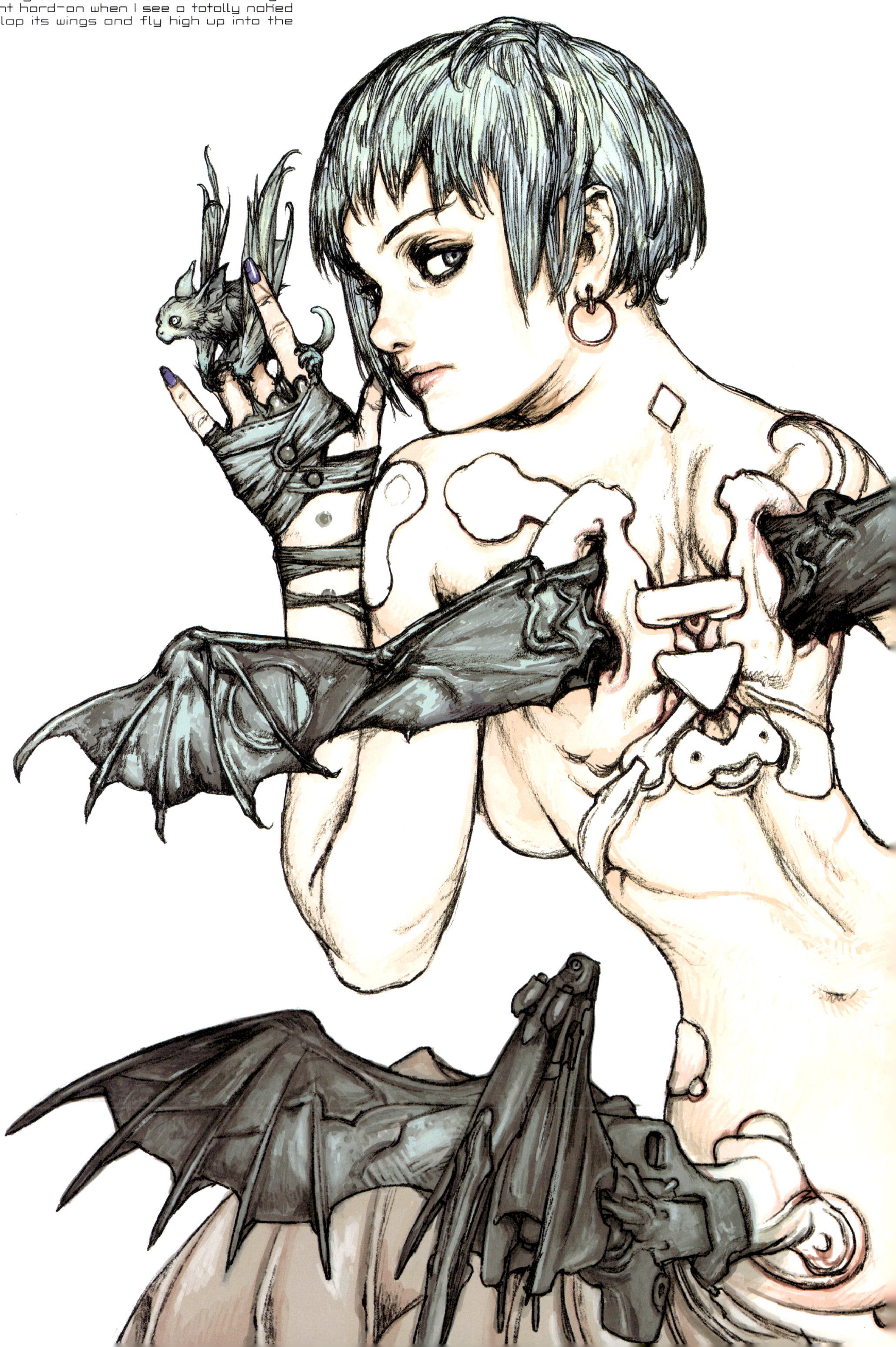

浴衣や和服に萌えるとかはとりたててない。ないが勿論嫌いとかでもない。
脱がせられるのなら、なおいい。
和服は洋服に比べると、さまざまな部位へのアクセスが早くて、そこはいいものだ。

I don't get particularly aroused by yukata or formal Japanese wear. But, of course, I don't dislike them. But what I really like is the process of undressing. Compared to western clothes, Japanese clothes allow quick access to various parts, and that is what makes them nice.

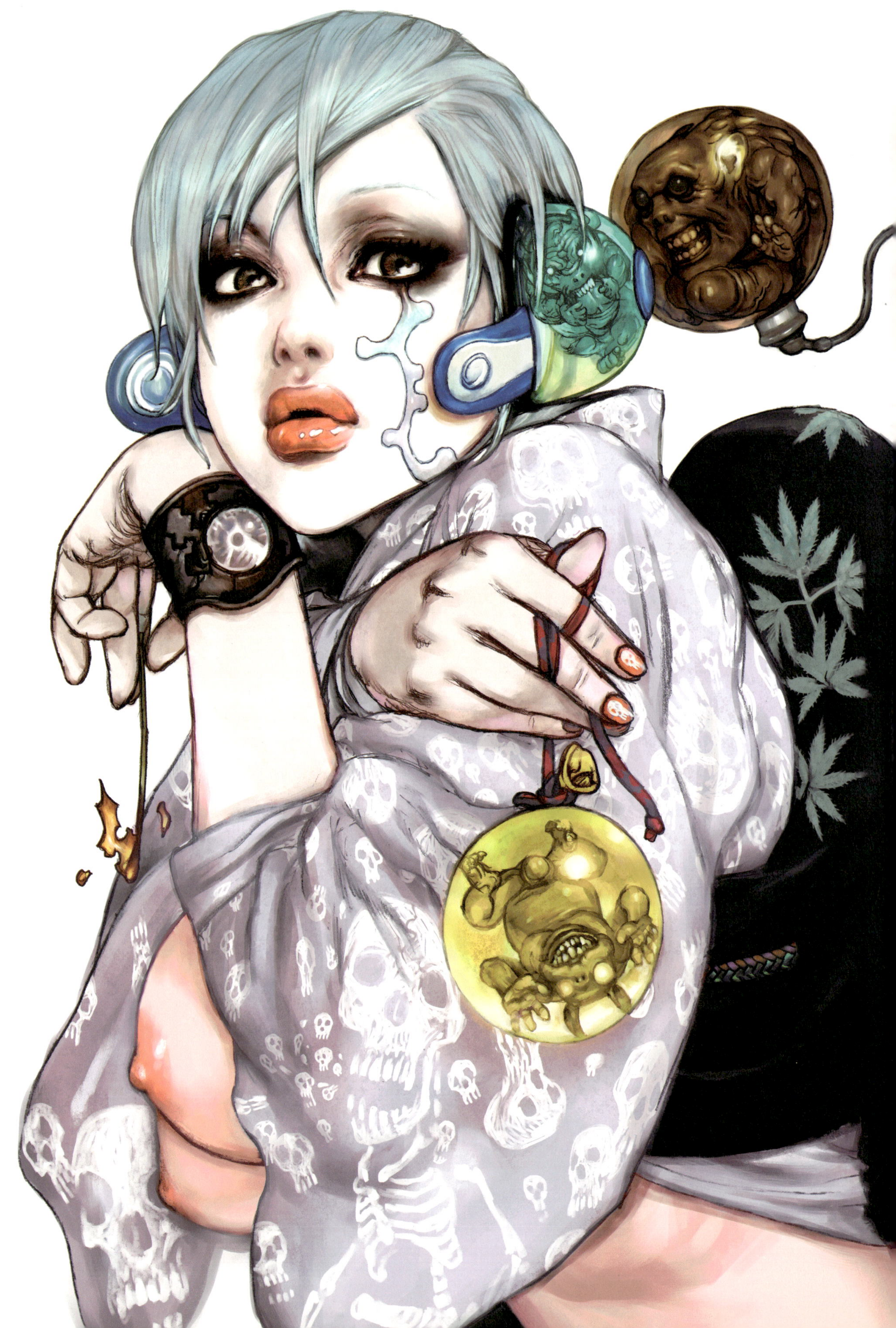

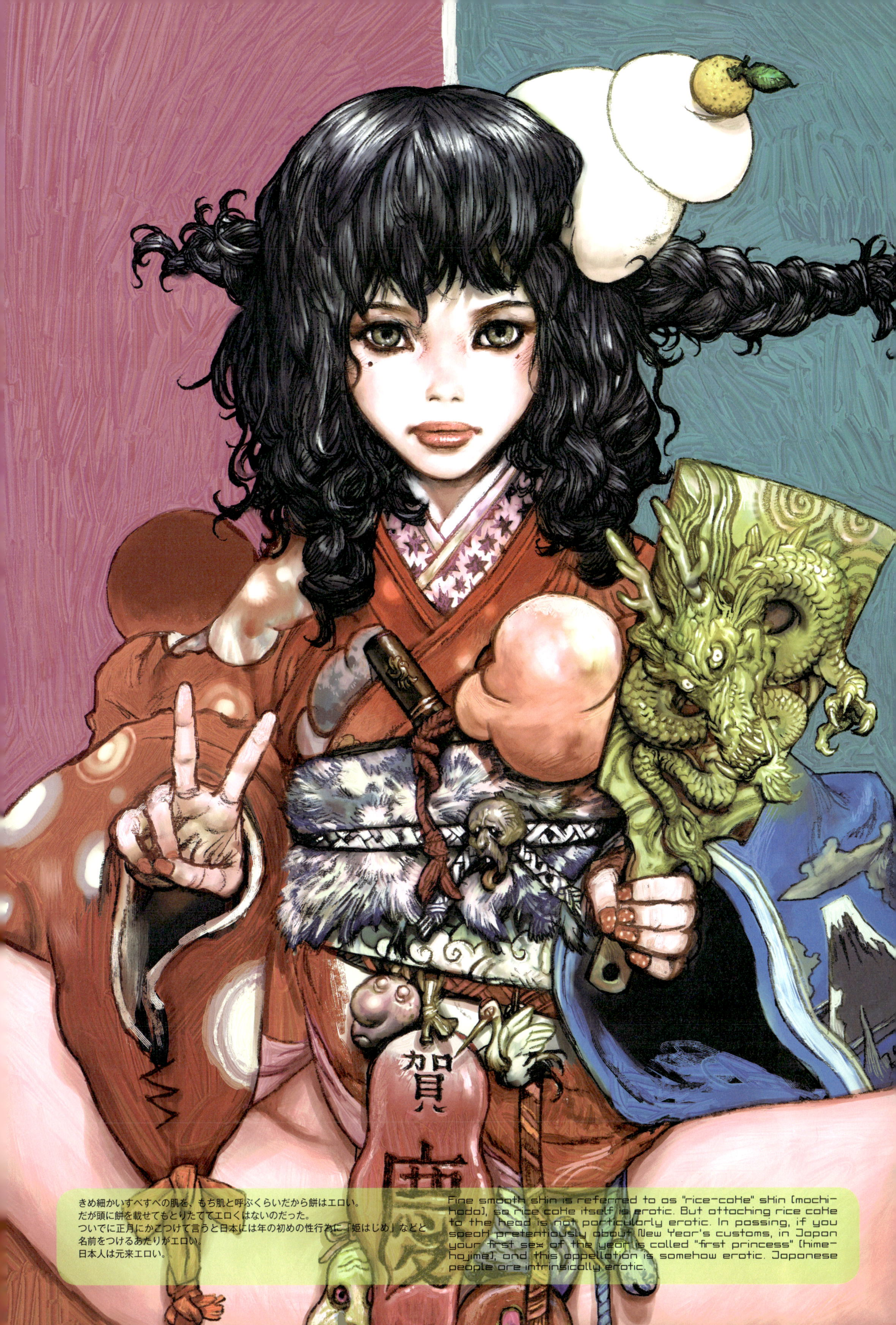

きめ細かいすべすべの肌を、もち肌と呼ぶくらいだから餅はエロい。
だが頭に餅を載せてもとりたててエロくはないのだった。
ついでに正月にかこつけて言うと日本には年の初めの性行為に「姫はじめ」などと名前をつけるあたりがエロい。
日本人は元来エロい。

Fine smooth skin is referred to as "rice-cake" skin [mochi-hada], so rice cake itself is erotic. But attaching rice cake to the head is not particularly erotic. In passing, if you speak pretentiously about New Year's customs, in Japan your first sex of the year is called "first princess" [hime-hajime], and this appellation is somehow erotic. Japanese people are intrinsically erotic.

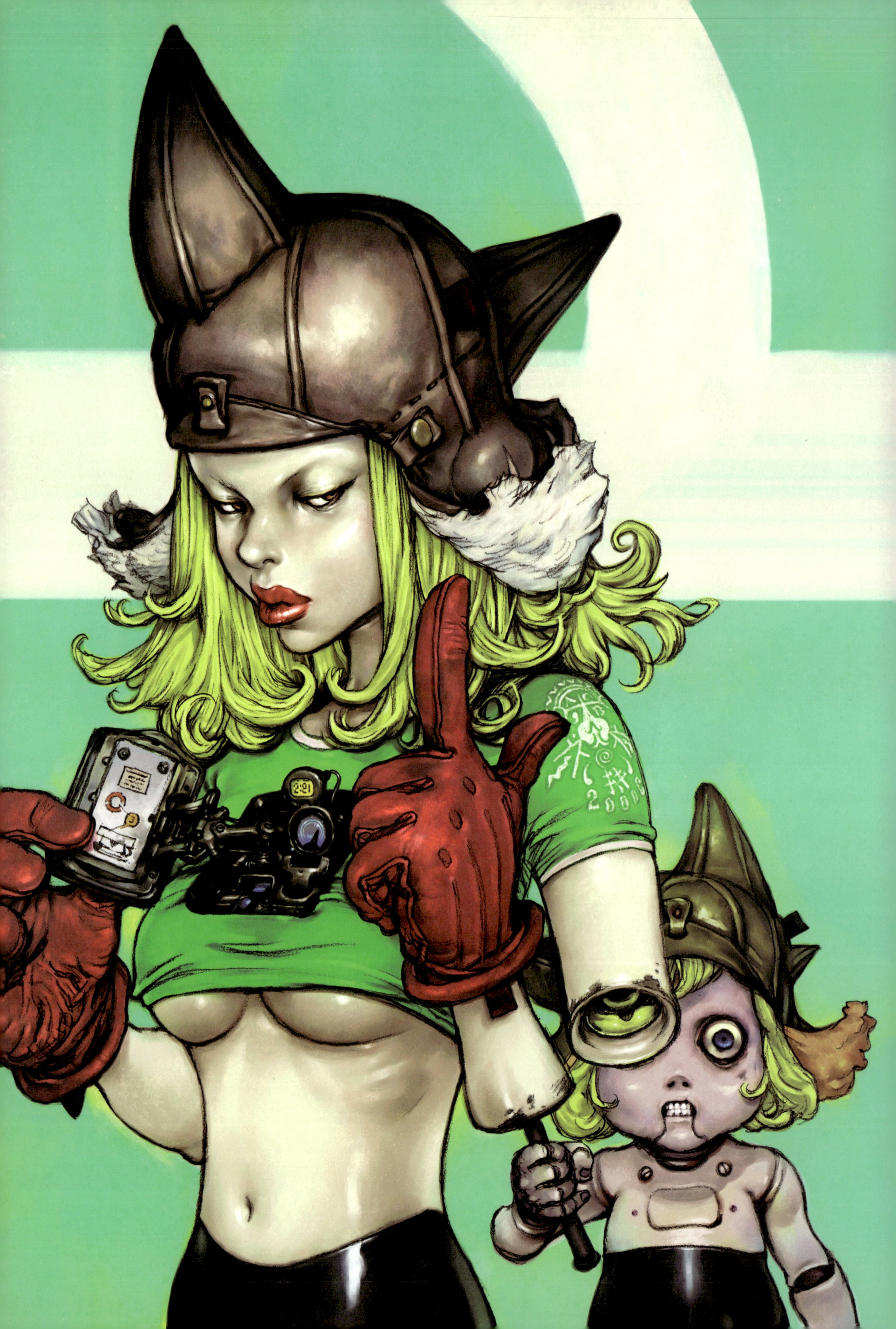

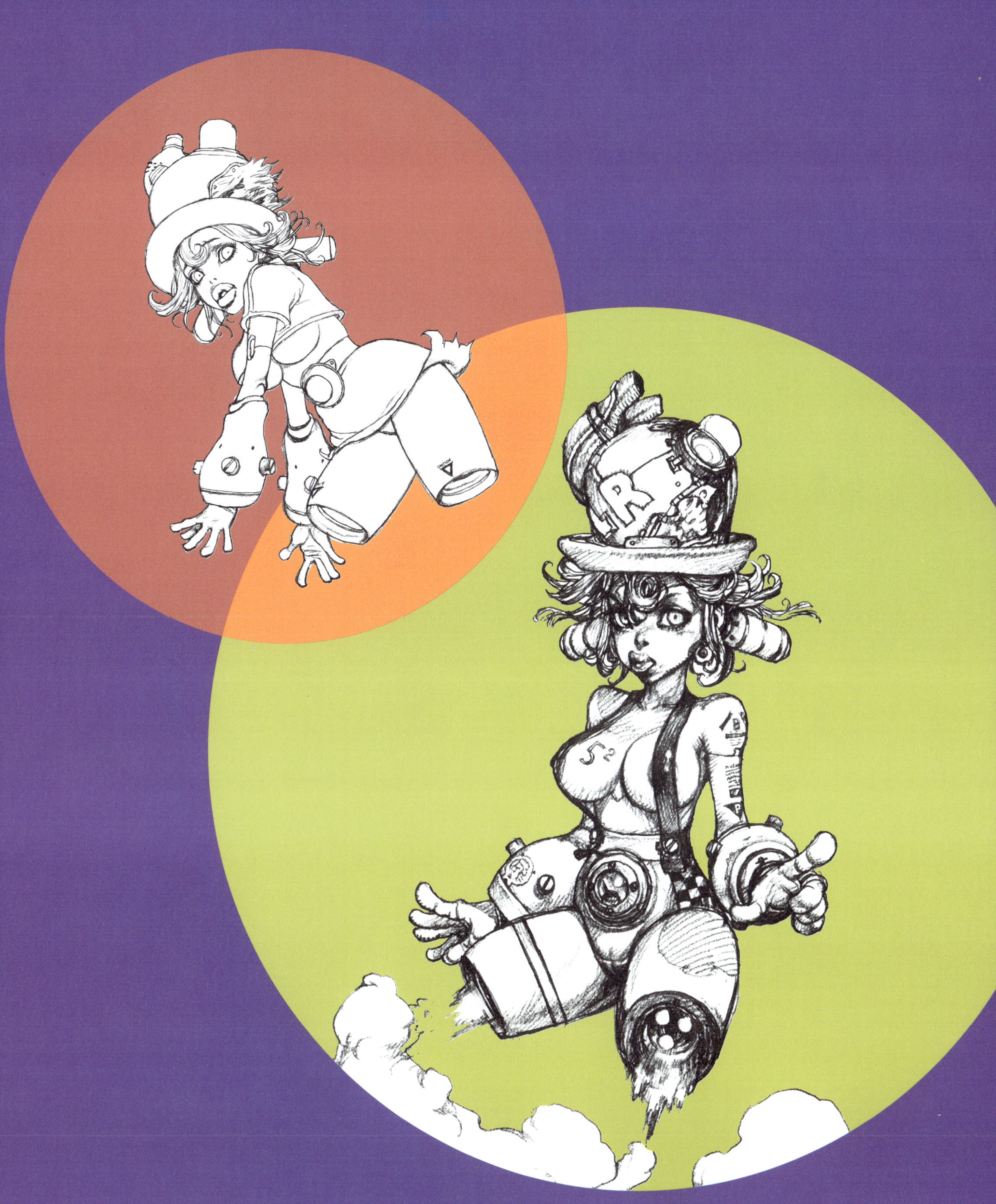

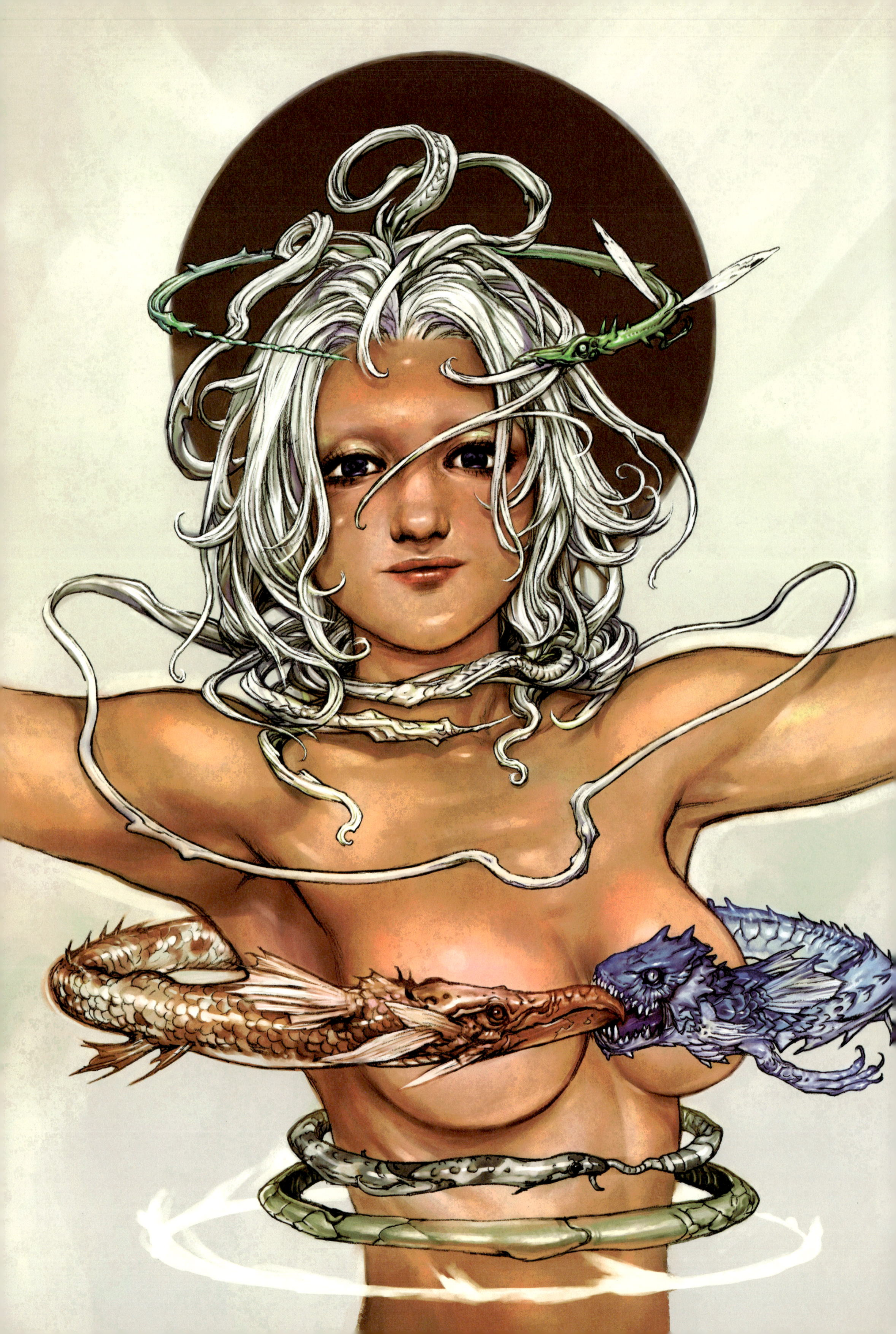

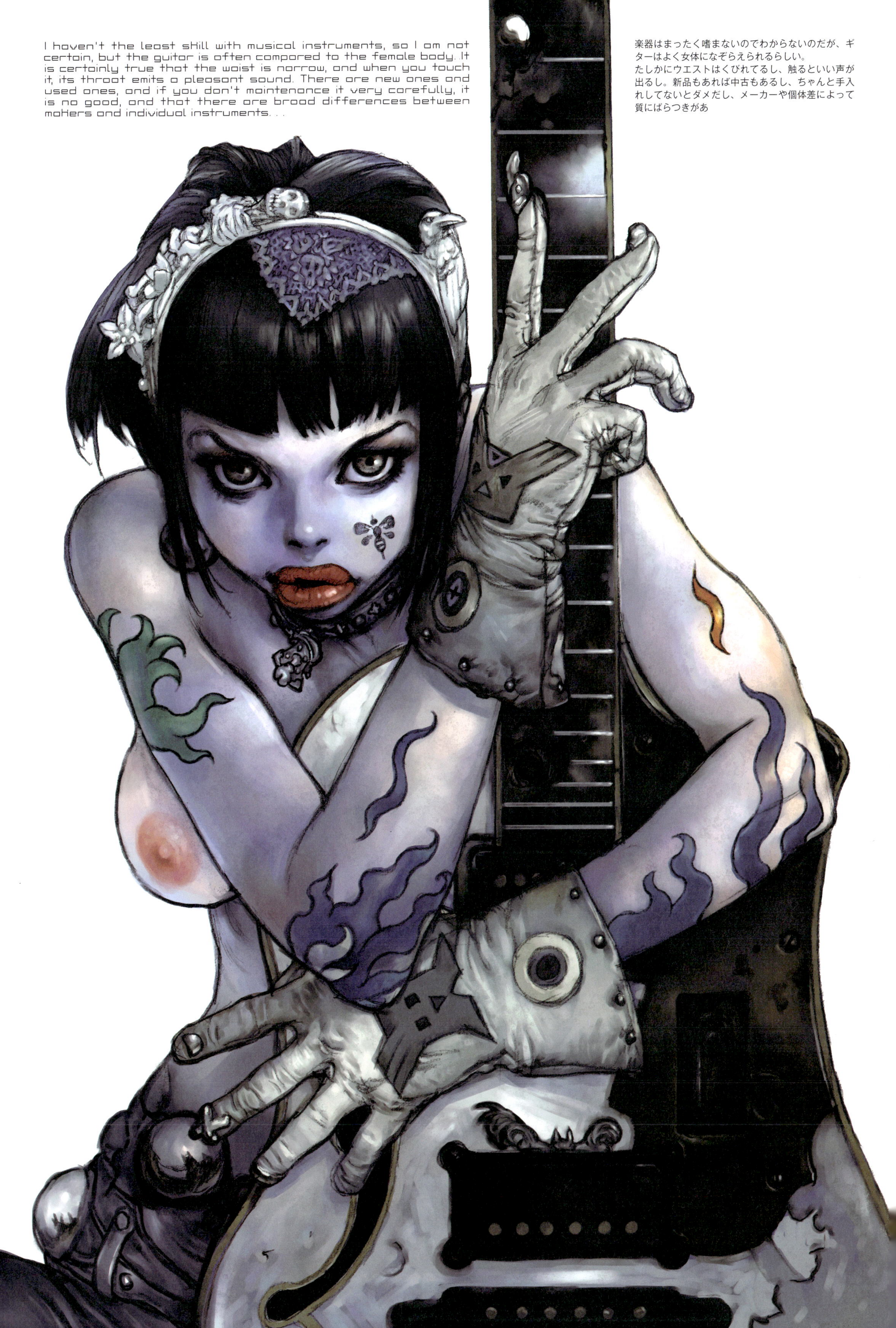

I haven't the least skill with musical instruments, so I am not certain, but the guitar is often compared to the female body. It is certainly true that the waist is narrow, and when you touch it, its throat emits a pleasant sound. There are new ones and used ones, and if you don't maintenance it very carefully, it is no good, and that there are broad differences between makers and individual instruments. . .

楽器はまったく嗜まないのでわからないのだが、ギターはよく女体になぞらえられるらしい。
たしかにウエストはくびれてるし、触るといい声が出るし。新品もあれば中古もあるし、ちゃんと手入れしてないとダメだし、メーカーや個体差によって質にばらつきがあ叩いて！ぶって！蹴って蹴って！！！！！
うそです。痛いの禁止。焦らされるのはいいが痛いのはダメ。

Strike me! Sock me! Kick me, Kick!!!!! No way! Pain is forbidden. Something that makes me nervous is OK, but pain is no good.

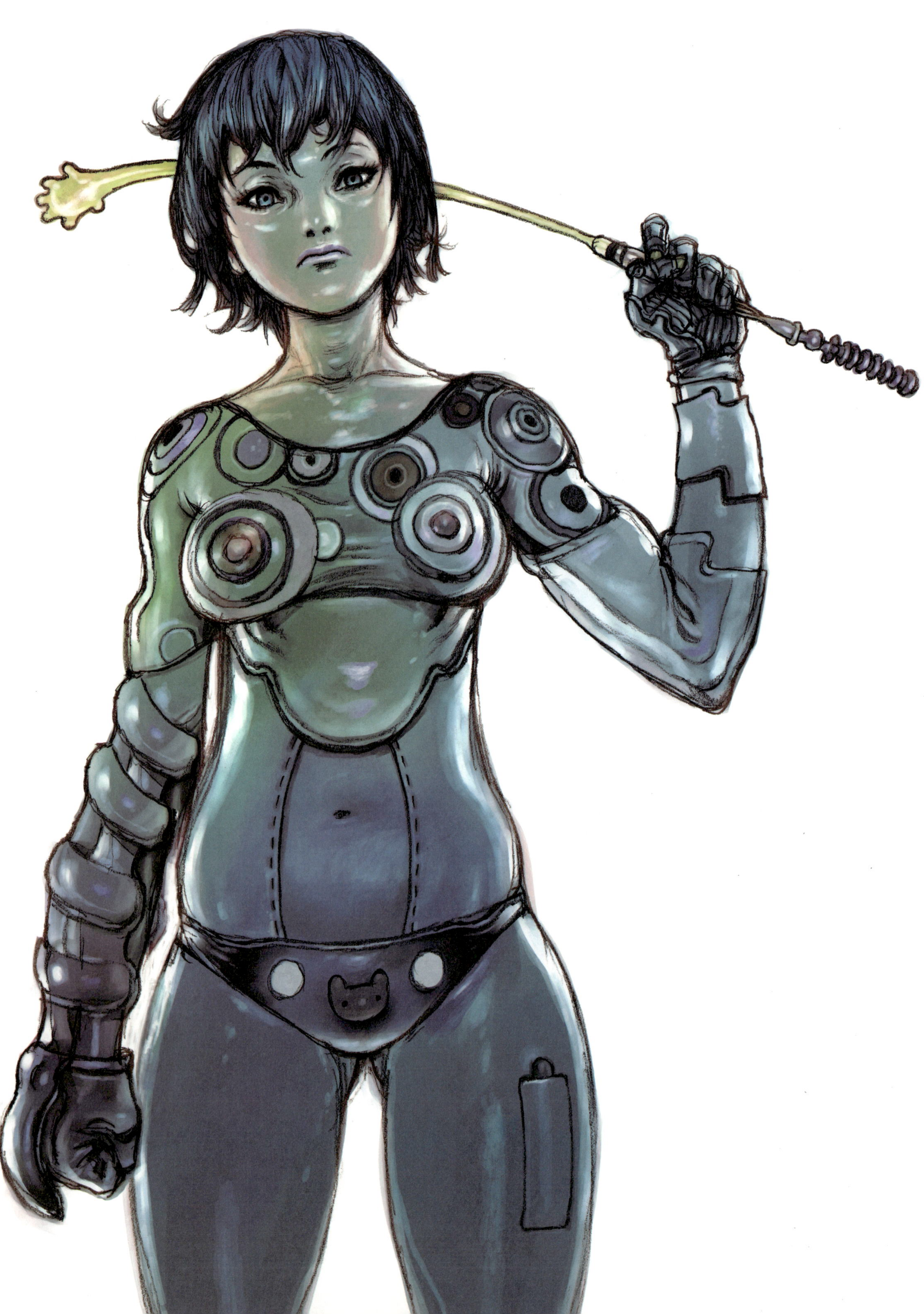

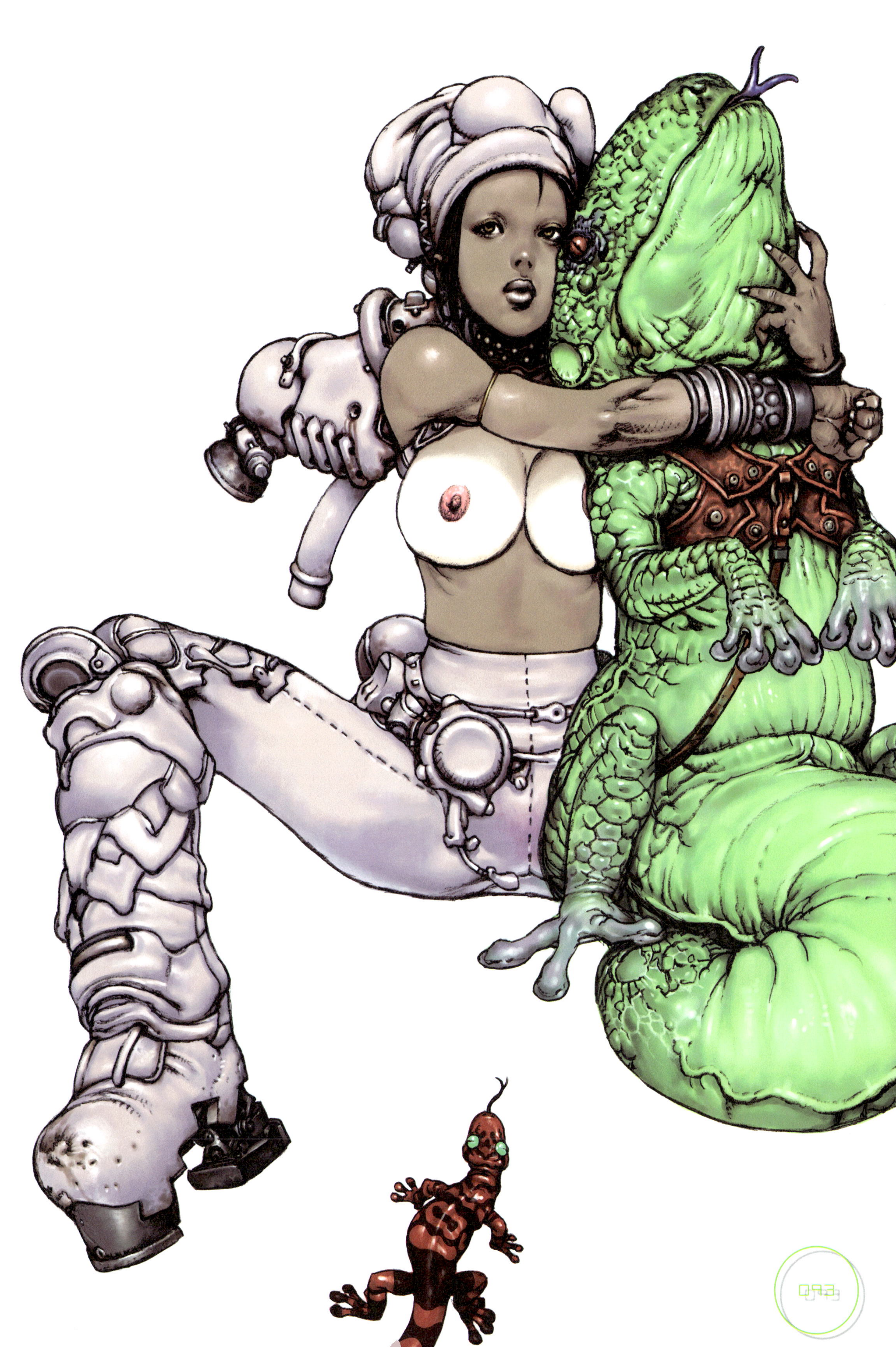

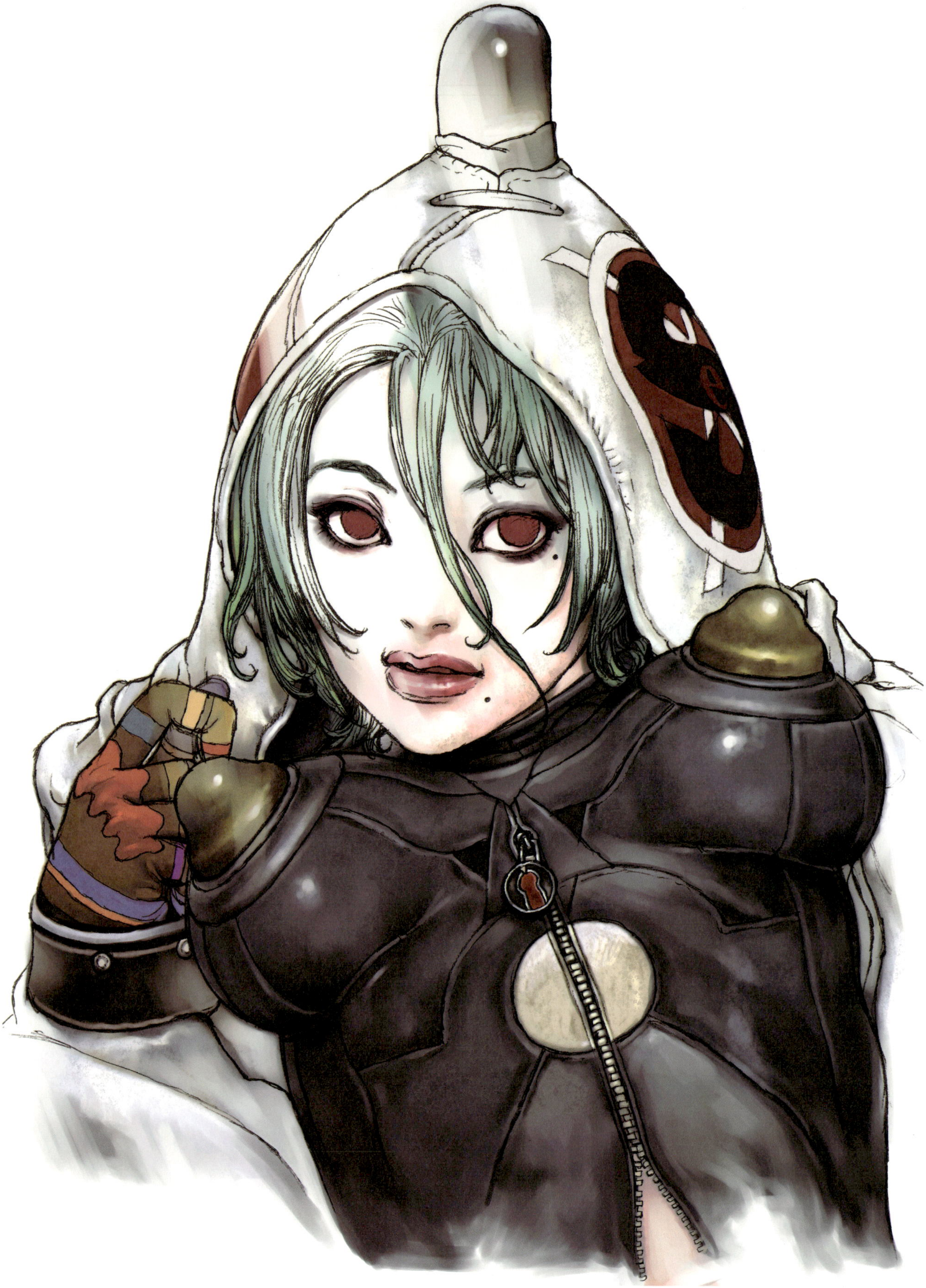

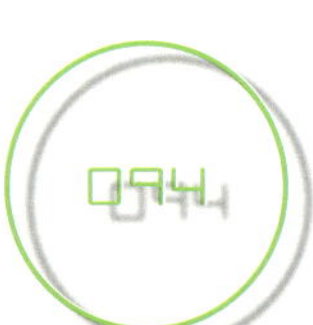

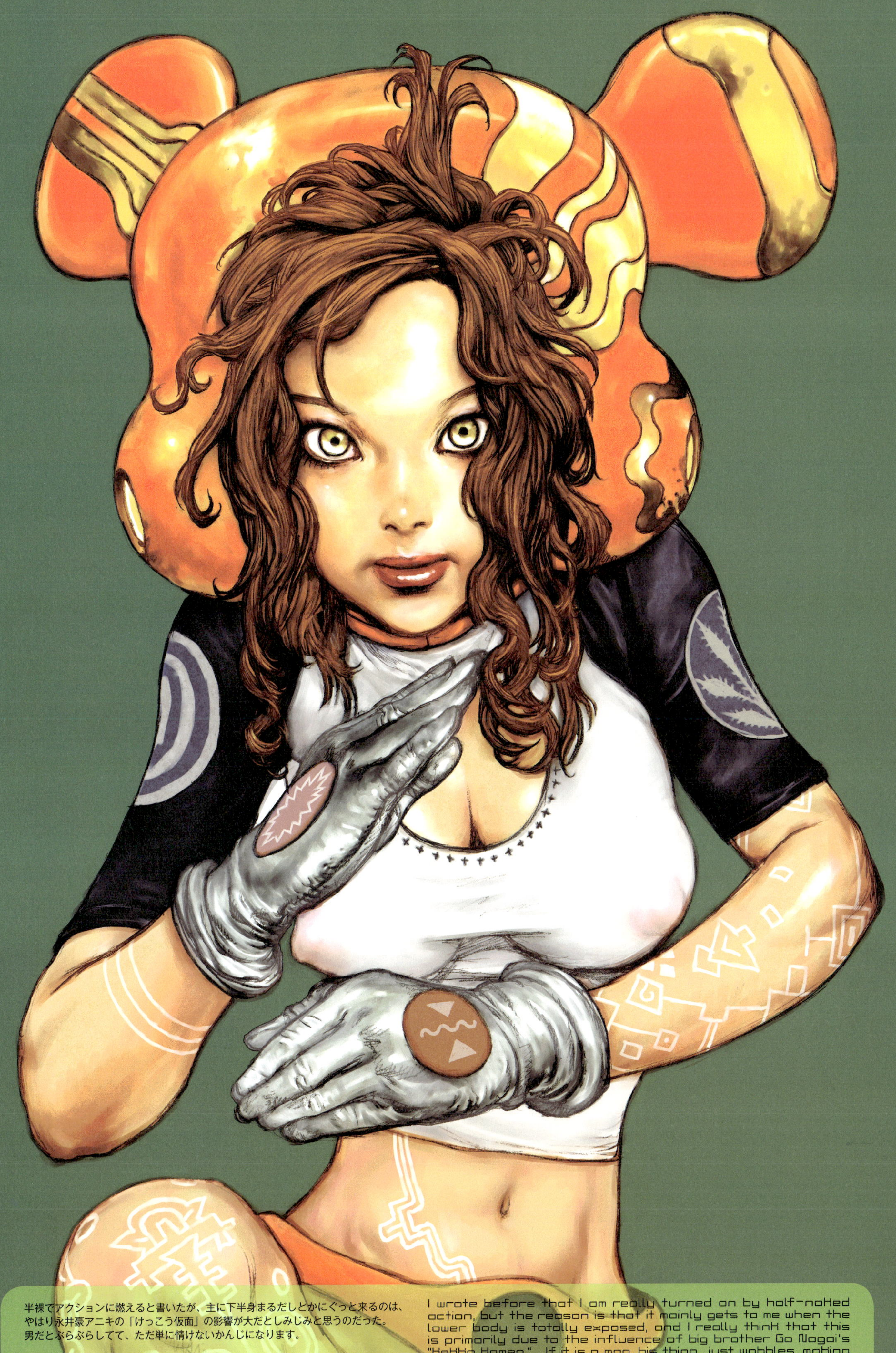

半裸でアクションに燃えると書いたが、主に下半身まるだしとかにぐっと来るのは、やはり永井豪アニキの「けっこう仮面」の影響が大だとしみじみと思うのだった。男だとぶらぶらしてて、ただ単に情けないかんじになります。

I wrote before that I am really turned on by half-naked action, but the reason is that it mainly gets to me when the lower body is totally exposed, and I really think that this is primarily due to the influence of big brother Go Nagai's "KeKKo Kamen." If it is a man, his thing just wobbles, making him look pitiful.

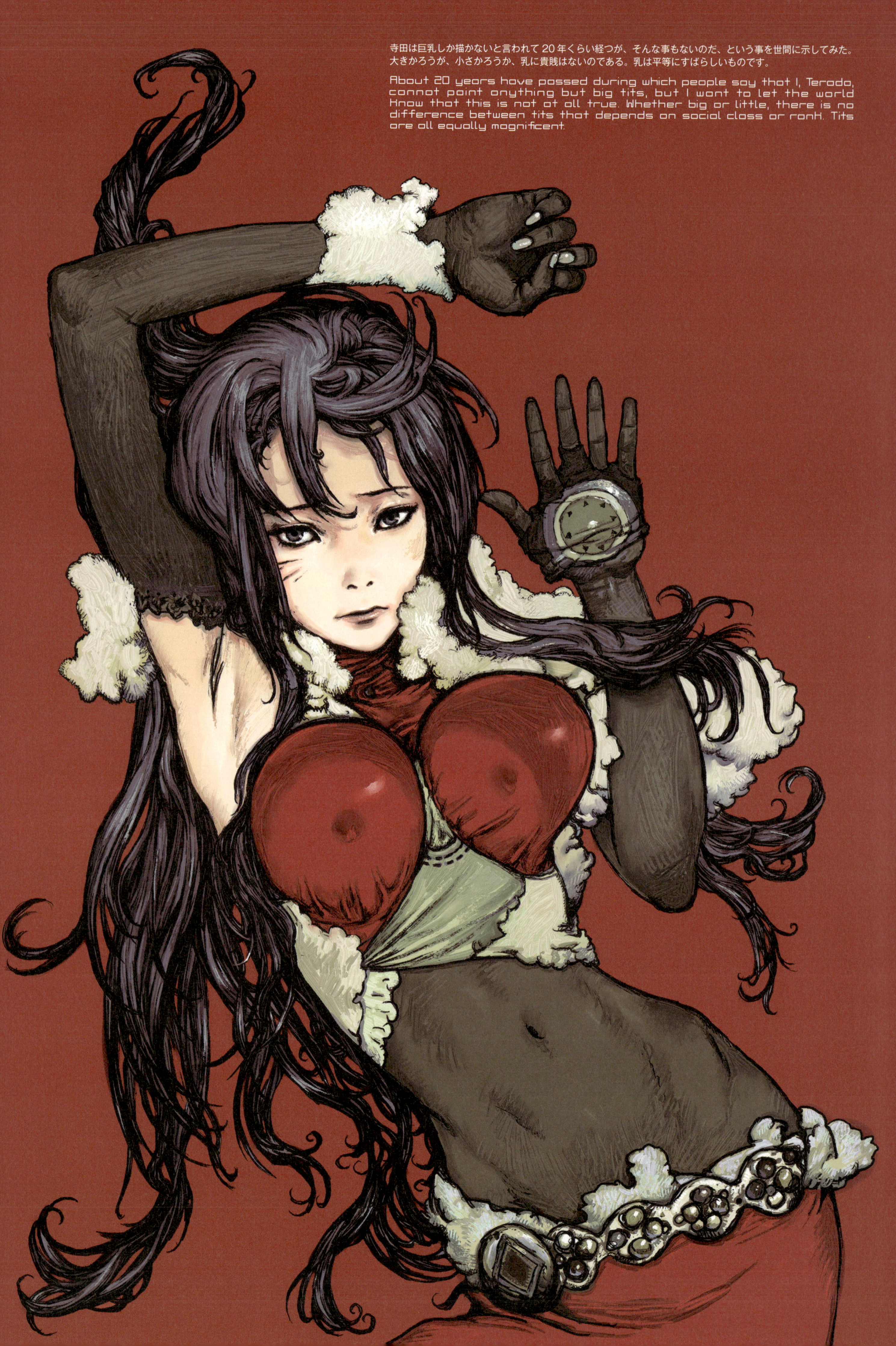

寺田は巨乳しか描かないと言われて20年くらい経つが、そんな事もないのだ、という事を世間に示してみた。大きかろうが、小さかろうか、乳に貴賤はないのである。乳は平等にすばらしいものです。

About 20 years have passed during which people say that I, Terada, cannot paint anything but big tits, but I want to let the world know that this is not at all true. Whether big or little, there is no difference between tits that depends on social class or rank. Tits are all equally magnificent.

ちょっとお尻つきだし気味にしゃがむポーズも好きだ。

I like poses in which the ass is shown just a bit in a squatting pose.

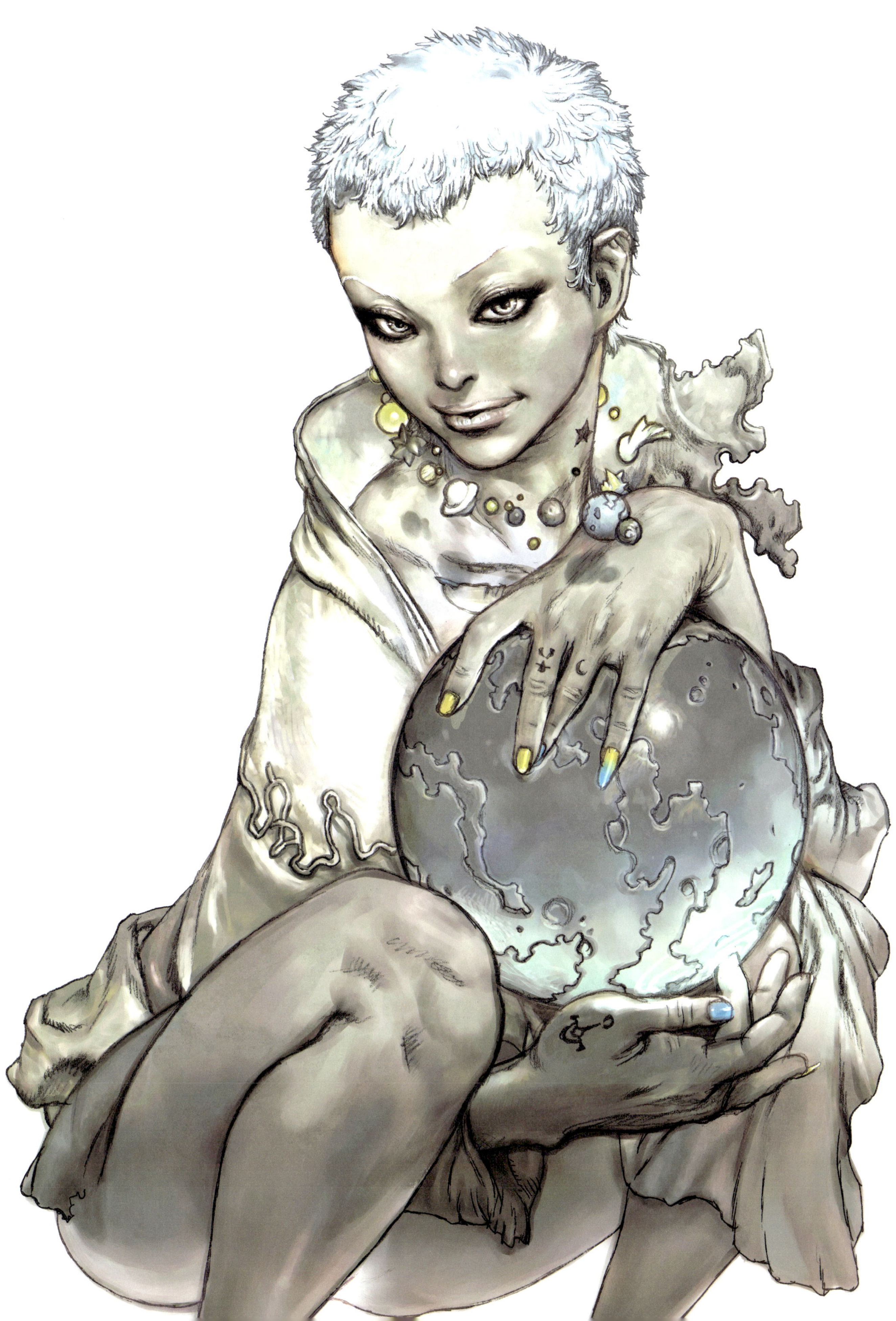

とにかくなにかを咥えさせたかったので。メリークリスマス！

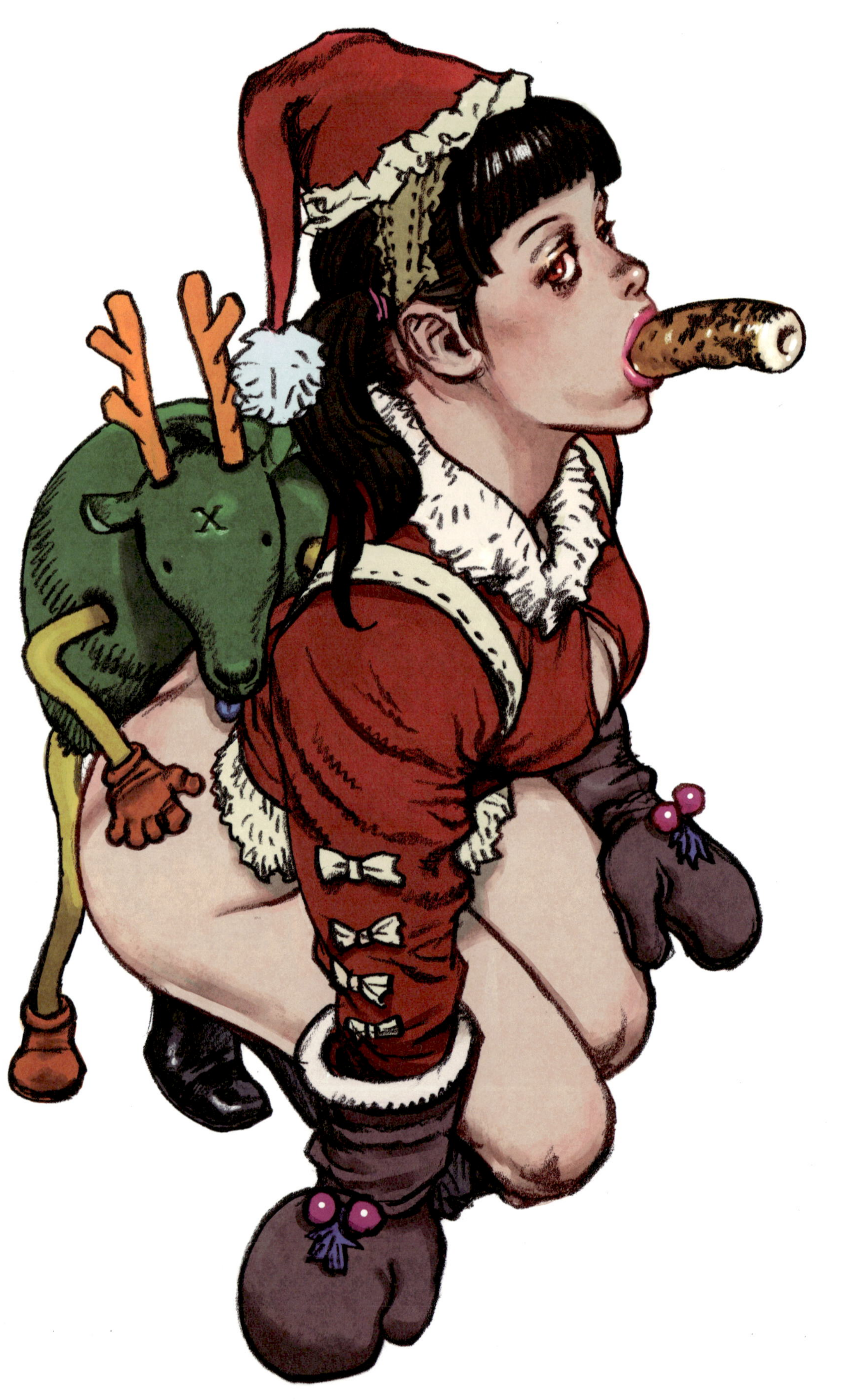

I just wanted to put something in her mouth. Merry Christmas!

日本ではいつのまにかクリスマスが、さかりのついたカップルがセックスする夜の代名詞になって久しい。
とりあえずなにかにかこつけて性行為に及ぼうとする、その姿勢がすばらしいと思う。諸君も頑張って欲しい。
クリスマスや正月や誕生日は言うに及ばず、友達の結婚式、法事、大学受験、あらゆる局面でかこつけてエロを追求していただきたいと思います。

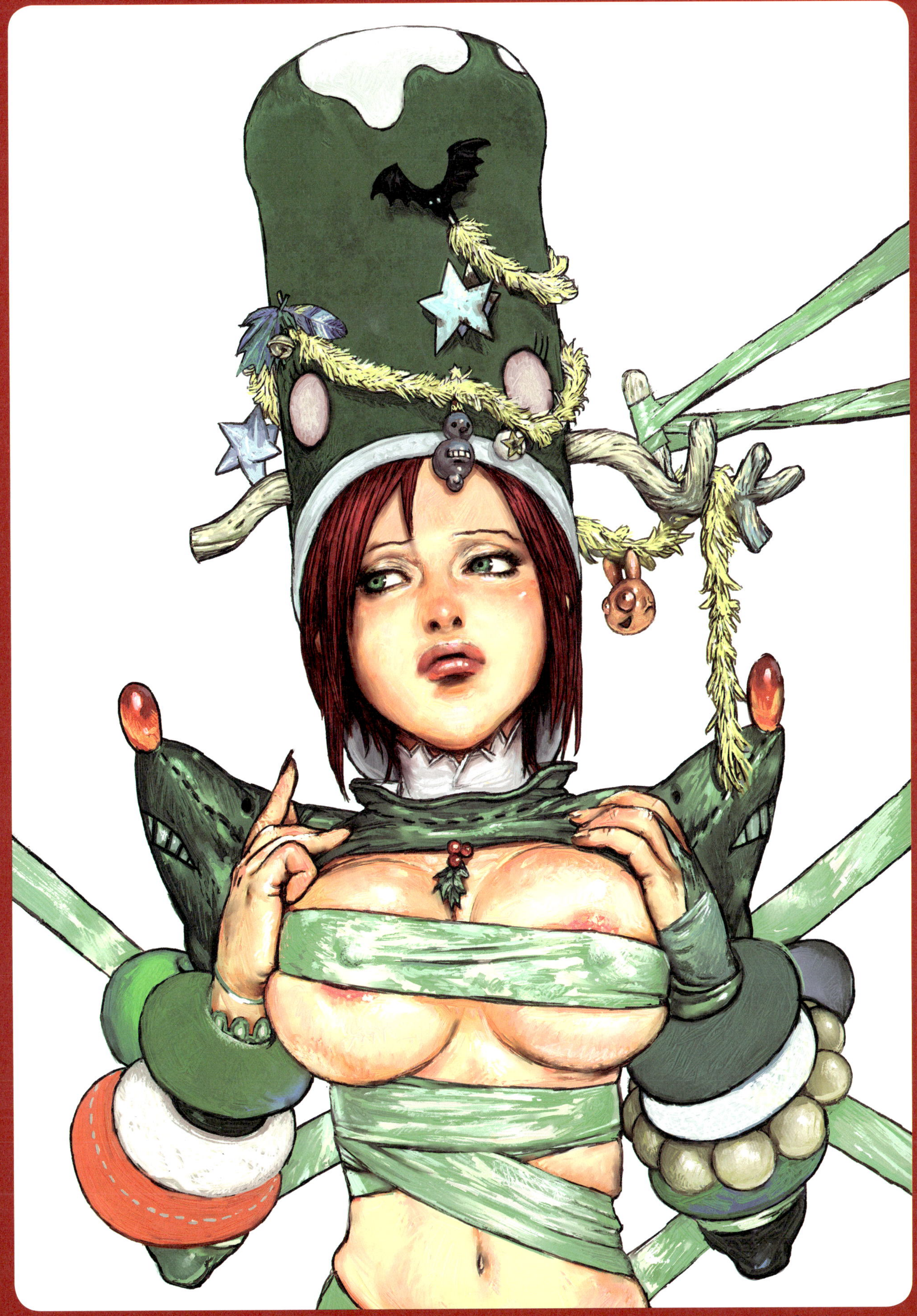

Without anybody taking special note, since some time back, Christmas has come to mean a night for having sex by couples in heat. But, at least, I think that the stance of making it a reason for having sex is wonderful. I do hope that you will all give it your best efforts. I hope that people will make anything and everything a chance for pursuing eroticism, at not only Christmas, New Year's and birthdays, but at the weddings for friends, their funerals, and their university entrance examinations, too.

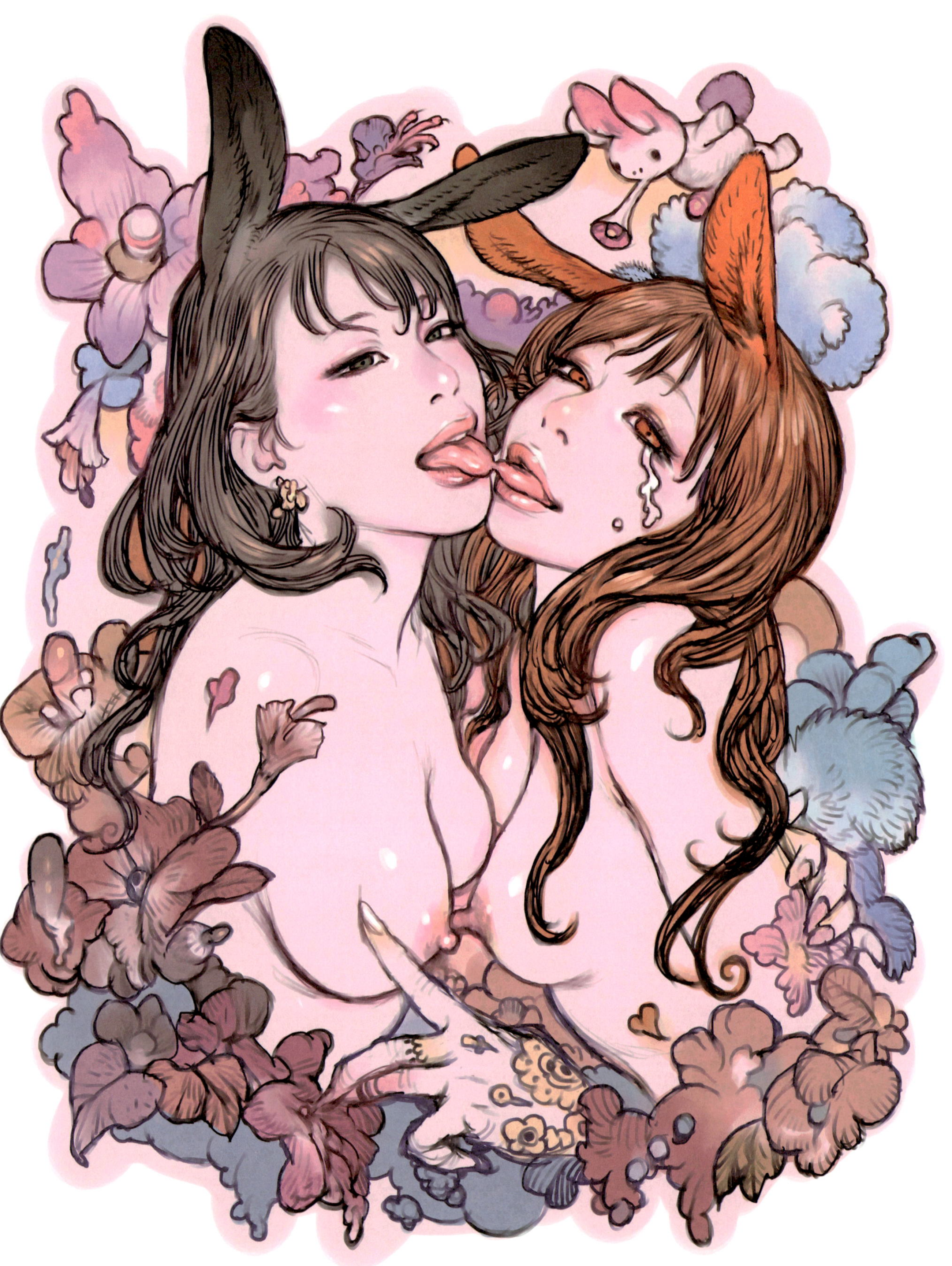

初めて行ったストリップ劇場は渋谷の道頓堀劇場だった。1980年代の終わり頃だったか。想像してたより淫猥さがなくて、変なハナシ健康的にすら思えておもしろかった。
抜くための風俗があたりまえにある現代に、ただひたすら行儀よく、座って女の子のハダカを見るためだけの空間で、うながされて手拍子とかみんなで打ちつつ、あったかい空気に満ちていたよ。
この絵はともだちのストリップ嬢の周年記念用に描いたんだった。

The first strip show that I ever went to was at the Dotonbori Theatre in Shibuya. I think it was around the end of the 1980s. There was far less sensuality than I had expected, and strange to say, I even found it healthy and amusing.
Today when whorehouses for getting your rocks off is the norm, in a space where one simply sat politely and viewed naked girls, who encouraged everybody there to applaud, the air was filled to overflowing with a pleasant warmth.
I painted this picture for a friend who is a stripper in celebration of her anniversary.

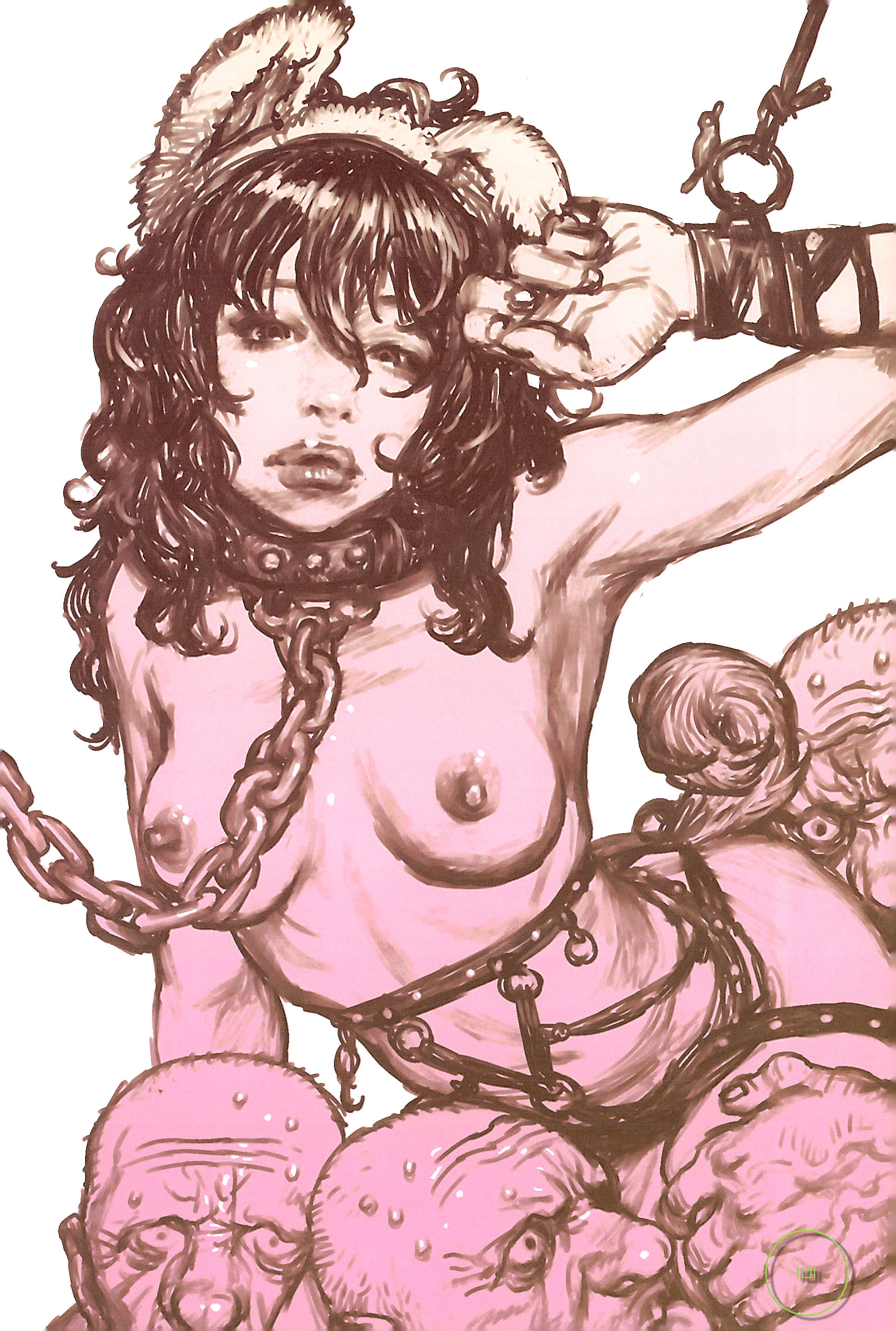

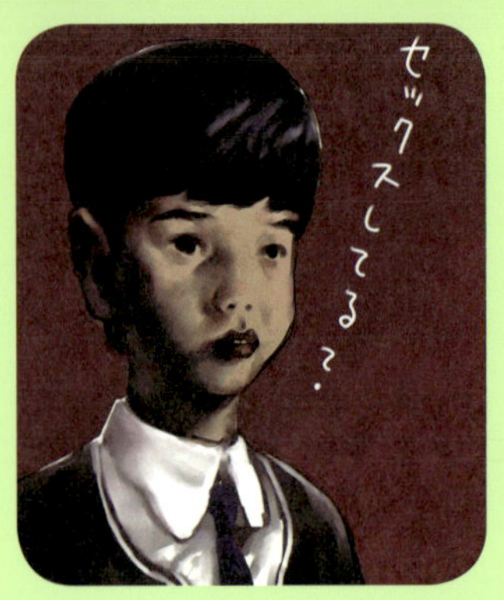

オレのオレによるオレのためのエロは
世のためヒトのためだった！

オレのエロガキ時代は、現代のようにネットがあるでなし、アダルトビデオすらない時代です。映画館で死ぬほどエロい（と想像してた）にっかつロマンポルノは かかってましたが、まさか青っパナ垂らした小学生が観に行けるワケじゃなし。エロガキ仲間と町を彷徨っては、団地の屋上や、工場ちかくの野っ原のハズレに雨風に打たれてカピカピになってるエロマンガ雑誌を見つけ出して、取り囲んでハアハア言ってただけです。
身悶えしまくった、ある日私は天啓に打たれました。あっ！ オカズがないなら自分で描けばいいんじゃん！ 自分の発想 に小躍りした私は早速ラクガキ用の広告紙の裏側に、たいへんな体位でまぐわう男女のスーパーエロい絵を描きました！
おお！　すごい！　ぜんぜんエロくないどころか、人間かコレ！！？？　だ、だめだこんなんじゃ！ とあわてて描き直しましたが、もちろん描ける技術もデッサン力も知識もないので酷い絵が生まれては消えました。そんなわけで第１次おかず自作計画は灰燼に帰したのです。悔しい。
いつかオレの手でオレによるオレのためのオレのオカズを！ と思い続けて幾十年。なんか絵は描けるようになったんですけど、なんでですかね。自分の絵はちーっっともエロくない。抜けない。やっぱりダメだー。それでも絵を見てくれた人の中には、寺田の絵はエロいよ、などと言ってくれるへんた、、奇特な方も出てきてくださいまして。まあ人様に喜んでもらえるエロでいいか！ と私は思いました！
あとなんでエロでメカなのか？ と訊かれたんですが、そんなのオレにもわかんない！ とはいえ鉄腕アトムがいて、キカイダーがいて、セクサロイドがいたニッポンのマンガで育ったのは大きいかも！
でもエロは分析しちゃいけないし、わからないからこそリビドーは無条件に亢進するんじゃないかと思ったり！
エロもメカも地球を救うといいなあ。暴力もエロも人間の本能ならば、エロのほうを支持したい私です。
エロ万歳！！！

寺田克也
岡山県玉野市生まれ
エロいラクガキが趣味です。
http://cacazan.com/

My eroticism that is made by me for myself is also for the world and all the people in it!

When I was an erotic kid, there was no Internet like there is today and there weren't even any 'adult videos.' At the movie houses, they showed the Nikkatsu Romantic Porno movies and I felt like (at least I imagined) that they must be excruciatingly Erotic, but there was no way that a snot-nosed grade school kid like me could get in to see them. My erotic buddies and I roamed the streets, and when we found erotic comic books (manga) on the roofs of apartment houses, or in fields near factories, we would surround them and simply sign in ecstasy and writhe in fruitless lust.
Then one day, I was struck by a flash from the blue. Hey! Since there was nothing to get our teeth into, couldn't I just draw some myself?! I was overjoyed at the idea, and immediately took a piece of advertising paper with the backside usable for graffiti, and I drew a picture of a man and a woman entwined in an extreme pose. Wow! Great!
But it looked to me like it wasn't the least bit erotic, and it even made me question whether it even looked like human beings! So I decided it wouldn't do at all! And I impatiently redrew it. But since I, of course, had no drawing or composition skills or knowledge, ugly pictures were born and disappeared one after another. As a result, my first attempts at creating ended in ashes. I was pissed off.
So I spent ten some years hoping that someday I would succeed in creating food for my own lust by my own hand. I finally gained the ability to one way or another paint pictures, but somehow I felt that they were not at all erotic. I began to think that it was impossible for me to pull through this impasse in the final analysis.
Even so, among the people who viewed my pictures, there were commendable individuals who claimed that they were, indeed, erotic. So, after all, I felt that if people enjoyed my eroticism, then it must be OK.
There were also people who asked me why I combined eroticism with mechanisms, but I don't even understand why I do it myself.
But that said, the fact that I grew up with such Japanese manga characters as Tetsuwan Atom (called Astro Boy in English), and Kikaider, and Sexaroid is likely a big factor!
But, then eroticism should never be picked apart and analyzed, and it is for this very reason, I think, that I go on unconditionally pressing forward.
How nice it would be if Eroticism and mechanisms could save the world. If both violence and eroticism are human instincts, I want to support Eroticism all the way.
Viva Eroticism!!!

Katsuya Terada
Born in Tamano City, Okayama Prefecture
I enjoy drawing erotic graffiti.
http://cacazan.com/

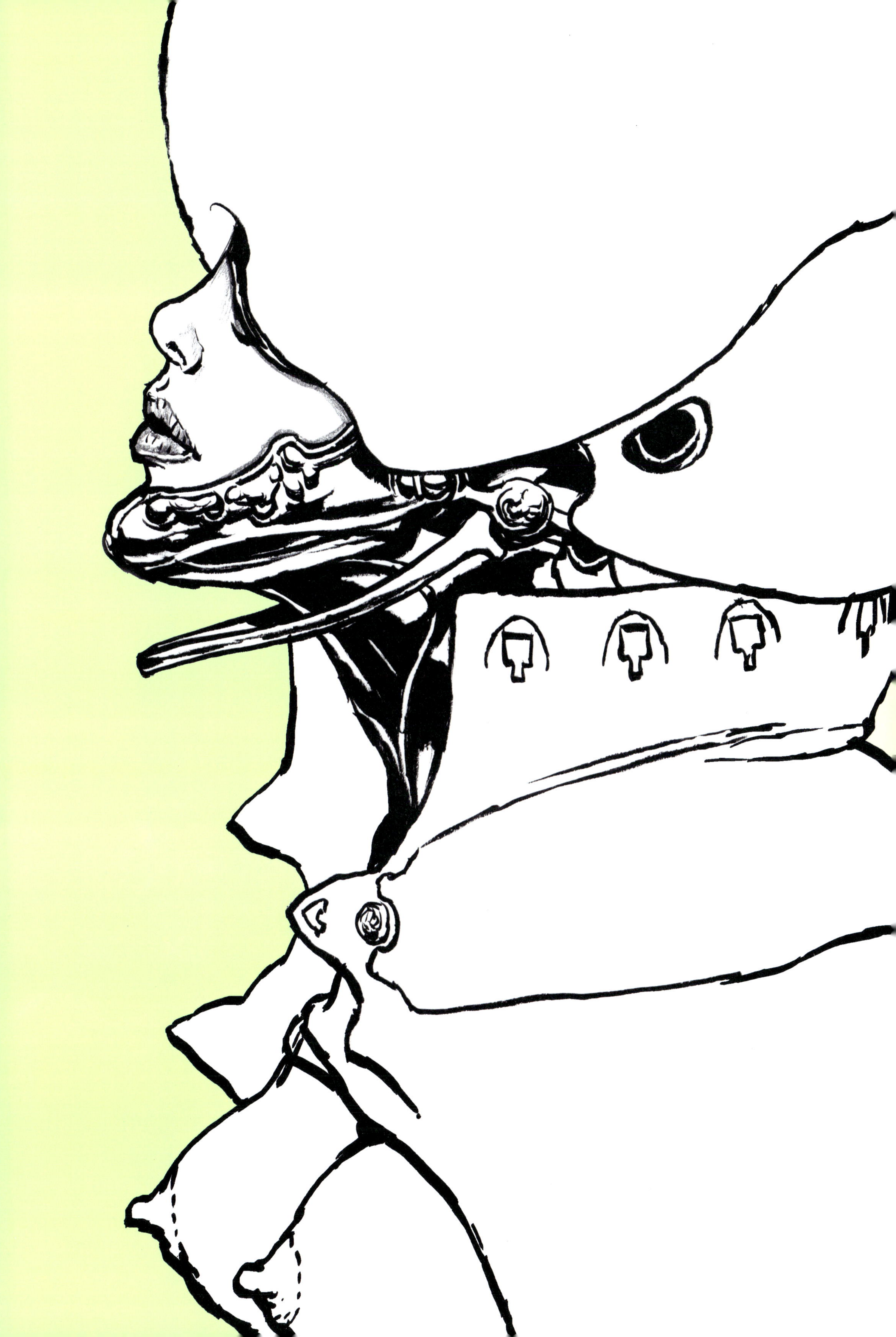

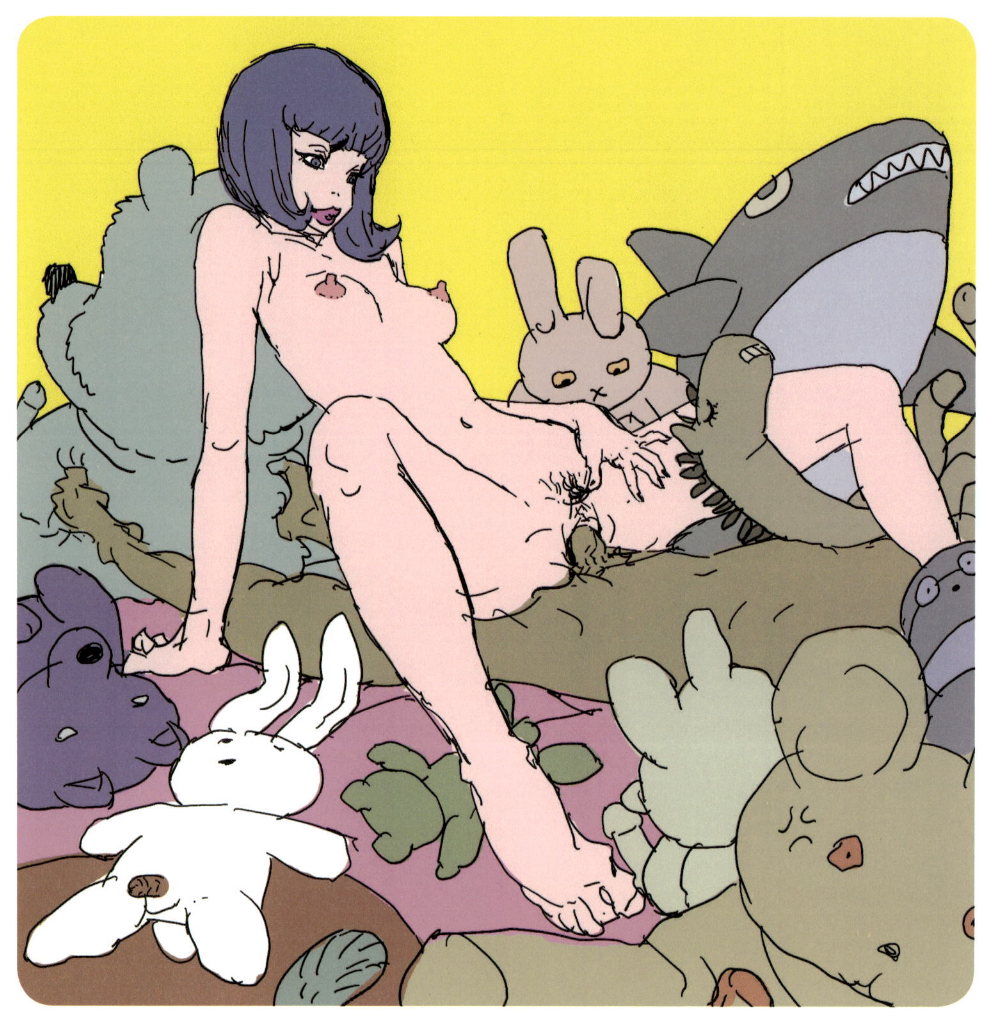

KATSUYA TERADA'S EROTIC ENGINEERING

Special Thanks: Kosuke Kawamura, Hajime Sorayama and Iiniku Ushijima
Book Design: Mayumi Kubota & Azusa Nakai of Uptight Co., Ltd.
Editor: Kenichi Kawai
Translation: Dan Kenny

Publisher: Kenichi Kawai
Published by Éditions Treville Co., Ltd.
804, 4-3-27 Shibuya Shibuya-Ku, Tokyo Japan 150-0002
Phone: +81-3-6418-5968, Fax: +81-3-3498-5176
E-mail: info@editions-treville.com
URL: http://www.editions-treville.net
Manufactured in Japan

寺田克也
エロ×メカ

初版発行：2014年3月31日

著者：寺田克也

協力：河村康輔、空山基、うしじまいい肉
ブックデザイン：窪田真弓、中井梓左（株式会社アップタイト）
編集：川合健一
翻訳：ダン・ケニー

発行者：川合健一
発行：株式会社エディシオン・トレヴィル
東京都渋谷区渋谷4-3-27 青山コーポラス804 〒150-0002
電話：03-6418-5968／ファックス：03-3498-5176
E-mail: info@editions-treville.com
URL: http://www.editions-treville.net

発売：株式会社河出書房新社
東京都渋谷区千駄ヶ谷2-32-2 〒151-0051
電話：03-3404-1201（営業）

印刷製本：シナノ書籍印刷株式会社

乱丁落丁本はエディシオン・トレヴィルにてお取り替え致します。
ISBN 978-4-309-92008-5

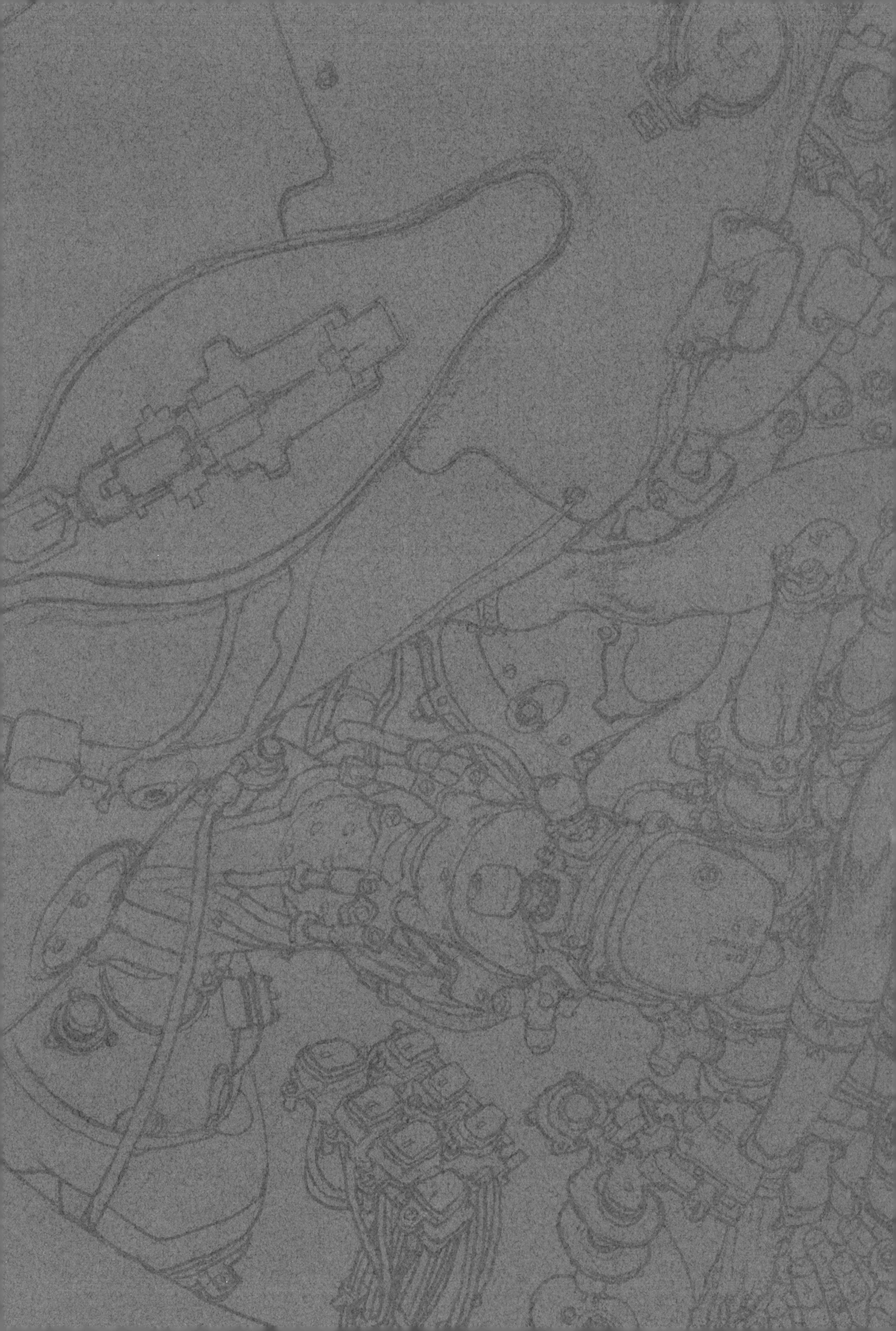